M. 89.

THE GOLDEN LAND

The new Cape Town rising from the old along the reclaimed
shore of Table Bay.

THE
GOLDEN LAND

A Background to South Africa

by

JULIAN MOCKFORD

WITH THIRTY-FIVE PHOTOGRAPHS

LONDON
ADAM AND CHARLES BLACK

FIRST PUBLISHED 1949
BY A. AND C. BLACK LIMITED
4, 5 AND 6 SOHO SQUARE LONDON W.1
REPRINTED 1951

MADE IN GREAT BRITAIN
PRINTED BY WESTERN PRINTING SERVICES LIMITED BRISTOL

CONTENTS

ACKNOWLEDGEMENTS

Of the photographs in this book, the South African State Information Office has given permission for the reproduction of Nos. 3, 5, 6, 16, 22 and 25; and the South African Railways for the remaining twenty-nine.

ILLUSTRATIONS

vii

PREFACE

AFRICA, IN its greater part, is still a continent for travellers rather than for tourists; but South Africa, with which this book is chiefly concerned, has elaborate facilities both for tourists and for immigrants who wish to settle there.

By the term South Africa I mean the Union of South Africa, made up of two former British colonies (the Cape of Good Hope and Natal) and two former Boer republics (the Transvaal and Orange Free State); and by the term Southern Africa I mean all Africa south of the Equator.

Swaziland, Basutoland and the Bechuanaland Protectorate, which includes the Kalahari Desert, are not politically part of the Union, but they are part of the same landscape and they interlock with it commercially, racially and socially.

But the former German colony of South-West Africa became a part of the Union in 1949 after having been administered by the Union Government for a generation by virtue of a League of Nations mandate given to it after the first great German war.

The Rhodesias are not part of the Union.

But all of these places are dealt with or touched on in the pages that follow, as are the great African holdings of the Western European countries—for instance, the Belgian Congo and Portugal's Angola and Mozambique.

They are South Africa's good neighbours and form her setting. All wrestle with the same problems as they cultivate and develop Africa and the Bantu peoples. The common pool of those problems—social, scientific, agricultural, pastoral, medical, veterinary—provides practical scope, non-political, for the functioning of a form of Pan-Africanism or African Pact.

The Union of South Africa itself is a completely independent country, and, as such, is a member nation of the Commonwealth to which it is voluntarily linked by the traditional symbol of the Crown. But the British Government has no more say in the Union's affairs than the Union has in the affairs of Canada.

Those who wish to obtain particular information about South Africa—whether as prospective tourists, traders or immigrants—may do so from the Union's overseas offices in such cities as London, Paris, Brussels, The Hague, Lisbon, Rome, Athens, Stockholm, Washington, New York, Canberra, Ottawa, Rio de Janeiro and Buenos Aires.

Aeroplanes and ships connect Great Britain, the Americas, and Europe with South Africa; and these transport facilities are steadily being improved after their dislocation during the second great German war. By air, travellers can get from Europe or America to South Africa in two or three days; by sea, in two or three weeks.

The great majority of sun-seekers, however, remain faithful to the ocean liners, the nearest thing to Utopia (for the passengers!) man has yet devised. Most passengers find the journey all too short, for life on a liner cutting through the deep blue of the Atlantic or the Indian Ocean is a very lovely thing, remote from the care and routine of the workaday world, and therefore not lightly to be put aside.

The enterprising go down one side of Africa and come up the other side. By doing so they double their ports of call. In the Atlantic they encounter such charming islands as Madeira, Teneriffe, or St. Helena; in the Indian Ocean they are on the fringe of the East in such Arab-influenced places as Zanzibar and Dar-es-Salaam, whose very names are poetry.

There are ships aplenty on the South African beat, both British and foreign. Some keep to one ocean or the other; others use both to circle Africa. Some go on a special cruise for tourists, who can thus budget for their entire holiday and work on a carefully prepared schedule of shore trips. Others shuttle regularly. And from Cape Town trains or aeroplanes take passengers to whatever regions they may have set their heart upon.

Unless his time is unlimited, the wise traveller does not set his heart on too many places, for by insisting on seeing too much he may well see too little. The African sub-continent is vast and varied, and even the hardiest, quite indefatigable traveller cannot hope to see it all in a few weeks or even a few months. So he must be discerning and not too greedy, choosing those places that he most wishes to visit and letting the rest go with a sigh.

South Africa House in Trafalgar Square, like other offices representing the Union overseas, has special departments to help and advise those who are contemplating a holiday or business trip to South Africa, where a transplanted Europe provides comfort and company cheek by jowl with the primitive Bantu tribes, such as the Zulus and the Swazis, and the herds of big game that still roam the veld for the arrow of the Bushman and the bullet of the European hunter.

Between that transplanted Europe and the Africa of David Livingstone your traveller, however, must make some kind of choice. He does not have to make a drastic decision either for the one or the other, for they intermingle rather conveniently for his delight; but he does have to decide whether his time will be spent mostly in the big towns, which we may call transplanted Europe, or in the game country and the native territories, which we may call the real Africa.

Rudyard Kipling, in his *Something of Myself*, calls the Cape of Good Hope a "glorious land", to which he gladly gave much of his "life and love". For many years he wintered there with his wife and children. The outward journey was always a "great joy", and, on the forest-clad mountain-slope where they lived as neighbours of Cecil Rhodes, "the children throve" and the "colour, light, and half-oriental manners of the land bound chains round our hearts for years to come".

But the Cape is only a corner of the sub-continent, and

others give their heart to sub-tropical Natal, that sometimes
seems a bright slice of India and sometimes Darkest Africa
itself; or to the multi-coloured hills of Basutoland, where the
blanketed tribesmen roam on ponies, for there is only one
mile of railway in their domains; or to Swaziland, which is a
Switzerland without snows; or to the Great Karoo, where
Olive Schreiner's *African Farm* still shimmers in the boiling
mirage that is always lifting the distant koppies into the sky;
or to the Northern Transvaal, with its baobabs and fever-
trees, its mysterious white rain-goddess, whom Rider
Haggard turned into *She*, and its "great grey-green greasy
Limpopo River" of the *Just-so Stories*.

There is so much to love in this strangely patterned land,
but to each man his own fancy. It may be a landscape in the
Kruger National Park—a landscape enlivened with giraffe,
elephant, buffalo, kudu, and waterbuck; a landscape gay
with the gold of marula plums and mimosa blossoms; it may
be the plant-smothered hothouse of the Zambezi, where the
Victoria Falls crash in a white wonder to the sunken river-
bed, only to shoot above themselves again as sun- or moonlit
spray and rainbows; or it may be the great towers and walls
that suddenly startle the onlooker in the Rhodesian bush—
the Zimbabwe Ruins, ghost-filled beneath the dazzle of the
stars.

Somewhere in that immense panorama there is a valley,
a plain, or a hill-top for everybody; but to find it one must
sometimes leave the *train de luxe*, the cushioned hotel. Even
so, only the mildest kind of trekking (in hired motor-cars)
is necessary.

There is no real "roughing it" for the traveller in South
Africa and the Rhodesias nowadays. His way is made easy
for him everywhere by paternal Governments that for years
have been gently nursing tourists from all parts of the world.
Nor need he bother about rates of exchange and languages.
For the South African or Rhodesian pound, which he buys
at par with the English pound, he will get value that will
surprise him very agreeably; and although he will hear

languages that he will not understand, Afrikaans and the Bantu tongues, his English will be understood everywhere.

Freed of the language trials and the currency tribulations of foreign countries, your traveller in Southern Africa is able, therefore, to concern himself entirely with the pleasant scenes and peoples beneath the sun he now shares with them. If he is a fisherman, he will find excellent sport in both the rivers and the seas; if he is a swimmer, he will be thrilled with the transparent combers that break and cream upon such endless beaches as those of Muizenberg and Durban and all the south coast of Natal; if he is a mountaineer, he will find climbs worthy of his skill up the Drakensberg peaks that pierce the rain-clouds at Mont-aux-Sources; if he is a botanist or an artist, there is the rich profusion of wild flowers at Caledon and Hermanus; if he is a golfer, there are courses for him everywhere.

As for those who travel "for to admire and for to see", there is all the variety of scene from dry desert to the damp, hot forests of the sub-tropics, and the beehive-shaped kraals where Africa dances to the drums and wild chants of Shaka's forebears.

CHAPTER I

VOYAGE OF REDISCOVERY

I

MY ORDERS were to uproot myself from Baker Street and go to South Africa. London's sun, so often niggardly, was tricking the autumn leaves of Regent's Park into pure Johannesburg gold. Breeze-stirred, they shone in the stripped branches of many trees, in the air as they fell, and upon the long lawns of the pleasure gardens. Of all the cities in the world, London is the most difficult to quit.

Dick Whittington tried but could not leave it. To say that he retraced his footsteps because Bow Bells smote his ear, prophesying fame and fortune, is merely to embroider the simple truth: Dick Whittington could not bear the thought of leaving London, though he starved there. For him London was life, even on a diet of crusts. Its receding outline made him slacken his pace and pause: he tried to turn his back upon it so that his eyes would not be troubled by the sight of what he loved; but, neglecting to stop his ears, its sounds still stirred his homesick soul, and he ran gladly back into its smoke. Beyond its borders lay the wilderness and outer darkness and a sort of suicide—and Dick rejected them in favour of coffee-houses and cosy light and stirring life. The Mother City is like that to all her children, whether her own or adopted. Her own know no other, though they journey in many lands; and the strangers who come to her from far horizons, hot with travel-lust, wander no more—or, if they must, they do so with reluctant feet.

For a decade I had subsisted on London's crises and crusts; but now the initial gaiety prompted by my marching orders died in my heart. If only it had been drizzling and

foggy and cold, I might have given her the laugh; but with
the liquid gold of this sunshine upon her—the softest sunshine in the world—all I could summon, to put a bold
front on it, was what the Russians call a crimson smile.
Between the bright red of the buses, I taxied through streets
which I had seen filled and flowing with the pageantry of
coronation and victory; and, in the intervening years, I had
seen them filled with the ruins and filth of death from the
trembling air. Now the streets were swift with normal life,
life as we have made it, on rubber wheels and rubber-heels.
I raced past the familiar faces and the familiar buildings of
a daily circle that was in process of being broken for me;
and from the West End and the City, by way of a varied
circumference embracing such dissimilar points as Bond
Street and Billingsgate, I shot off at a tangent to London
River and Southward-ho! From a Bond Street tower tumbled
a sweet carillon of sentimental song; at Billingsgate, traffic-
confused, the fish-porters gave harsh cries and curses while,
upon their flat, hard hats, they balanced London's supper
—Thames-borne, sea-fresh, malodorous.

My ship was resting in an oblong of water somewhere in
that maze of canals, locks and harbours which give muscles
and meaning to London River. It is impossible to grasp
their intricate pattern for nothing less resembling a pattern
was ever seen. They seem to create higgledy-piggledy in
terms of a surrealist's nightmare; yet they function with the
perfect precision of a chronometer. They have grown with
the apparent carelessness of a tree's multiplying branches
—each putting forth, however, for a real purpose. Slowly,
generation by generation, they, too, have come into being
—year by year and century by century since the days when
the Romans loosed commerce up and down the river through
the walled magic of Londinium.

I went aboard the *Umtali*, a small, snug steamer named
after a Rhodesian town, and looked out over the West
India Docks. The Midas touch of the sun gave gilded
beauty even to that grimly utilitarian scene, wherein ship-

ping activity is the only thing that matters beneath the vasty sky, whether by day or by night. On the wharves, pigmies against their background of cargo-shifting cranes and the high flanks of ships, pot-bellied men in bowler hats— stevedores, chandlers and other such landlubbers—gestured genial farewells to captains and pursers. Lock gates opened and shut, and the *Umtali* picked her way through this puzzling dockland to the free water of London River, then at flood-tide. As the pilot nosed her downstream, I felt glad that it was in this fashion, on the back of Old Man Thames, that I was leaving London and England. From the left bank blew the mixed aroma of an endless variety of cargoes; from the right bank, as the river pythoned widely seawards, a veritable platoon of tall chimney-stacks breathed broad, parallel bars of black smoke over the low, flat smudge of industrialism and towards that lovely county known as the Garden of England.

In every direction there was a Turner ready for painting. The evening, red and gold, put a chill into the breeze, sucked a miasma from the river and drew dragon-like clouds about the sun. Soon the heavens were glorified with many colours, gentle and bold, and the gathering gloom was divided along the western skyline by two gigantic spear-blades of watermelon red. The red spears glowed triumphantly above the darkening river, alive with tugs and barges, which flattered the size of the *Umtali*. She steamed importantly past the little home-tied fellows on her long voyage to the meeting place of the Atlantic and Indian Oceans. The red spears seemed to cool until they were red no more, but deepest indigo, then slate. As the river and its dark banks became pricked with points of light—red, green, white, lemon—the lamps of the *Umtali* shone in friendly response. One from her bridge chattered in dots and dashes to a speeding tug, which drew alongside. The pilot clambered down a rope ladder from the *Umtali* to the tug, from whose deck he waved us God-speed. Then the tug snorted like a hippopotamus, splashed away from us, and turned

and churned into the upstream blackness. The pilot left to
us the estuary and the wide, wide world. We were footloose
and the Atlantic Ocean was ours; but for him, why, London
River and London Town held all that made life dear.

2

After the shattering years of the second great German
war, I was returning to South Africa to see what it was all
about. New political forces were being loosed about the
world like thunderbolts from Europe and Asia. Their
farthest vibrations made the sensitive skin of the Whiteman tingle, down there in Africa, south of the equator, but
especially in the Union compounded of the two former Boer
Republics, the Transvaal and the Orange Free State, and
the two former British colonies, Natal and the Cape of Good
Hope. The good hopes of the Whiteman, after battling for
his slice of Africa for three centuries, suddenly became less
rosy as the Europe of his fathers seemed determined to
inflict upon itself the death of a thousand cuts. The Whiteman, alone in the African jungle, discovered himself out
on Europe's remotest limb, perched precariously, listening
to a frightening orchestration of death-rattles from the
West, of war-cries from the East, and of a new, semi-
educated mumbo-jumbo from the surrounding Bantu whose
young idea he was teaching how to shoot.

In addition, the backsheesh-wail of famine-cursed India
pitched itself to a shrill hymn of hate which her many
emigrant-sons in Africa re-echoed into the Tree of Empire,
wherein the Whiteman sat and wondered; and this Indian
hate-call cut across the deep diaphragm of Africa's talking
drums like an unexpected rip-tide of sound and fury.
Could the Whiteman's position in Africa be as insecure
as it seemed from the viewpoint of London? I hoped
to find an answer to that question in the course of my
voyage of rediscovery. From the debating halls of the

United Nations, in London, in Paris and in New York, White South Africa appeared to be on the spot. But, before admitting that it was so, I wanted to examine South Africa on the spot in the sense of the older colloquialism—to see and hear South Africa again, *in loco*, the South Africa I had lived in for the greater part of my life.

Above the Thames estuary the stars pointed the way down the English Channel. Then, in the night watches, a cluster of lights to starboard marked shell-scarred Dover, from where, at times, I had witnessed the Battle of Britain and the long-range duel between English and German shore guns. And, as I thought of the deep tunnels in the chalk cliffs where the citizens of Dover went to cover when air-bombing became intense, it reminded me, for some oblique reason, of Peter Moor, the young German soldier who, early in the century, had passed this same way as his troopship carried him from Hamburg to the deserts of South-West Africa. His mind had been stirred by the sight of the white cliffs of Dover, for they symbolised for him the England he envied. At that time England was at the very zenith of her might and majesty, but, curiously enough, it was not her wealth and power that the German soldier pondered—it was her wisdom and character:

"We stood at the starboard rail", he recalled later,[1] "and looked over to the coast of England, which rose mighty, steep, and rugged out of the water not far off; and we watched the fishing-boats which, with their gray and black sails, lay in great numbers on the broad, ever-moving ocean. . . . While I stood there the staff physician passed me, and with him the first lieutenant of the marines. They stood a while at the railing not far from me, and I heard the first lieutenant say to the other man: 'We seamen think differently about the Englishmen from the people who live inland. We meet them in all the ports of the world and we know that they are the most respectable of all the peoples. There behind the high chalk cliffs dwells the first

[1] Gustav Frenssen, *Peter Moor's Journey to South-West Africa* (Constable, 1908).

nation of the earth,—distinguished, wise, brave, united, and
rich. As for us—well, one of their qualities, bravery, we
have had for ages; one other, riches, we are slowly acquiring.
Whether we ever acquire the others—that is our life
problem.' I wondered over that speech, but afterwards the
old African settlers, whom I came to know, also spoke with
the greatest respect of the English."

Alas, this prayer or prophecy was in vain. Germany's
war against Europe, begun in 1870, was to be twice resumed,
in 1914 and in 1939, after the young German soldiers had
been blooded in their massacre of the Hereros in South-
West Africa. And the England that lay in the darkness
beyond Dover, like the Continent in the darkness on our
port bow, had been bludgeoned to death-point by the same
German soldiers and their sons—in search, not of the higher
wisdom, but of the lower tribal domination through yet
another and greater massacre. Then across England's
bleeding body, the fighting done, passed the shadows of
wings: not the wings of Death but the wings of international
vultures, long-sighted, far-smelling, that had flown out of
the morning of victory; but this particular feast was not yet,
not yet; so they flew on till they came to roost in the branches
of the uno tree—and there they sit, waiting and watching
for another human slaughter, casual or sanctioned. Out of
Germany—so clever in small things, so stupid in great—
the beaks of the vultures had torn off strips of flesh; but her
body has life in it yet. And as the young German would
expect—the young German soldier who pondered the white
cliffs of Dover on his voyage to South-West Africa—it will
be England, if any of all the nations of the world, who will
play the good Samaritan to Germany and bind up her self
inflicted wounds and the wounds inflicted by the vultures.

The cluster of lights marking Dover became watery and
vague, then vanished. It was a sign that I must be content
to leave her in the ship's wake and look forward to the land
of my present purpose. The *Umtali* glowed about me, alone
in the black wastes of the sea. The light of no other craft

was visible. It was a luxury, after London's eternal press of people, to find solitude again and to commune with the mighty deep and the myriad stars: they gave no answer unless I desired an answer—and then they gave the answer I desired! I could not tell where sea met sky—save very roughly by the end of the downward sweep of the hard, bright stars. How many they were, these northern stars, now that they were not hidden by the fogs and mists of London; but the southern stars would be bigger and brighter, no doubt, once we got a sight of them beyond the equator.

The ship rolled with the unashamed ungainliness of a waddling duck, as if smugly assenting to my belief that, once south of the line, the ocean would be bluer—or was it greener?—and the skies wider, just as, once I was ashore in South Africa, everything would be gayer, more free, happier, healthier, wealthier, more plentiful—especially food, with lovelier, sun-filled landscapes, with girls more golden, and men more godlike and bronzed in the creaming, emerald-transparent surf. Out of this darkness of benighted England, crippled by two great German wars, out of a ruined Europe in the depths of the returned Dark Ages, there would emerge for me the bright jewel of South Africa, the white light of reason and joy playing upon each of its many smiling facets. And fruit, of course—an endless variety of citrus and deciduous fruits, fruits from the temperate zone of the Cape and tropical fruits from the oven-warm belt of coastal Natal and the low-lying lands of the Northern Transvaal. It would be a case, after Seven Lean Years, of eat, drink and be merry for tomorrow—well, tomorrow Europe might die.

3

Through the window of my cabin on the promenade deck there appeared one day the most delicate dawn I had ever seen. Its colours were beyond a painter's powers to depict. They were of such rare quality that only a fine lyricist would have dared to transpose them and the rapture they engendered into a musical pattern of measured words. In the middle of all these flower-like colours of sea and land, sky and cloud, there rose up the great mountainous bulk of the Grand Canary, with the town of Las Palmas lying along the unbroken mirror of the bay we were entering. There was nothing for me to do, since lyrics are quite beyond me, except stand and stare; and as I stood and stared the colours changed with a magic more subtle and, I imagine, more marvellous than the spectacular variations of the Northern Lights, the much-studied Aurora Borealis. It was a moving aquatint, a Japanese painting on silk, constantly evolving.

As dawn became day, the colours lost their supreme delicacy; and when the sun shook off his misty veils, he revealed the mountains in all their stark nakedness, their ribs showing where the rain and the wind had washed away their covering of vegetation and soil. It was a startling transformation, from dreamlike fantasy to harsh reality. In the full glare of the merciless sun, the island had become the skeleton of an island, an island stripped of its good earth, its flesh, so that its rock formations, its bones, were laid bare. But when I went ashore—a safe course steered for me between the little boats piled high with bananas, oranges, cigars and linen—I found that the fertility of the foothills and valleys, with their blossoms and grapes, their vegetable gardens and orchards, made me forget the creeping desiccation of the mountain slopes. Desolation was descending from the hilltops, but in the valleys and plains below the Spaniards and coloured folk of the island, untroubled, continued with their cultivation and with their buying and selling in the market place.

The dazzle in the air heralded a latitude where the sun was lord. Even the smooth, shallow sea played sycophant to him, sedulously flashing back his blinding smile. I welcomed him as an old familiar, for I had never wor-

shipped him. Though I had respected him, I had feared
him for the deadly thrust of his swords of light. Sun-worship
is a religion of the northern hemisphere where he shows his
face with comparative infrequency; in the southern hemisphere, he is too constantly on show to be taken seriously as
a god. There the moon, with her fickle moods and phases
as she grows from sickle to shield, is a likely goddess for
sun-blinded, sun-heated Africans who can look upon her
cold light and find it good for body and mind and spirit.
In the sun there is naked strength; while in the shadow-
marked moon there is witchery. But after my long absence
from the South African sun and a surfeit of fog and cloud,
I gladly acknowledged his glory as he struck at Las Palmas
and rejoiced to be in his presence once again. Intoxicated
by his light and warmth, I began to ask myself why I had
left his lands to live in the lands which he spurned. He
provided a climate and way of life which, always attractive,
seemed doubly so in retrospect through ten years of European hardship and horror in a deepening twilight of Western
civilisation.

Now I could lift up my face to the sun and forget. Well,
if I could not forget, at least I could lift up my face to the
sun. And for that day in Las Palmas and for the two following days as we steamed south again, this sun-ecstasy filled
me: then I felt the sun's fever in my blood and his sword-
points in my eyes. Quickly I retreated to the shadowy, air-
cooled sanctuary of my cabin; but it was too late. Vertigo
unsteadied my legs, and a sharp pain knifed me from the
eyes to the nape of my neck. I knew from experience of it
in Rhodesia, South Africa, Mauritius and the Seychelles
that it is impossible to reply to a sunstroke; so I fell back
upon my bunk and stayed there for several days, putting
cold compresses over my eyes and temples, and quenching
the fever in my veins with iced drinks of fresh lemon. Also
I kept the shutter up so that I could not see the glare on the
water nor the vibrating mirage of the boiling air.

It was the cry of "Whales!" that brought me to the

deck again; but all I could see was a porpoise bouncing off the waves. And for day after weary day we scanned the seascape for signs of life, but no sign could I see save the occasional purposefulness of the porpoise. We entered the tropics, and still the ocean had nothing to offer for a divertissement. I circled the deck, morning and afternoon, describing an inner circle to the outer circle of the sea. Never before had I noticed, though I had crossed the Pacific, the Indian Ocean and the Atlantic, the smallness of the circumscribed sea in which a ship moves. Observing now, I discovered myself to be the centre of a watery disc that appeared to move forward, with dull monotony, on each rotation of the propeller. It was an absurdly little disc—a mere quoit of grey cut from the ocean; and beyond its rim there was nothing but the steel-grey of an ever-open, arching sky. All this was nothing but maddeningly modernistic decoration—flawless, flat, clean, lifeless.

Then billowing white clouds came sailing about us, and, with the clouds came life. Familiar birds and strange birds —casual gulls and long-necked, long-legged geese in careful formation—flew up to and away from the ship, coming from and returning to their haunts along the West Coast of Equatorial Africa. And as if they were the first wonders of a new creation, they were succeeded by other forms of life —life, this time, from out of the ocean itself. Whales floated into view to starboard and to port, blowing fountains of spray into the sunshine. Tunny-fish and barracuda, in large schools, shot gleaming from wave-crest to trough. Some paced it with the ship, others leapt into the air, high and higher, where they double-somersaulted and crashed back into their breath-giving element.

Then came more birds, a few swallows, which, after fluttering and darting about the boat-deck for an hour, turned towards the coast to search out their summer resort. In Regent's Park, just before leaving London, I had watched some swallows at their aerobatics, and thought to myself that they were limbering up for their long flight from the

The cable-car swinging to its station on top of Table Mountain, with Lion's Head towering above the Atlantic Ocean.

Wearing the fez of the Faithful, a Malay tailor of Cape Town who, in the evening, might share in the semi-religious ordeal of the slashing sword.

Cape Coloured folk picking and packing grapes in a vineyard at Paarl, centre of the Peninsula's wine country.

English winter to the African summer. Perhaps these swallows, skimming for a while between mast and smoke-stack, were from that very flight; and perhaps I should meet them again on the plains of the Orange Free State or the highveld of the Transvaal.

From daybreak to sundown, on this day, the flying-fish exploded in dozens from the flanks of the waves and darted in glistening flurries along the troughs until they hit the water again. Porpoises were also present. With the white, majestic clouds paradoxically enlarging our world as they crowded into the faintly blue sky; with whales spouting and the barracudas flinging themselves so high into the air that they fell out of control; with the tunnies almost rubbing themselves against the *Umtali* as they bucked their way from stern to stem; with the birds reminding me, as they sped over these wastes, that they were better travellers than men; with all this life and movement suddenly loosed within the circumscribed disc of our voyage, I felt on better terms with the reluctant ocean that I had crossed so often. The old Atlantic could still do its stuff, and I felt quite absurdly pleased with it.

4

Each night I scanned the skies for the bigger moon and the brighter stars I knew so well—and the Southern Cross and the Milky Way. But if your youth lies behind you, it may be difficult and even dangerous to revisit the glimpses of the moon. You and they, in all probability, have changed too much. I recalled Leonard Merrick's Conrad who went in search of his Youth and the middle-aged woman in the film *Carnet de Bal* who, widowed, hurried to her home-town to find the several suitors whose honeyed, passionate words still echoed from her girlhood. The bright illusions of yesterday become dusty disappointments if we turn again to touch them; but the tropical moon, the Southern Cross and the Milky Way were surely not illusions, and so I took courage and scanned the skies night after night. But the moon, when at last she swam into our ken, seemed anaemic and listless, like a lovelorn girl, not radiant and laughing, like a shining bride. As for the Milky Way, which my memory pictured as the Great White Way of the Heavens, it was discernible only as a vague, hardly traceable discoloration of an unfiery firmament.

But there was still the Southern Cross, and for this I watched, patiently, anxiously, peering along the southern skyline night after night. As we rolled towards the Cape, it would, I hoped, come swinging into the sky, a glorious sign and symbol that God was still in his high heaven and that all was well in the southern world. Night after night I looked, but it was not there, until I began to fear that my eyes were blear and their sight blighted. However, I comforted myself by blaming the low-lying clouds and by calculating that, at this time of the year, the Southern Cross hung at its lowest level. One night, however, the Southern Cross did show up precisely at the off-south position I had plotted for it. Its four main brilliants were dull, as if they needed polishing, and no different from the few and disappointing stars overhead. About me the small circle of sea, forbidding and unsympathetic, was black as India ink and, as I scratched my head in bewilderment, an absurd rhyme came unexpectedly jingling out of the long-stored music-box of my earliest memories :

> If all the world were paper,
> And all the sea were ink,
> It would make a poor old man like me
> Scratch his head and think!

So now I thought that this dull, distant shadow of the Southern Cross was indeed a sign and symbol for me—not the bright sign I had hoped for, but a sad and solemn signal that he who expecteth nothing shall not be disappointed. If heaven itself could hang out no lamps of welcome for me, I must not blame South Africa, of the earth earthy, if miracles no longer grew there for casual plucking. Carefully I conned over my notions of the country we were approaching —the country I knew better than any other. It was a new country; a Whiteman's country; a country of great opportunity; a country with a great future; a country of beautiful landscapes, of golden beaches, of joyous hunting, of fertile farms; a country whose spacious homes were silently serviced by cheerful, willing blacks; a country of plenty which had been and still was a Promised Land for Europe's displaced or misplaced, for the hemmed-in and thwarted, whether Dutch, English, German or any other; a country of health, liberty and happiness, of hope, enterprise and fortune. After Europe's Valley of the Shadow of Death, South Africa's open uplands of sunshine and the breath of life.

And that was why the new trekkers were spilling out of Europe and heading overland and by sea for the unshackled, golden life in Africa below the line. Kenya, Rhodesia, South Africa—there a man might still live in freedom and rear a family free from fear and want. Indeed, the new migration had begun, it seemed; an army of settlers was on the march, so that the swallows and cranes, doing their routine flight down Africa, could not fail to notice the many little ships upon the high seas and the dust-raising caravans spluttering along the Cairo-to-Cape highway of adventure. After van Riebeeck's seventeenth-century Dutchmen and van der Stel's French Huguenots, the British settlers of the early nineteenth century, the Boer Voortrekkers, and Cecil Rhodes's Pioneers of the nineties, here came the political refugees and fortuné-hunters from the Hitler-wrought abomination of desolation. Would they find the South Africa of their dreams? And would my South Africa still be there? The pale reflection of the Southern Cross, showing itself so miserably above the inky sea, warned me and warned me again to put a leash upon my leaping hopes.

Meanwhile, far away to port, out of sight, lay the Congo

and Angola. And as we waddled on through their latitudes, I thought of the dazzling days I had spent traversing those lands, and visiting some of their uninhabited, unused bays. I remembered the Congo anthills as things of wonder. After all, they were the first skyscrapers in the world. Wherever I had looked in the Congo, there they were, immense, multitudinous. Fifteen, twenty, thirty feet high, they are fantastic castles in comparison with whose architecture Germany's medieval castles are prim and formal. From a large base they taper gracefully like the Eiffel Tower; they lurch awry like the Leaning Tower of Pisa; they pile up and up in zones like the modern miracles of Manhattan.

Below them, caverns and tunnels honeycomb the earth where the indefatigable termites bite deep and deeper into the bowels of Mother Nature. The stacking of Egypt's pyramids and the piling up of Rhodesia's Zimbabwe were less wonderful than the excavating and the building of these self-contained, water-supplied, many-walled cities. So complex and gigantic are they that some Europeans living among them in the Congo cannot believe that they are the result of white-ant energy. No, they will tell you, they are all deserted now, these saliva-cemented skyscrapers; the termites bustling about on their crust and throwing up a new storey are late-comers making use of the deserted metropolis planned and constructed by a race of giant-ants that has disappeared off the face of the earth, perhaps wiped out by disease, perhaps annihilated by new climatic conditions, perhaps consumed by ant-eaters, human, bestial, reptilian, during a prolonged famine in what has been so often a hunger-country.

When I repeated this theory to a spectacled, bearded entomologist in the *Umtali's* smoking-room, he threw back his splendid head and roared with laughter. The termites, still very much extant, undoubtedly had made these hills, as could be proved quite easily by a scientific examination of the old ones and the new. But they were right, these

amateur theorists, when they said that the deserted skyscrapers were very old. Several hundreds of years, they had
said? Well, they were being unduly cautious, there. These
great termite-nests, deserted, grown over with grass, bush
and aged trees, were thousands of years old, tens of thousands, a million.

Then, as the days and nights tumbled over each other,
we were paralleling South-West Africa, so that I thought
again of Peter Moor, the young German soldier who had
gone to fight the Hereros, leaving the corpses of some of his
friends upon the desert sand for the vultures and the jackals
and the ants. But by then he and they had done much
slaughter among the Hereros and driven the rest of the tribe
deep into the bush to die of hunger and thirst. This is how
he noted the flight of a nation that he and his comrades had
caused:

"Somewhere about midnight, as we were trotting up a
slowly ascending wagon trail, the Berliner raised his hand
and pointed to the right in front of us across a clearing.
Not five hundred yards from us, low on the ground, were
glowing several little covered fires, like cat's eyes in the
dark among the bushes. . . . I saw tracks of innumerable
children's feet, and among them those of full-grown feet.
Great troops of children, led by their mothers, had passed
over the road here. . . . The thought went through my
head: 'There lies a people, with all its children and all its
possessions, hard pressed on all sides by the horrible, deadly
lead, and condemned to death,' and it sent cold shudders
down my back. . . . We learned to our great amazement that
the enemy had withdrawn, was indeed in wild flight. . . .
The enemy had fled to the east with their whole enormous
mass,—women, children and herds. . . . How deeply the
wild, proud, sorrowful people had humbled themselves in
the terror of death! Wherever I turned my eyes lay their
goods in quantities: oxen and horses, goats and dogs,
blankets and skins. And there lay the wounded and the old,
women and children. A number of babies lay helplessly

languishing by mothers whose breasts hung down long and
flabby. Others were lying alone, still living, with eyes and
noses full of flies. Somebody sent out our black drivers and
I think they helped them to die. . . .

"Then came the news that the enemy, after overcoming
and passing the great stretch of waterless country, where
thousands of them had perished, were situated far to the
east on the further side of the sand field by some miserable
water-holes. The general decided to follow them thither,
to attack them and force them to go northward into thirst
and death, so that the colony would be left in peace and
quiet for all time. . . . At night we would see here and there
to the east of us the burning grass which they had set on
fire, and the fires of the single tribes which had detached
themselves from the main body and were trying to break
through to the west, to their old home, in order to escape a
cruel death from thirst. Scouting parties were sent out to
prevent their getting through. . . .

"Along the path lay many little burnt-out fires, and near
them all sorts of abandoned goods belonging to the enemy
or stolen by them, especially clothes and saddles and
Christian books which the missionaries had given or sold
them. The whole way was bestrewn with cattle which had
fallen dead. We had reached the path of the enemy's flight.
. . . From a hill we saw two mighty clouds of dust moving
rapidly to the north and north-east, toward certain death
from thirst."

Since then the South Africans, led by Generals Botha and
Smuts, had driven the German colonists out of their towns
and off their farms, driven them without much slaughter
into the bush, not to die of hunger and thirst but to surren-
der. Since then, in the course of a generation, the remnants
of the Hereros, emerging from the bush, have multiplied
and prospered; but to them, proud and even surly savages,
a Whiteman is a Whiteman, whether German, British or
Dutch, and a Whiteman is the enemy. By one of the minor
ironies of history, therefore, the Hereros, either not com-

prehending or being by nature ungrateful, have airily suggested that the United Nations should dispossess their
rescuers from their position of administrators of the vast
South-West, inhabited by many tribes, in order that they,
the Hereros, may possess the whole territory and be lords
over far more than they can possibly survey. For my part,
they can have it, anybody can have it, for South-West
Africa, diamonds and karakuls notwithstanding, is to me a
land of sin, sand, sorrow and sore eyes. It has lashings of
lebensraum between the desert and the unsown. Indeed the
United Nations, so cramped in their New York head-
quarters, might do very much worse than to build upon its
sand their modern Tower of Babel.

5

Belated by gale-lashed Cape rollers, we tumbled towards
Table Bay all anxious about the weather: not on account of
the fierce wind and heavy seas but lest clouds and rain might
spoil our view of Table Mountain. As we drew close, the
sun was clear of cloud; but a low cloudbank lifted itself
slowly above the skyline, straight ahead, with a dark mass
beneath it which at first puzzled us and then delighted us
as somebody exclaimed, "It's the Mountain!" The cloud,
flat and thin, like a pancake, was the rock's tablecloth; and
soon the rock itself, with bare, gaunt flanks, became clear
to the eye, its main surface throwing back at us the light of
the sun and its gorges and crevices being marked by
shadow.

To the left, Devil's Peak stood clear of all cloud save for
a whisp rising in a thin column, like smoke from a forest
fire—or from the reeking pipes of the Devil and van Hunks,
the pirate. The Devil and van Hunks? Yes; and here is the
story:[1]

[1] Ian D. Colvin, *South Africa* (Jack, incorporated with Nelson in 1917).

"Then van Hunks took the bag by its two bottom corners, and shook its contents on to a large flat stone. People say that there were eight pounds, no less, of strong tobacco, damp with rum, as sailors like it. He divided the heap into two equal parts. . . . Puff, puff, puff. A cloud of smoke was now about them; it swirled and eddied as it rose. It leaped the gulf from the Peak to the Mountain and clung to its rocky sides. It covered the top like a cloth. . . . The wind tossed the huge cloud in savage glee till it rocked and split and fell in fragments on the town. The burghers coughed and choked and drank brandy within closed doors, and said never had there been such a south-easter. . . . But van Hunks' face only took a darker purple while the stranger's grew first pale and then green. There was a damp clammy sweat upon his brow. 'Ugh!' he groaned at last, 'the fumes of hell are nothing to this.' 'Baccy a bit strong?' said the Dutchman, with a chuckle. . . . A blaze of lightning came at the same moment, making the cloud look like a pyramid of fire. There followed a dreadful smell of sulphur. Then the mist swept down upon the place. There was a cry, and when it rolled away there was no stranger and no van Hunks; but only a spot scorched bare of herbage. . . . And if you want any proof of my story, to this day the place is called the Devil's Peak. And when there is an ordinary south-easter, an old citizen will remark that the Devil is smoking today. But when it is a black south-easter, blowing great guns and tumbling cloud, then, he will say, it is the Devil and van Hunks."

To the right, perpendicularly serrated at regular intervals, I could see the wall divided into and known as the Twelve Apostles. Sloping gently away, shoulder to shoulder, the Twelve Apostles support Table Mountain and keep it in position, like an outsize architectural buttress to a medieval building. From our point of approach, Lion's Head, balancing Devil's Peak on the opposite side of Table Mountain, was dwarfed and indiscernible against the massive background of its betters. At first its invisibility was a puzzle; but binoculars solved it as they brought into focus its tapering head and its rump, called Signal's Hill, foreshortened into insignificance. I felt a slight pang of regret that Lion's Head had come off so badly in this stage-setting for our approach. Its lower altitude entitled it, by courtesy, to a lion's share of the ocular angles—and its name should have counted for something; but the *Umtali* was not interested in lines of vision but only in coming safely to harbour at this Cape of Storms. My regret was personal, for of the mountainous trinity—Devil's Peak, the Table and Lion's Head—my favourite was, and always had been, Lion's Head. Perhaps I am prejudiced, for, as a Cape Town schoolboy, I roamed its friendly sides and climbed over its shoulders for the swimming at Sea Point, Clifton and Camp's Bay; but as the Twelve Apostles disappeared and the ship was piloted into Table Bay, the angles fell true for Cape Town's heraldic badge—the outline of its mountainous trinity—and I thought again, as I cast a critical eye over the town's magnificent setting, that Lion's Head is friendlier than its two more austere companions. It may lack their solemn solidity, their massive dignity; but it possesses graceful contours and a variety of charming aspects, a most amiable personality and, what is even more rare in rocks, a quality that I identify as a sense of fun.

Low over the bay swept hundreds of seagulls, and hundreds of others bobbed up and down in the choppy water; high up the slopes of the mountains, as white as the seagulls in the sun, stood row upon row of houses as if resting before climbing still higher through the heath and the pines. We all felt elated, after our anxiety about the weather, at this sight of South Africa's Mother City, resplendent in the afternoon light. The long, lonely drag of the Atlantic lay behind us, and, gratefully, I rested my eyes upon the Whiteman's gateway to his African domains—the historic gateway of discovery which allowed him to outflank the equatorial jungles and fevers to secure his foothold upon the Dark Continent. It remains his chief African gateway, though now his aeroplanes are flying regularly over the equatorial belt, direct to the Transvaal plateau; but cargo and the great majority of travellers still come this way to the far south. And they will continue to do so, I imagine, into the indefinite future, newer and larger aeroplanes notwithstanding. The harbour, newly walled against stormy seas, snuggles against the city itself, from which, at the moment, it is only separated by a level stretch of ground reclaimed from a segment of the curving bay. Upon this new area of land, created by Dutch engineers from the East Indies (who pumped the shelving sea-bed up on to the shore) the town-planners are now busy, determined to make good use of a second chance to build their city. The long, concrete pier, finding itself on dry land, has gracefully disappeared. Now the big ships tie up where the pier used to be, virtually at the foot of Adderley Street, the main street bisecting the city, and actually at the end of its extension, known as King's Way since His Majesty King George VI entered Cape Town by that route on February 17th, 1947, in his capacity of King of the Union of South Africa.

Cape Town, therefore, like the true Mother City she is, embraces you as you arrive. Strangers and sons are equally caught up into her unaffected but affecting welcome. I could feel her easy hospitality even before we tied up. It was in the air. I was exhilarated by the general atmosphere of joy that we all now breathed, but, in a quite maddening way, Merrick's Conrad unobtrusively joined me where I stood clutching the deck-rail and whispered his sad disillusionments in my ear.

Still, the Table Mountain trinity and the Mother City, seen in this perfect way, had given me a good beginning, a reassuring beginning. The good-natured bustle on the wharf, the coloured porters with their eager help and smiling faces, the brilliant light over everything, the changing colours of the tablecloth under the rays of the setting sun— all were reminiscent of a happier past. But as the eye was keenly appreciating these things (both because their unaltered appearance momentarily rubbed out chaotically changed Europe and because, in any case, they were delightful in themselves) the ear was filled with a chanting which was something quite new—foreign, one might almost say—in this place: it was the hearty, harmonised chanting of Bantu dock-hands. Ten years before there were no Bantu tribesmen working as far south as this—there never had been any, except for a few imported slaves. The Kafir wars of the Cape's far eastern border had kept them, in the early part of the nineteenth century, six hundred miles away from Table Bay.

Then the diamond mines had drawn them to Kimberley for the wages of hard work, regularly performed—something utterly unknown before to Bantu men. But in the Cape Peninsula their muscles were not needed as there were the pure-bred Malays and the mixed Coloured People, compounded of Hottentots, Malays, West Coast Negroes, East Coast Bantu and Europeans. As the Dutch colonists serviced the ships of the Dutch East India Company and planted their gardens, orchards and vineyards, a tiny new race sprang into existence around them—God's step-children as the South African novelist, Sarah Gertrude Millin, calls them. I had long heard the warning, "The Bantu are coming", a political cry; but, here they were, in the very Mother City of White South Africa—they had come a long way since the border wars had kept them in their place and prevented their trespassing in lands where they had never set foot. And they were chanting below me, as they manhandled bales and shouldered railway trucks into position, with all the sonorous zest which makes the air of their tribal villages vibrate when custom or mood demands it. Was their presence here a portent, I wondered, as I raised my hat to all I could see and hear and greeted it with a comprehensive "South Africa, I presume?"

6

POSTSCRIPT

The stranger to Cape Town should make a bee-line for
the Visitors' Information Bureau of the Cape Peninsula
Publicity Association; and the Travel Department of the
South African Railways. They are both conveniently situated
in Adderley Street. Between them, they have all the answers
to the questions of those who wish to see as much as possible
in the time at their disposal. In the Visitors' Information
Bureau are reading and writing rooms; and, apart from
personal advice on sightseeing and shopping, accommodation and education, residential and social amenities, there
are free guide-books and maps of Cape Town and the
Peninsula.

There is plenty to see in Cape Town before going farther
afield—the Michaelis Gallery of Dutch and Flemish paintings, the Koopmans de Wet House of antique Cape furniture, Government Avenue and the Botanical Gardens, the
star-shaped Castle built by the Dutch East India Company,
the views from the top of Table Mountain, whose height of
3,500 feet is won in the swinging comfort of a cable-car,
the beauties of the mountain roads that converge at Kloof
Nek, the exquisite loveliness of Kirstenbosch where a
botanist's dream comes true, Groote Schuur—the house that
Rhodes built, and Lord Charles Somerset's shooting box
where one takes tea while resting the eyes on the Twelve
Apostles above and Camp's Bay below.

Cape Town's other official name is Kaapstad, the Afrikaans version, for South Africa is a country of two languages,
two capitals (Cape Town the legislative: Pretoria the
administrative) and two flags. Originally it was called
simply De Kaap. That was in the days of its founding in
1652 by Jan van Riebeeck of the Dutch East India Company. De Kaap served then as a halfway house on the sea-
roads to India and the Far East. "The Tavern of the Seas"
is its nickname. It was still fulfilling its role of a halfway
house in the 1940–45 war when a million and more soldiers,

sailors and airmen of the United Nations in their hundreds of ships paused for shelter and food.

Nearly half a million people make up the city's mixed population. The census of 1946 revealed the following racial proportions—Europeans 214,201; Coloured (or mixed race) 197,484; Asiatics 7,959; Natives (or Bantu) 34,408. They are scattered round the base of Table Mountain and its neighbours—Devil's Peak (3,300 feet) on the east and Lion's Head (2,175 feet) on the west. They represent the cultural extremes of primitive Africa, of the mystic East, and of transplanted Europe.

Above them towers not only Table Mountain but its human brother, General Smuts, who, though small in physical stature, is one of the world's landmarks—a mountain of a man. Going on for eighty, he still spurns the cable-car, the easy way, but toils to the summit of Table Mountain on his own feet. Up there, in dedicating a war memorial to his fellow mountaineers, he said, "Table Mountain was their cathedral, where they heard subtler music and saw wider visions and were inspired with a loftier spirit. Here in life they breathed the great air: here in death their memory will fill the upper spaces."

CHAPTER II

"SOUTH AFRICA, I PRESUME?"

I

STANLEY'S FAMOUS phrase as he advanced on Dr. Livingstone was not, of course, a genuine query but merely Victorian courtesy practised in the timeless African jungle. Contrariwise, my adaptation of it, as I approached South Africa, was not a polite, geographical greeting: it was an anxious question that I asked myself. From the protective framework of the Whiteman's school, the Whiteman's office, the Whiteman's club, the Whiteman's home, I had been familiar with a South Africa of the Whiteman's making, perhaps of the Whiteman's imagination. Would it still be that South Africa, or had that South Africa dissolved with the mirage of a romantic yesterday? So I went ashore doubtfully, cautiously, like a stranger in a strange land.

Certainly it is a strange if interesting family that the Mother City of South Africa has begot. That I saw at once. Part White, part Coloured, part Malay, part Indian, part Black, it is a lively family, which swarms round the slopes of the mountains and spills over the Cape Flats. The presence of this mixed humanity, talking English, Afrikaans and Xosa, is a fact transcending all others in importance about Cape Town. Even before the recent arrival of the Bantu's advance party, the city's Malays and Coloured People gave it a pattern and a character which I had found fascinating in the early years of the Union, established in 1910. In those days, however, the Cape Coloured People were much more in the background; and Cape Town's Whites took their services and their state of virtual serfdom very much for granted. The Whites occupied the foreground, a very generous foreground where they had plenty of elbow-room.

When they wanted things done for them, they beckoned
to Coloured persons in the shadows who promptly skipped
forward. And when the tasks were done, the Coloured
persons faded magically back into the shadows. Or so it
seemed if you were a permanent resident of Cape Town,
busy with your own life, your daily routine and having,
therefore, a personal, limited view of the world developing
out of the early settlements of the Dutch East India Company. It was a small but distinctly new world; and as I
observed this new world on the first day of my return to it,
I was surprised by the ubiquity of the Coloureds. As a
community, obviously they had multiplied and pushed one
another into the foreground. Whites and Coloureds were
jostling each other in the streets and crowding together on
to tram-cars, buses and into trains. Under the hot sun, they
were mingling in the city's workaday life.

Thinking that, as I had come straight from all-white
London, I might be exaggerating this intermingling of the
two main parts of the population, I checked what I saw with
White residents. I fully expected, remembering the limited
view of those who move by routine along the same daily
beat between home and office, that they would say I was
mistaken; but, instead, they fully confirmed my impression
of a society crowding in upon itself at the main places where
it worked and moved. They were fully conscious of it and
rather downcast about it. They, the Mother City's children,
felt that their style was being cramped by God's step-
children. The stepchildren were now everywhere. And not
only were they everywhere, but they were demanding
everything. From being a boon they were becoming a
burden. For generations they had enjoyed the privilege of
the franchise, but, as their earning capacity remained low,
they contributed only a trifling amount to government
treasuries, so that the Whites had to pay for the houses and
the education of the Coloureds and, indeed, for all the
civilised amenities required by their growing community—
a community as numerous as Cape Town's White com-

munity. Whole suburbs were changing their character as the result of the Whites moving out as the Coloureds crowded in. I visited some of these suburbs and at least two of them had been fashionable and select twenty years before: now the Coloureds were flooding in after an unnoticed period of quiet infiltration.

The few Whites who remain are the last survivors of a prosperous, house-proud upper class. One such survivor, an old friend of mine, said to me as I dined at his home one night, "We are just a little island of Europeans here in a rising sea of Coloureds". He spoke a trifle sadly but with a fatalism which for a South African is reckoned a kind of defeatism in this context; but, for the most part, his approach to the subject was direct, matter-of-fact, topographical. At times he might have been a real estate agent discussing the monetary value of suburban property. He named streets and even particular houses: he pointed in their direction; and then, with a sweep of the hand, he described the living streams of the Coloureds, overflowing from their main pool, and traced the local lines along which they were moving. "So you see," he concluded, with unintentional drama, "we are surrounded." Despite this phraseology, he was not suggesting that he was being hemmed in by a hostile people; but he was saying quite clearly that he was being hemmed in by the Coloured People. Born and bred in Cape Town, where he had been in business all his adult life, he knew the Coloured People well, understood their virtues and failings, and sympathised with them in their hard struggle for a place for themselves between a master-race of Whites and the great southward-surging mass of Blacks. But, for the moment, he was considering his own position, the position of his family, and the position of his relatives and friends. They did not want to be hemmed in by the Coloureds; they did not want to be cut off from their former neighbours by a widening belt of Coloureds; quite naturally, they wanted, on the contrary, to be living in the midst of fellow Whites, with whom they could easily exchange visits, whose children would be going to and coming from school together, whose lives ran together in the normal order of things.

The Coloureds, however, must live somewhere besides in District Six, that festering slum which, slowly, systematically, is being cleared and rebuilt. The narrow, unhealthy alleyways with their filthy, overcrowded houses are being replaced by great blocks of flats. They tower up from the hillside, lifting their heads high above the squalor and dilapidation of the old Coloured quarter, where vice and disease have flourished in the past and still flourish, rotting the heart and perishing the soul of a between-folk already psychologically unbalanced. They breed fast, like all slum dwellers, and find it difficult to uproot themselves from the mucky backyards, the malodorous, melancholy huddle of insanitary houses and tenements, from the hideous streets which have been their home, their town, their all as the years have fallen away between three wars—the Boer War and the two great German wars. But the overflow of their population, even against the personal wish of individuals clinging to the old familiar places of District Six, was inevitable, and so the Coloureds spread out into the great emptiness of the Cape Flats, building themselves *pondokkies*, shacks, of wattle trees, galvanised iron and sacking; while others, not penurious but earning regular wages, moved by groups of families into houses—some jerry-built for them and by them, others vacated by Whites transferring to new homes. The Whites, also increasing, established new suburbs on sites adjacent to areas occupied by Coloureds; and so a double movement developed in which the resulting pattern tends to resemble a tangle of white and coloured twine.

2

To simplify this informal pattern, excellent municipal townships for the Coloureds have been and are being built

c

in the wattle-smothered, sandy Cape Flats. Into the well-designed houses, built on curving streets with schools and shopping centres adequately provided, are moving the denizens of the *pondokkies*, those displaced by the systematic slum clearance schemes in District Six, and those who are hiving off from the parental home. A great sorting out is thus going on under a master plan which may be summed up by borrowing the term coined by the late General Hertzog, the two-stream policy, though it was applied by him to the altogether different problem of balancing the political claims and aspirations of the two main sections of the White population, the British South Africans and the Afrikaners. This two-stream policy is not political, in that sense, but social in the simplest meaning of that word. It seeks, in a practical way, to provide a partially separate way of life for Coloureds and Whites, to give home space for each, and thus to eliminate the human friction set up by neighbours of different clans, different colours, different temperaments, and different social classes, thrown together higgledy-piggledy in an expanding population.

From these townships on the Cape Flats fast and frequent trains transport the Coloureds to their places of work in and around Cape Town; but the master plan envisages industrial areas, already plotted, out on the Cape Flats, paralleling the townships. This would save the Coloureds time, expense and fatigue in their daily travel, prevent congestion in Cape Town and thus eliminate excessive intermingling and confusion.

There are special housing schemes for the Malays, whose old, picturesque quarter of early Dutch style, high-verandaed houses, is being cleaned up in its slummy parts on the lower, townward slope of Signal Hill, and being extended, higher up, in the form of many-storeyed blocks of flats. And there are other schemes, again, for the Bantu, who, even when disallowed railway tickets by the authorities who do not want them to leave their own Transkei reserves, walk hundreds of miles to secure jobs in the widening spiral of

Cape Town employment. The Malays, as the fez and the yashmak proclaim, are Mohammedans who, in consequence, live very much within themselves; and, although speaking what might almost be described as a sub-dialect of Afrikaans, they maintain, in modified form, the customs and traditions, the social habits and creeds, the superstitions, cooking recipes and dress styles they brought with them from the East, whence they arrived as slaves and political prisoners in the seventeenth century.

The Bantu, on the other hand, like the Coloureds, are, for the most part, Christians, with the background and customs of the Transkei tribes. They, too, have their social customs, their way of cooking, and their method of life; and all these different notions and habits have to be taken into the calculations of those devising the details of the master plan. It is a gigantic task, all this, and costs far more than the Cape Town ratepayers can afford; but the Provincial Government contributes its share of the costs by paying for and running the schools, while the Union Government pays the largest share of all out of the central Treasury. But the provision of these capital funds is becoming an increasing strain on the resources of the three treasuries, municipal, provincial and national, which depend on the Whites for the taxes gathered to fill them each year. The answer to this serious difficulty has yet to be found.

Some ask higher wages for the Coloureds so that they will, as a community, move economically upward to the income level from which taxes may be drained off. Others say this will kill the industries to which the Coloureds are being recruited as factory-hands on an ever-rising scale. The middle way seems to be the one along which a solution may be found, opinion crystallising to support the view that the industries benefiting by cheap labour must contribute to the cost of providing their workers with sub-economic houses. This, it is argued, may not be the final answer, but it may serve during a long interim period before South Africa can possibly arrive at the logical point of a fair and open labour field for all, equal pay being given for equal work, and no favours to any one section, no matter what their class, colour or creed.

The Millennium is not yet—anywhere in the world; and the evidence of history seems to suggest that the Millennium must come to Europe, America, and Asia before it comes to Africa, with so much of it still uncivilised, with scarcely any of it enlightened, and with its lagging at the barbaric end of Man's straggling column of march to the perhaps mythical land of freedom and plenty.

Despite my harshly drawn outline of the social shape of Cape Town, the Coloureds and the Malays get a great deal of fun out of their lives, which are easy and carefree in comparison with the lives of great masses of workers in Europe and Asia and even in the United States, judging from what I have seen in such cities as Chicago and Detroit. They are still play-children in a world which elsewhere has so largely had the spirit of play knocked out of it. To them the thrumming guitar is the sound of earthly paradise and they sing and dance to its rhythms with a wild joy. Although the Malays and Coloureds are separate communities, they merge by miscegenation in the outer fringes of their communities, a practice which the leaders and elders of both frown upon.

Miscegenation with Whites also occurs, though the social taboo against such a casual liaison is so powerful that it is comparatively rare and then more or less secret and a disallowed topic of polite conversation. The children of such love affairs are usually of a lighter complexion than the ordinary Coloured person, and sometimes so much so that, given the right set of circumstances, they pass as Whites and take their places in and even marry into the White community. To make the pass is to be a success, in the opinion of the Coloureds. It means going from the lower to the higher class, from the under- to the over-privileged. When such a passing takes place, the fortunate one's Coloured relatives and Coloured parent, according to their own strict code of loyalty, do not give him or her away; and, in order that they may not even do so unintentionally, they recognise their "White" son or daughter, brother or sister no more. Apparently unseeing, they pass one another in the street without greeting one another. This is not an easy exercise in restraint, as family feeling among them is strongly affectionate and they are passionately attached to their homes.

3

The Coloureds, as a people, align themselves with the Whites and not with the Blacks, or with the Malays—or with the Indians who, like the Bantu, are more in evidence in Cape Town than they used to be; but, thus far, the Indians do not form a settled community as they are not allowed to stay there longer than a special permit specifies. Thereafter they must return whence they came—Natal, usually—and apply for another permit. This they resent, arguing that, since they are nationals of the Union by birth or naturalisation, they should be allowed to move freely about the country, from one Province to another, to wherever their work may take them; but the Whites—and in this they probably would be supported by the Coloureds and the Malays—oppose giving them the right of permanent residence. The present racial composition already makes for a complicated social pattern and they are unwilling to face the extra difficulty of providing a way of life for the Indians who, therefore, are migrants, readily finding work as waiters in Cape Town's numerous hotels.

The Malays are often tailors, carpenters and masons, while the Cape Coloureds are fishermen, farm hands and factory workers. Having the vote, they are a factor in the general elections, while several of their own folk are members of the municipal council. These members will be more numerous when the new Coloured townships are occupied, for then various units, scattered in predominantly White constituencies, will be massed together in such a way that they will have an almost all-Coloured franchise in those localities—another advantage which these new suburbs will have for them. Those I visited in their new houses were extremely pleased with them and their modern appurtenances of heat, light, water and sanitation; and they were already vying with one another as planters of kitchen and flower gardens.

The Bantu, too, told me they were well satisfied with the rooms given them in great blocks of flats with communal dining rooms and kitchens in adjacent halls; but they present special problems as they regard themselves as migrants—they are practically all men who come to earn wages for a while and then return to their homes and families in the Transkei. They are apt to be homesick and difficult —rather like new boys at boarding school for the first time. These Bantu newcomers, however, are obviously the fore-runners of a settled community of Blacks: they will, in the course of a few years, become a permanent part of Cape Town's developing industrial life, and where the men of the Transkei go their womenfolk will follow—if need be, on foot.

Perched higher up Signal Hill, the Malays are already accustomed to the modern flats which have replaced, in many cases, their old homes in the streets lower down. Their only complaint is that, although it is within a very short distance of the centre of Cape Town, it is something of a stiff climb on a hot summer's day; the justice of this com-plaint is admitted, and some suitable mode of transport will be organised for them as soon as supplies and finances are available to the Whites.

"The Malay Quarter", writes a Cape Town journalist,[1] "is like a gappy mouth now—like a mouth with several teeth missing. There is a shabbiness about the place, but you forget it in the laughter and the singing of the Cape

[1] Tom Macdonald in the June 1947 number of *Milady*, Cape Town.

Malays. . . . The old houses seem to lean towards you like a welcome. . . . They are symbols of the lost art of a simple and delightful architecture. . . . Surely, there is nothing in the tapestry of Cape Town which has more romance than a Malay bridal coach, the four white horses wearing ostrich feather plumes, the coachman with his quaint headdress and, beside him, the little fellow wearing white gloves. And, of course, the most gracious picture of all, the bride in white. Some brides have four bridal dresses. The bridal coach brings a white light to the dingy street. In the Quarter you will find stables in dim courtyards. Somebody is always cleaning the brasses that jingle on the harness of white horses. . . . The Malay is the fellow with the everlasting guitar. His songs are rich in rhythms. He listens to Arabic in his mosque but his home language is Afrikaans. The fellows are lounging against the street-corners in groups— they seem to be always there. The streets are alive with children. . . . Whence came all the fig trees? You find them all over the place. They grow in cobbled yards. They are good for hanging out the washing. Every day is washing day in the Quarter; washing hanging out in yards, from window-sills and in passages. Never at any time of the day is any street without colour if it is only for the fez. . . . You will see streams of old men, bearded, with bent backs, all going the same way to a mosque. And there is glory in the robes of the priests. Colour everywhere in the strong sunlight, in the women's dresses, in curtains and draperies. The young girls have lovely features. The children have warm faces. Step down into a basement and see the Malay tailors at their work. They are deft tailors—craftsmen who have not lost the pride in work. Slip into an alleyway and into a carpenter's shop, rich with the smell of wood, rich, too, in pride of work. The very hands that fashion the furniture pieces have the colour of the wood they handle. . . . In the Quarter you find chickens everywhere—perched on the windows and the stoeps, white specks in the shadows. . . . And when the moon is full, like the harvest moon the

other night, the fascination is complete. The gaps are softened. The grime is washed away by the moonlight. There
is something of the mystery of the Arabian Nights in this
old-world corner. You can feel that at any time as you turn
a corner you may meet Ali Baba—but you wouldn't be
surprised to find Aladdin."

One night I myself climbed to the old Malay quarter,
rainswept and dark, to witness the mysterious sword trial.
Along a narrow alley I groped my way to an open doorway
through which yellow light streamed. It was the house I
was seeking. A smiling Malay, well dressed, a black fez
upon his head, guided me to a narrow, spiral staircase up
whose wooden boards I assisted myself by hand-hoists
along its rail. The upper room, dimly lit, was filled with an
eager crowd of Malays and Whites who, like myself, had
come to see what terrors and mysteries the *khalifah* had to
offer; and it was filled, too, with an indefinable incense of
the East, neither pleasant nor unpleasant, but usefully
persistent as a counter to the odour of mixed humanity,
herded together in this ramshackle yet ill-ventilated room.
Tambourines began to murmur and then, in company with
the guitars, to talk with repetitive phraseology and the
tempo of the human heart-beat. One's blood and mind
were soon throbbing within the easy, inevitable ebb and
flow of their primitive rhythms. The musicians sat cross-
legged behind a high open screen, half altar, half rack,
upon which reposed, tier above tier, a curious assortment of
long pins, three-pronged spikes, and a variety of long swords.
Beside these instruments of spirit-discipline and flesh-
control, stood the calif, the *khalifah*, an old, short, wiry
Malay, part priest, part gymnast: his body swayed to the
swing of the orchestra, whose brief but endlessly repeated
melody was sometimes lifted from its monotony by male
voices rising up in sudden fervent cadences as the soul of
some worshipper, now here, now there, was stirred. Sitting
on the floor in two parallel lines before the sword-rack, and
facing one another, were the disciples of the cult, adjusting

their minds and bodies to the music and preparing themselves by silent prayer for the ordeal by self-torture which
they so ardently wished to undergo. This was the test of the
spirit by the play of sword upon flesh.

The lithe little priest or acolyte of the sacred swords
allowed the disciples to sway and pray for some time before
putting them to the first tests. Then, when he felt that they
had been caught up into the protective arms of their gods,
he handed two of them a pair of treble-toothed spikes. They
rose to grasp a spike in each hand and these, as they danced
in a slow circle throwing the balance of their weight from
one foot to the other, they plunged against their belly,
shielded only by a cotton shirt. They did so on a major
beat of the short, echoing refrain. Then two other disciples
had given into their right hands long, light, slightly curving
swords: with these they wove flashing figures above their
heads before whipping the razor-sharp blades downwards
—downwards against the tender-skinned inner side of their
left arms. Again the stroke synchronised with a major beat of
the music. Others had long pins thrust through their cheeks
and ears, or bore the steady weight of heavy blades against
their necks, or stood, barefoot, upon the sharp edge of a
sabre.

If faith brought them through these tortures unscathed,
bodily cunning at least contributed something towards their
safety. On the downward thrust of the treble-toothed spikes,
the belly was drawn in to harden the muscles and to give
with the impact instead of opposing it too suddenly. As the
sword reached the end of its stroke, the arm was lowered
to travel with instead of against its blade. I do not pretend
to know the whole technique of these spectacular tricks,
but I imagine the skin may resist three prongs, equally
angled, whereas, in all probability, one straight point would
bite deep into the flesh; and by a play of the fingers, the
skin of the inner side of the arm may be kept loose and not
tautened so that it is merely depressed on the first light
touch of the edge—and the sword, by skilful timing, is

lifted before laceration is possible; the soles of the feet, if placed firmly and evenly upon the sword's blade, will remain uncut through counter-balance—especially if they have been strengthened by washing them in a solution of alum.

And so on; but I do not lay down the law on these matters, for I do not know it; and I would say that even with such tricks as these, the *khalifah's* sword-play is still an ordeal which not many of us would care to undergo— an ordeal requiring great discipline of mind and body, accurate calculation, confidence in hand and heart. If it is not a miracle, neither is it a fake. Blood runs, as I saw it run in that upper room of the Malay Quarter, if the hand of the swordsman shakes or his leg trembles. I can well believe that long contemplation, to free the mind from the distractions of daily life, and a prayer-fortified spirit to strengthen the weak flesh, are helpful to those who practise this curious cult.

There are other strange cults among the Malays— fortune-telling, magic for lovers, necromancy, voodooism. But all that is only the dark side of the lives of these thirty thousand worshippers of Allah and followers of Mahomet; and there is much light for them. As a Cape Town author[1] reminds us, "tomorrow the sun will break warmly over the flat-roofed houses with their high stoeps, and from the minaret the priest will call the Faithful to prayer. Then you will hear the cobbled streets resounding to the clatter of the wooden sandals called kamparangs. . . . Well-shaped, clear-cut features and black, oblique eyes, delicate hands and small feet, rounded foreheads; by these signs you may distinguish the Malays. The women have fine teeth in spite of their fondness for sweets. They wear the gold earrings prettily in their oiled, straight, black hair. Some cling to the yashmak—all women who follow the teachings of Mahomet strictly should go veiled—but there are many who have abandoned the custom. The men can appear extremely

[1] Lawrence G. Green in *So Few are Free* (Timmins, Cape Town, 1946).

well dressed on occasion. . . . The Cape was the convict station of the East; but the Malays were mainly political prisoners rather than criminals, and there were men of royal blood among them. . . . Some of Cape Town's first restaurants were started by Malays, and you can still see cafés where the food has a decidedly Oriental flavour, where *kabobs* of mutton are served with rice, and where queer sweets, gaily coloured, are displayed in the windows. Malay coachmen won renown as safe and expert drivers. For years the Rogge Bay fishery was ruled by them, and the Malay fish-hawker with his conical hat and two baskets slung across his shoulders on a bamboo yoke was a familiar sight in Cape Town up to the middle of last century. . . . Cape Town sends more pilgrims to Mecca than any other Muslim community of the same size in the world. A wharf in Table Bay Docks, when the pilgrims arrive or depart, becomes a brilliant rival to Baghdad; a parade of coloured silk and headdresses worn by massed thousands of well-wishers struggling to kiss the cheeks of the pilgrims and send them away with the double hand-clasp of Islam. . . . The songs of the Malays, those peculiar to the Cape Malays that is to say, are called *gommaliedjies*. Some are songs that were known in Holland centuries ago; forgotten there, they are kept alive by Malays whose ancestors heard Dutch sailors singing them at the Tavern of the Seas. Guitars and drums beat out the rhythm of these old tunes from the Netherlands and the East Indies."

4

Despite racial complications, which approximate to class complications elsewhere in the world, the Whites hold themselves lucky to be living in Cape Town—and in the Cape generally. That was always so, but they do so more consciously today when their newspapers, radio, and news-reels, their kinsfolk returning home from England and

visitors from Europe all tell of the severe tribulations of the
peoples overseas who are desperately struggling amid the
ruinous consequences of war. They do what they can to
help Great Britain to regain her economic health, just as
they did what they could to reinforce Great Britain's fighting
forces in both German wars. Their record of living and dying
for the British or Commonwealth cause in this generation
of sustained world crisis, their record in war and peace, bears
comparison with the record of the United Kingdom itself
or with the records of Canada, Australia and New Zealand.
While their conscience is clear, therefore, there is nothing
smug or boastful about their conduct, but only a regret that
their sacrifices and help could and can be only on a scale
commensurate with their small size as a community—and
that holds good, of course, not only for the Whites of Cape
Town but for the South Africans as a tiny nation occupying
a large country in company with four times as many non-
Whites.

But they would be either fools, or not be human at all,
if they did not enjoy, despite the European crisis, the
beauties and benefits of their own country in which it is
their lot and duty to live. Mortification of their flesh and
chastisement of their spirit would be of no possible service
to Europe, so they run like Greek athletes in the sun and on
the sand of their beaches, laughing in the spray blown from
the green-bodied, cream-crested combers crashing in from
the cold, westerly Atlantic and from the warm, easterly
Indian Ocean. Gratefully they eat the many fruits that grow
and ripen in their fertile valleys at Constantia and Paarl and
Stellenbosch, at Wellington and Ceres, and drink the wine
that they make where their labourers thread the hillside
vineyards, picking heavy bunches of black, white, and purple
grapes. Fruits are plentiful; whether peach or pineapple,
pomegranate or plum, melon, tangerine, apricot or orange,
strawberry, grapefruit, lemon, apple, pear, or nectarine.
And others come to their tables from the Northern Transvaal
and Natal—mango, banana, avocado, lichi, pawpaw.

Out of their seas are dragged heavy net-loads of fish of all varieties, from the spiny crawfish to the oily snoek, fish with formidable names such as musselcracker, kabeljauw and seventy-four. From their hinterland come mutton, beef, venison, or buck as they call it, partridge, guinea-fowl and quail. Milk, cheeses of many kinds, butter, honey, eggs—all these are produced in such quantities that there is an abundance of them for the Whites; but there is not an abundance of them for export, partly because South Africa, as a whole, is a poor agricultural country, partly because of the limited White manpower applying itself to agricultural and pastoral pursuits, and partly because the Blacks, traditionally content with maize, kafir-corn, sour milk and an occasional feast of beef, are acquiring a taste for the Whiteman's foods; but, while eating such things as bread, cheese, butter, vegetables, fruit and meat more regularly, and drinking tea and coffee with sugar and milk, they are doing very little themselves, in their own reserves, to increase the production of these foods, with the exception of beef. And, with the competitive drag of industrialism, White farmers find it more and more difficult to obtain Black labourers.

However, this is a problem which hardly touches the life of the average individual in Cape Town: for him that is a national problem for the politicians and economists to solve as they talk and talk, from January to June, in the classically designed Houses of Parliament which show themselves through the oak-trees of Government Avenue, an extension of Adderley Street, linking the town with the Botanical Gardens. The original oak-trees of this restful avenue, which is reserved for pedestrians, were planted by Simon van der Stel, one of the early Dutch Governors of the Cape, and so were the Gardens, in which grow plants and trees from all parts of the world; and in the central streets and squares of Cape Town, the simple lines and plain surfaces of certain houses and buildings, with their parts nobly pro-portioned, remind us, here and there among the taller modern blocks, of Holland's Golden Age, the age of her East India Company, whose wealth gave her colonial officials and free burghers the opportunity of building and living spaciously.

"Building in South Africa", state the authorities,[1] "had a propitious beginning. The early Dutch settlers brought with them a deep-rooted and flourishing cultural and craft tradition. They came from a land then at the zenith of its commercial power, and were equipped with the organising ability and acumen proper to the dawning mercantile age. ... At that stage building took on the character of permanence. The small community, centred at the Castle, now expanded rapidly beyond its immediate confines. An attractive and imaginative layout for the houses, public buildings and gardens gave an impetus to building of an appropriate civic character, while the villages and farmhouses, spread over the broad and fertile lands of the peninsula, developed a style and a technique in building in keeping with a magnificent setting. ... The Revocation of the Edict of Nantes brought Huguenot refugees to the colony. Well qualified technically, industrious and creative, they made a distinctive contribution in a period of widespread architectural activity. ... The direct stylistic influences were thus the gabled and shuttered brick houses of Holland (with their cleanly organised interiors), and the late Baroque architecture of Europe. ... But considerable difference in climatic conditions, in material resources and in the nature of the colonial settlement called for a rapid modification in technique, and as a consequence, in design approach. Thus the impossibility of producing hard weathering facing bricks meant a great restriction in the use of such face-bricks as could be imported, while the plastering of the exterior surfaces of buildings became a necessity. Malay slaves, brought from the East, proved excellent craftsmen and established a tradition for good workmanship which persists to the present day.

[1] South African authors and editors of the October 1944 number of *The Architectural Review* (London).

"The greater freedom in design which plaster allowed led to sweeping changes in the shaping of the gable, and to its dominance in the horizontal composition natural to farm buildings. In fact, all the elements taken over from the architecture of Holland were used in pure and modified form, but in a new context. Gable, window, stoep, doorway and loft, though bearing a family resemblance to their prototypes, took on a different functional significance. The formative process is clearly to be seen in the use of local reeds for thatching, of indigenous yellow wood and stink-wood for some purposes and imported teak for other, of standard size panes from Europe, of local 'stock' bricks for walling and imported 'klompjes' for special work. . . . The temperate climate generally gave the opportunity for outdoor living, hence the development of the oak-shaded stoep which, incidentally, was used for a generous hospitality. Spells of hot weather encouraged the use of thatch for roofing and shuttered, widely disposed windows for the lofty spacious interiors. . . . The dominant farmhouse was usually flanked by the wine cellar, the slave quarters and the stables, and these, together with carefully treated adjuncts such as slave bell towers, pigeon houses and enclosing walls, formed a complex which the designers were particularly adept in grouping and siting. . . .

"The town houses of the burghers of Cape Town, the public buildings and the churches, though by no means stereotyped, reached a degree of uniformity in fundamentals without which neither harmony nor monumentality is possible in city planning. The general scale, however, was homely, varying, in the houses, from the two-storeyed formal and lofty façades of those of the wealthier citizens, to the more modest single-storeyed type which the majority of townsfolk built for themselves. The simplicity of the wall surfaces of the latter was offset by gaily moulded parapets, capable of infinite variety. Eventually all were flat-roofed, as a necessary precaution against the ravages of fire. Undoubtedly, the town as a whole gained in appearance in

the final result. Today the atmosphere of historic Cape
Town has, of course, been largely dissipated in the rapid
growth of the modern city. It is a loss all the way along the
line. The spaciousness of layout and the firm and imaginative handling of simple building forms and materials are
qualities singularly lacking in the Cape Town of today.
It is possible that the extension of the city on to a new
fore-shore, made possible by a large-scale reclamation
scheme, will bring back a generous approach to land
use and to civic amenity so characteristic of the original
settlers."

Some of those free burghers, brought to the Cape at
the end of the eighteenth century, were, as already stated,
French Huguenots, whose skilled craftsmen influenced the
Dutch architecture by adorning it with frescoes and decorative ironwork; and they introduced the double-storeyed
houses, with a railinged balcony above the veranda, which
are such a feature of the old streets running up from the city
to the area known as the Gardens at the residential end of
Government Avenue. These balconied houses, sometimes
semi-detached or in rows, with flower gardens about them,
made it occur to me that there is much about Cape Town
reminiscent of New Orleans, with its early French influence
still upon it, its special foods, it warm, lazy summer, and
its Coloured-folk, laughing good-humouredly as they do
the chores for the Whites. On one of the overhanging
balconies a Whiteman and his wife may be seen being served
with tea by a Coloured-girl whose head is covered with a
bright scarf; in the garden a Coloured-man goes slowly
about his work. In a neighbouring garden a Coloured
nurse is playing with two White children. Through the
streets a horse-drawn fish-cart rumbles, heralded by un-
musical but far-travelling blasts from a horn blown by a
Malay fishmonger. Past him flash large American and
small British motor-cars, driven by White businessmen or
their wives out on a shopping expedition; and he is over-
taken by a Malay-driven hansom cab, its horse a-jingle,

Said to be the work of Captain Louis Michel Thibault, a member of the Dutch East India Company's garrison, it graces an inner court of Cape Town Castle, and marks the golden period of the Mother City's architecture.

Europeans and Africans building blocks of flats near Cape
Town to provide accommodation for Bantu migrants from
the Siskei and Transkei Reserves.

its ears stuck through a high-pointed, wide-brimmed hat of woven straw. In a kitchen, White mistress and Coloured cook-girl discuss the day's purchases and the night's dinner; and, occasionally, as both a ritual and a treat, the main dish will be prepared from a recipe favoured by the early Dutch colonists and originating, probably, from the Malays and the East Indies. Such dishes are apt to be spiced, curried, or served with a highly seasoned sauce. They please a slow palate, but may quarrel with a weak stomach. Once you begin with them, they are hard to leave off. Indigestion forgotten, the memory of their varied aromas and flavours lingers on and, in due season, demands more.

5

"I am dizzy with beauty!" exclaimed an English visitor to me when I asked him how he had enjoyed his day's motoring round the mountains. The scenery of the Cape Peninsula, both in form and colour, is undoubtedly very beautiful, with an exhilarating, almost intoxicating effect upon the senses. Framed by aquamarine sky and deep blue sea, its vistas of mountain and forest, valley and farmland are strongly Italian; and the climbing vineyards complete the comparison. The artists of the Cape, whether born amid these scenes or coming to them from Great Britain, never tire of painting the brilliant colours of the enormous cloud formations which pile up against the mountain summits, the steep slopes covered with unique silver trees of glittering leaves or close-packed bushes of red and white heather, the deep valleys filled with orchards and white-gabled Dutch homesteads, the high, stark crags, the surf-pounded coast of beach and rock seen beyond a tall straight aloe, and the fascinating, strange flowers of the countryside.

Concerning the country's flora, General Smuts, a botanist when not a politician or soldier or philosopher, makes the

D

following dramatic comment: "We have two distinct floras in South Africa; the one, the South African flora, which covers most of sub-tropical Africa and is clearly of tropical origin; the other, a temperate flora, found only in the south-west of the Cape Province on the seaward side of the first great mountain barrier, with outliers extending to the north along the mountain systems into the tropics. The two floras are, apparently, quite different and distinct and are engaged in a mortal conflict with each other, in which the temperate or Cape flora is slowly losing ground. This Cape flora forms, indeed, a problem of profound and baffling interest. . . . This flora points not only to a southern origin, but to an origin even farther south than the ancient Gondwanaland is commonly supposed to have extended. May we not venture the suggestion that the Cape temperate flora is the survival of an Antarctic and sub-Antarctic flora which has perished in the climatic changes of the past? That, at any rate, would account for its marked differences from our sub-tropical South African flora."[1]

The Peninsula, however, is only a small part of the Cape, which is by far the largest Province of the Union. To the east its flat, arid, semi-desert of Namaqualand merges, beyond the Orange River, with the sin, sand, sorrow and sore eyes of the still vaster territory of South-West Africa. To the north, above the Hex River Mountains, the Little Karoo and the Great Karoo form two level steps leading to the still higher plateau of the Orange Free State. While the Little Karoo has its moments, the Great Karoo, to me at any rate, is almost frightening in its flat-faced ugliness; but those who live there say they love it and extol its beauty. This illusion of beauty is given, I imagine, by the magic of its sunsets, wonderfully coloured through the dust-particles of an otherwise crystal-clear atmosphere. But a lovely sunset is one thing and a lovely landscape quite another; and nobody who has beheld the full beauty of the Peninsula

---

[1] Address by General J. C. Smuts before the British Association for the Advancement of Science, on 6 July 1925.

could seriously argue in favour of the pancake flatness of the Karoo, covered with dusty, knee-high scrub, riverless, featureless, dry and dreary, spanned for the greater part of the year by a sky so faintly blue that it seems to have been bleached by the pitiless sun to the greyness of a burnished steel.

The Great Karoo may be kind to its sheep, who thrive upon an unvaried diet of its shrub, but it is cruel to the human eye, for it reduces the richly endowed world to its lowest possible denominator—the light of day over an empty level of scrubby earth. This is not scenery, beautiful or otherwise—it is desolation, bare and hopeless. I can well believe that a hermit's soul might flourish here, for nothing else will—except the short-lived desert flower, which opens trustingly after the rain if there is any rain, and the small, carefully irrigated garden about the well on the sheep rancher's homestead.

This tableland does, however, have its celestial views, for besides the sunsets it has low-hung, sparkling stars and a moon so brilliant one can read by it as it sheds its softening silver over the harsh countenance of the Karoo; and, besides providing uncultivated, untended pastures for sheep, each of which requires from two to ten acres for its annual sustenance, it has an air so dry that consumptives can not only live but regain their health by breathing it.

If the Cape is not all Peninsula, neither is it all Namaqualand and Karoo. Eastwards from the Peninsula, along the coastal belt lying between the mountains and the sea, lies the hinterland of the port-towns of Port Elizabeth and East London; and this great area around George, Grahamstown, Kingwilliamstown and Queenstown, tamed by the 1820 settlers, the settlers who had been rendered jobless by England's switch-over to the industrialism of machines, is both lovely to look upon and generous in its agricultural and pastoral rewards. I sometimes think it is a great pity that the Whiteman did not concentrate his South African energies upon the coastal belt from Cape Town to a few

miles north of Durban, leaving the vast inland plateau of
the Transvaal and the Orange Free State to the Blacks. The
high Drakensberg Mountains, dividing the Cape and Natal
from the Orange Free State and the Transvaal would then
have been like a curving wall, paralleling the south-east
coast and separating the Whites from the Blacks. When the
Whiteman barred the southward path of the Blacks, they
were nomadic and fleeing from the terror of the Zulu warlords. To have turned them inland, through the mountains
to the empty pastures of the interior, would have been
comparatively easy.

Instead the Whiteman cut himself in two, and the Dutch
half assumed the form of the Voortrekkers, who turned
away from the easterly, coastal advance and, instead, directed
their hooded wagons, drawn by teams of sixteen oxen,
through the barrier of the Drakensberg and onwards
through the antelope-swarming plains beyond the Orange
River and the Vaal River. This dispersal of a few Whites
over a vaster area than they could fully utilise or adequately
control allowed, paradoxically, a wider dispersal of the
Blacks and the beginnings of an intermingling of the two
races which has continued ever since in increasingly complicated convolutions. That intermingling, both in the coastal
belt and on the plateau, can never now be stopped: it must
go on, and all that the Whites can do, if they so desire, is
to try and modify it here and there, to slow it down when
they believe this necessary, and to control it in an effort to
prevent racial confusion and chaos. The *territorial* segrega-
tionalists have spoken up far too late: it becomes more and
more plain that nothing really effective and comprehensive
can be done now to give reality to their dream.

6

POSTSCRIPT

Visitors to Cape Town without their own cars can make use of the streamlined road-coaches which do a variety of morning and all-day tours. Enquiries and reservations should be made at the South African Railways coach-office in the Visitors' Information Bureau. The following are among the tours scheduled throughout the week:

Cape Point via Chapman's Peak. Leading along the spectacular Marine Drive, the route to Cape Point skirts the Atlantic as it passes the suburbs of Sea Point, Bantry Bay, Clifton-on-Sea and Camps Bay. Past the Twelve Apostles, it continues to the village of Llandudno and on to Hout Bay. Then the road climbs the side of Chapman's Peak, revealing views of the ocean far below, and after passing the fishing hamlet of Kommetjie and the wireless station and lighthouse at Slangkop, it reaches "the fairest cape in the whole circumference of the globe". The return journey is through the many resorts on the False Bay coast, including the naval port of Simonstown, and Muizenberg —famed for its gently shelving beach and its surf-riding.

Paarl, Stellenbosch, Gordon's Bay and Somerset Strand. The road goes through two of the oldest settlements in South Africa. By way of the Table Bay foreshore and Bellville, it runs through Western Province farmlands on the way to Paarl, a town founded by the Huguenots and marked by Paarl Rock—said to be the largest solid block of granite in the world. Continuing through the Drakenstein Valley and Rhodes Fruit Farms, the road climbs Helshoogte before reaching Stellenbosch, a tree-shaded old-world town, tranquil since the far-off days when it was named after Simon van der Stel, one of the first Governors of the Cape. The tour continues via Somerset West to Gordon's Bay, a holiday resort at the foot of the Hottentots Holland mountains, and so back to Cape Town, passing the seaside resort of Somerset Strand.

Chapman's Peak and Muizenberg. This trip follows the

route from Cape Town to Chapman's Peak. Then, cutting across the Peninsula through the beautiful countryside of Noordhoek and Glen Valley, it reaches the False Bay coast at the resort of Fish Hoek, known for its safe bathing and delightful surroundings. The return trip traverses a chain of watering places, including Kalk Bay, St. James and Muizenberg. Then, crossing the Peninsula again, the route leads through the suburbs of Wynberg, Claremont and Rondebosch, and, high up on the mountainside, it passes the stately university buildings, and Groote Schuur (residence of the Prime Minister) before following the De Waal Drive, giving views of Cape Town and Table Bay.

Hout Bay and Groot Constantia. This tour enables those with only an hour or two to spare to see many of the beauties of the Cape Peninsula. First comes the drive through Sea Point, Bantry Bay, Clifton-on-Sea and Camps Bay; and then, after the long climb to Hout Bay Nek, the scenery changes to views of mountains and wooded valleys. Then the sea can be seen breaking on the beach at Hout Bay. The road continues along the back of Table Mountain through Constantia Nek to the Constantia Valley, famous for its wines. A visit is paid to Groot Constantia, probably the most famous of the old Dutch residences, where visitors may look over the homestead and the wine cellars.

Elgin and Fransch Hoek. This tour is through some of the finest scenery in the Cape. Proceeding through the heart of the fruit country, the road climbs Sir Lowry Pass, from where can be seen, far below, the seaside resorts of Gordon's Bay and Somerset Strand and, across the wide expanse of False Bay, the numerous holiday places on the farther side. After a stop at Elgin for luncheon, the trip continues through Viljoen's Pass, giving panoramic views of the surrounding country, and on to the grandeur of Franschhoek Pass. After going through Franschhoek Valley, the route leads to the Drakenstein Valley, patterned with fruit farms, before returning to Cape Town.

Ceres via Bain's Kloof and Michell's Pass. Awesome mountain passes mark this tour which follows the highway to Bellville and then, after passing Paarl and Wellington, ascends the nine-mile stretch up Bain's Kloof. Continuing through the Witte River Gorge, with its turrets and pinnacles and its maidenhair and other ferns, the road follows the river until the ascent of Michell's Pass is made. Near the top, Ceres is seen through the trees. A new national road through Du Toit's Kloof, flanked by thrilling landscapes, leads back to Cape Town.

CHAPTER III

SNAPSHOT OF A CONTINENT

I

WHILE TIPTOEING on Cape Point, the Union of South Africa balances upon its shoulders the top-heavy Dark Continent. South Africans are beginning to realise this only now, for in the past their lines of communication ran so surely from Cape Town to London, cleanly by-passing all the peoples and problems of Equatoria. As for Egypt and the other territories of the Far North, the restraining, guiding, strong hand of Great Britain, or France or Spain, was upon them. But Equatoria is beginning to shake out its Blacks upon the labour market of the Transvaal, and Europe's hand upon North Africa is no longer strong but palsied. So South Africans, who have twice in a generation crossed the equator to fight in East and North Africa, tend to shift the focus of their gaze from Europe to the bulky continent in which they live. Standing in Cape Town and pointing northwards, Cecil Rhodes earnestly told them in the nineties of last century, "Your hinterland lies there!" Today, with world influences again playing upon the Africa as scrambled by Rhodes, Kruger, Stanley and the others, the idea of a friendly Pan-Africanism is blown like a bright bubble from General Smuts's pipe of peace and goes floating over Table Mountain to the Mountains of the Moon.

For South Africans as for everybody else, it is a puzzling continent, this Africa whose great bulk divides the Atlantic Ocean from the Indian Ocean. Sometimes we think of it as a new land: that is because Europeans who settle in Africa find it undeveloped and cry it up as a land of golden opportunities. Sometimes we think of it as an old land: that is because the Old Testament pictures for us the civilisation that flowered in ancient Egypt: or because we think of the Queen of Sheba, and Cleopatra, and the invading Cæsars. The Roman legions waged wars with the barbarians along the North African coast as far as Libya and proud Carthage; but all that is left of their African Empire are ruins in the sand—ruins that still tell the tale of the Roman occupation, ruins that were magnificent cities set among fertile farms. Those Roman masterpieces of architecture stand stark and empty; and the fruitful farms are now a desolation of sun-scorched sand.

The North African coast, running unevenly from east to west, is the whole southern shore of the Mediterranean. But what we know as Mediterranean civilisation and culture —"the glory that was Greece and the grandeur that was Rome"—did not flower or prosper in North Africa. Africa would have none of it. The European invasion of North Africa did not succeed: European civilisation withered in the sun and either disappeared under the shifting sands or retreated whence it had come, across the Mediterranean to its northern shore.

North Africa, however, despite its unfriendliness to the outriders of European civilisation, is part of the framework of European civilisation. Just the east-to-west coast line of North Africa. The interior, all Africa running south from that coast line, remained apart, dark, barbaric, un-known. But, as from time immemorial, the Egyptians went on cultivating the long, narrow valley of the Nile, making green the lands fertilised by the muddy flood waters of the great river.

The Nile still comes flowing into the Mediterranean from the dark heart of savage Africa, from the Great Lakes of Central Africa, fed by several sources, from sources in Ethiopia, whose history is linked with the Queen of Sheba, with primitive Christianity, and with the legend of Prester John and his Kingdom of Monomotapa. And it is fed, this long, important river, the Nile, by equatorial snows, the mountain-caps of Central Africa: the snows that glisten in the sun above clouds clinging to the high flanks of the Mountains of the Moon.

Like a thin green finger, Egyptian cultivation runs southwards on either bank of the Nile—southwards until it is lost in the lush extravagance of the equatorial jungle. Seen from an aeroplane, Egypt looks like miles and miles of nothing with a river running down the middle. But that river nourishes a nation of eighteen million Egyptians, ruled from Cairo by their own king. The Sphinxes and towering pyramids and the richly furnished tombs of the Pharaohs remind King Farouk of a glorious past when Egypt was the very centre of the world, the treasure-chest of the human race, with its Alexandria as the seat of learning and culture; but the fellaheen tilling their gardens and irrigating them by means of a bucket swinging from a pivoted, weighted pole recall him to present-day realities. It is from Nile mud and from the enormous bodies of water stored in the Nile dams that his eighteen million subjects draw their sustenance.

Sharing the North African coast with the Egyptians are the romantic Arab tribes of Morocco, Algeria, Tunisia and Libya, with their Moorish cities and their domed and turreted mosques that claim for Islam all the lands running down from the imposing Atlas Mountains. They are picturesque in a flowing burnous that protects them from the hot rays of the desert sun; and picturesque in their lives, for, away from the towns and bazaars, they are pastoralists, living in tents and riding on horses or camels as they herd their sheep and goats from used-up grasslands to pastures new. All this is a transplanted Arabia from whose mosque-turret sounds the shrill cry of the muezzin calling Allah's faithful to prayer. Much of the colour and the romance of the Arabian Nights' Entertainments survives here in the spacious, fountain-cooled rooms of the sheiks and merchant princes, in the narrow streets of the poor, and in the bazaars where the goods of the world bring all men together to buy and sell. The coast of this land, known in olden times as the Barbary Coast, was once ravaged by pirates, rough and tough, who sought for booty and human prey in its harbours and trade routes, capturing merchandise from ships and warehouses and raiding ashore for slaves. At Ceuta and Tangier this coast moves north until it nearly touches Spain and Gibraltar; but southward lies the Sahara Desert, Africa's "Dead Heart" or mighty "Dust Bowl".

The Sahara Desert lies like a great barrier against migration; yet it is by no means just a sea of sand. Beyond the shifting dunes and the Thirst Land there are the grass and bush regions of the Sahara. Here wild animals thrive, and lone pastoralists roam with small herds of goats and cattle. European traders and settlers outflanked the grim Sahara wastes by sailing in ships round to the west coast of Africa—to Dakar, capital of French West Africa, Dakar with its red, onion-shaped cathedral, and with its hills of monkey-nuts, piled up on the wharves after being gathered in the farmlands of the hinterland. And missionaries and miners, hunters and dealers went to Sierra Leone, to the Ivory Coast, to the Gold Coast and to the savage lands that stretch away from the banks of the Niger River which flows down from fantastic Timbuctoo of the French Sudan.

Below Egypt is the British Sudan, watered by the Blue Nile from Lake Tana in Ethiopia, and the White Nile from the Great Lakes of Central Africa. The Central African jungle, with its dense forests and its malarial fever, forms another barrier to easy southward migration. From the West Coast to the East Coast, from the lands of the Negroes to the lands of the Bantu, right through the equatorial belt of the tropics, is Livingstone's Africa, Stanley's "Darkest Africa", the Africa of the ivory trade and the slave trade. And the direction of its present-day trade and life, as was the direction of the old ivory and slave trade, is westwards down the stream of the Congo River and eastwards from the Mountains of the Moon and the

Great Lakes to Mombasa and Zanzibar and Dar-es-Salaam —more Arab places from which Arab sailors in Arab dhows carry cloves and oils and ivory to the Red Sea and Arabia.

Here on the East Coast the Africans have assumed the Mohammedan fez and religion, and the long white garments of the Arabs; but inland, around the Great Lakes, in Kenya, Tanganyika, and Uganda, the Bantu tribes remain faithful to the spirits of their fathers, practising barbaric customs and strange tribal rituals. Through their tribal land sounds the "bush telegraph", the throbbing of the "talking drums"; and evidence of former cannibalism and present black magic survives in the symbolism of the witch-doctors and rain-makers.

In the Masai country the young men pierce the neck-artery of bullocks and suck the hot blood through a tube. In the deep dark forests of the Congo the pigmies live apart, remote and isolated from the rest of the human race; in its long-grass country stalk those African giants of the Watusi tribe—men and women standing seven feet in height—who can look over the tops of the longest grass; and in this equatorial belt, in inaccessible fastnesses, are the chest-thumping gorillas whose embrace can kill; and the secret societies of the Leopard-men and the Lion-men, who wear knives for nails and thus slash out the eyes and cut the throats of their victims; and the great herds of elephants and antelopes that roam the plains.

2

We have come half-way down Africa. Now, to be historically logical, we must go to the far south, to the Cape of Good Hope that is the toe of the African continent, and work our way northwards until we again come to the equator.

When the ancient Romans withdrew from North Africa,

no other Europeans seriously attempted to regain a foothold in Africa until three hundred years ago. Then it was
that men from Holland sailed into Table Bay and established
a fort, the Castle, at the foot of Table Mountain. The Dutch
blood was enriched with French Huguenot blood; and the
resultant race of Boers or Afrikaners was reinforced, over
a hundred years ago, with English settlers. The English
settlers moved up the coast to extend the Cape and a few,
even more adventurous than the rest, sailed into Durban's
landlocked harbour to found Natal; and the Boers trekked
in covered wagons through the coastal range of mountains
to establish the Orange Free State and the Transvaal.

This coastal range of mountains, the Drakensberg, is
the southern beginning of Africa's Great Divide. It is the
backbone of Africa. It runs from south to north until it
walls the Great Rift, a wide valley cupping extensive lakes
in Central Africa and crowned by volcanoes and snow-
capped peaks. This mountainous backbone is the Whiteman's chief hope in his modern endeavour to hold and extend his precarious footing in Africa. From the Cape, Natal,
the Orange Free State and the Transvaal, the outriders
of European civilisation—farmers and miners, traders and
officials—have climbed along this backbone into Rhodesia;
and other white settlers, scrambling on to that backbone
from the East Coast, have established themselves in the
healthy Kenya Highlands—and in the other British-con-
trolled territories which link up with Rhodesia and the
Union of South Africa. This mighty wedge, with its base
in the Cape and its point reaching as far as the Sudan, is
the Whiteman's Africa. On the healthy plains, lifted high
by this mountainous backbone, the South Africans, the
Rhodesians, and the Kenyans—helped by a scattering of
settlers and officials in Nyasaland, Tanganyika, and Uganda
—are building up a so-called Whiteman's country. That is
to say, they believe they are doing so, or some of them
believe they are doing so—or, at any rate, believed so
yesterday.

The great bulk of that white population is settled in the Union of South Africa, whose House of Assembly and Senate sit in Cape Town. Its administrative capital, however, is Pretoria, a thousand miles to the north, which is close to and virtually part of greater Johannesburg, the mining and commerical hub of Southern Africa. These cities, with the rapidly growing Durban, symbolise European civilisation in Africa at its highest level. But in the whole Union, with its fertile coastal belt of vineyards, fruit farms and sugarcane fields, and with its interior of sheep and cattle ranches and rich mines of all kinds, there are only two and a half million Europeans.

Patterned across the Union's varied landscape (which is five times as big as the area of Great Britain) are many tribes of the Bantu people—not Negroes, but of that branch of the negroid race that apparently has an admixture of Arab and Hamitic blood. These tribes speak different languages and have different customs; and, before the pacification of Africa by the Whiteman, they were engaged in fierce wars waged with spears and ox-hide shields. In their Native Territories, between the Whiteman's cities, the Bantu tribes—the Xosas,[1] the Basutos, the Swazis and the Zulus—still live in primitive style and with seasonal moments of barbaric splendour. The Zulu warriors still dance triumphantly to the singing and hand-clapping of their womenfolk; and the Swazi youths, at the thrilling ceremony of the First Fruits and of Rain Making, still kill a black bullock with their naked hands and chant their sacred songs about their Chief. In the Game Reserves, too, the Old Africa survives—the Africa of the lion and leopard, of the hippo and crocodile, of the elephant and rhino, of the giraffe, zebra and antelope. But the Natives, despite the survival of their tribal customs, are more and more becoming Christianised, civilised and urbanised. They are attracted to the Whiteman's farms and factories by the

---

[1] Otherwise spelt Khosa, which approximates to its pronunciation, in English at any rate.

boon of regular wages, by the desire to share in his knowledge and creature comforts.

It is the same story in South-West Africa, the former German possession that in 1949 became a fifth province of the Union—South-West Africa with its diamonds that rival those of Kimberley and with its cattle grasslands that disappear in the Kalahari Desert where the Bushmen, the pigmies of the south, live in grass nests as a strange survival of the Stone Age. And it is again the same story in Rhodesia (where the Great Zimbabwe Ruins remind us of the heights reached by the Bantu culture of a former era) and in the adjacent territories of the Congo, held by the Belgians, and of Angola and Mozambique, ruled by the Portuguese. Across the invisible borders of all these territories of the continent south of the equator run roads and railways, intermingling in a master design of transport. Along these roads, many of red soil hot beneath the sun, the ox-wagons of the Boers still trundle at the rate of sixteen miles a day; but along these roads, too, speed motor-cars and lorries, increasing the tempo of African development.

3

The exchange of services and goods between all these areas has been increased enormously under the pressure of world economics. A great intermingling is going on which tends to make the territorial borders theoretical, certainly political, rather than actual. The Bantu tribes straddle those borders; and there is a movement of Bantu workers from one territory to another; while from such important institutions as Onderstepoort, near Pretoria, the results of scientific research flow outwards to all corners of the sub-continent to combat animal disease and pests and to improve farming methods.

The Europeans living in all this area south of the equator are busy mining the wealth below the soil—copper in the

Congo and in Northern Rhodesia, gold in Southern Rhodesia and the Transvaal, diamonds in the Cape; and coal and iron, and in fact almost all base minerals. But there are only about three million Whites in all this area, as against fifty million Blacks; there are, in fact, not more than four million Europeans in the whole continent of Africa as against perhaps two hundred million Blacks, Arabs and Egyptians.

Africa is about five thousand miles in length from north to south, from Tunis to Cape Town; and not much less from west to east, from Dakar to Cape Guadafui in what used to be Italian Somaliland. Those vast distances, across the equator and sprawling into both northern and southern hemispheres, have for many generations, for thousands of years, kept one half of Africa from knowing how the other half lives. The beloved jungle of the explorers, the impenetrable jungle, has intensified the difficulties of travel, and so held Africa back, kept Africa in the past. But today that is all changing. The steamships of many nations, but notably those of Britain, have opened up the great coast of Africa, in the fever belt no less than in the healthy temperate zones. Smaller steamships nose their way along the Congo River, into the green heart of Central Africa, and down the Nile; and across the Great Lakes. Where the steamships cannot go, the primitive craft still ply—the one-sailed dhow and the long dugout canoe. You see them on the lakes, in shallow coastal lagoons, on the jungle-framed, crocodile-infested Niger. In this way, from all parts of the interior, the products of Africa are brought to the coast and thus made available to the markets of the world. And through that "impenetrable jungle" of Livingstone's and Stanley's Africa now run the Whiteman's motor roads and railways. Cecil Rhodes's dream of a Cape-to-Cairo railway remains a dream. Much of the railway has indeed been built; but there are gaps that have to be filled in by river steamer in the Congo, along the Lualaba, a tributary of the Congo River, by lake steamer across Lake Tanganyika and Lake Victoria

Ostriches, bred near Oudtshoorn for their feathers, being driven from kraal to paddock by a Cape Coloured farm-hand

European girls take a lunch-hour stroll in the gardens of the
City Hall, Port Elizabeth, while Cape Coloured folk enjoy
a rest on the benches.

Nyanza, by motor-car across Uganda, by river steamer on the Nile as it flows through the Sudan and Egypt. The Cape-to-Cairo motor road is the same sort of reality—that is to say, the motor-car, at certain points, must be ferried across unbridged rivers and lakes and manhandled over black quagmires of cotton soil and deep dry sand.

To east and west of the Cape-to-Cairo road and rail there is a double pattern of transport lines—motor roads and railways that link up with all parts of Africa's East and West Coasts. The oils and coffee and copper of the Congo, the gold of the Witwatersrand and the diamonds of Kimberley, the far-spread cocoa plantations of the Gold Coast, the rubber and groundnuts of the French Cameroons, the copper of Northern Rhodesia, are all part of a continental economy linked by motor roads and railways with the coast and so with the rest of the world across the Atlantic and Indian Oceans. And the cocoa plantations of the Gold Coast, most of them owned by the Africans themselves, give to the world a great proportion of the chocolate it eats.

Linking up with the motor roads and railways are the footpaths beaten across the veld by the Africans as they tramp from their kraals. In single file, they walk barefoot along these paths even though they possess boots. The boots, which they find harder on their feet than the footpath, they hang around their necks until they arrive at the railway station or the Whiteman's town: then they sit down by the wayside and put them on! Many of these Africans live in mosquito-infested areas where malaria is rife; many of them live in bush and game country cursed with the scissor-winged tsetse flies which kill off their cattle. Certain tsetse flies also give sleeping sickness to human beings.

The rivers that run through Africa—with the exception of the Nile, the Niger and the Congo—are not navigable. In the south, the Orange, the Vaal, the Limpopo—to mention only a few of them—are rainy season rivers. It has been said of South African rivers that if you fall into one of them you have to get up and dust yourself. There is

E

often truth in this jest, for in the dry season many of Africa's
rivers are without water; but in the rainy season they are
often raging torrents.

In the dry season, the face of the countryside—or the
veld ("felt") as South Africans call it—is scarred by sloots
and dongas which are rather like the wadis of North Africa.
These are watercourses which in the rainy season are
rushing streams and rivers in spate. The flood waters are
often red in colour, owing to the red soil and sand being
washed downstream. These muddy waters of the rainy
season, like the gaping dongas of the dry season, are signs
of a serious problem—soil erosion. At the mouths of the
larger rivers that run to the south-east coast the sea is
often red—red with South Africa's washed-out soil.

The Orange, the Vaal and the Limpopo are South Africa's
three most important rivers. The Orange forms the boundary between the Cape and the Orange Free State, and then
continues flowing westwards to the Atlantic Ocean; the
Vaal further north, forms the boundary between the Orange
Free State and the Transvaal before it forms a confluence
with the Orange River; and the Limpopo forms the
boundary between the Transvaal and Southern Rhodesia,
flowing eastwards through Portugal's Mozambique to
empty itself into the Indian Ocean. Further north is the
Zambesi River, whose course is broken by the majestic
Victoria Falls.

In periods of drought even these three big rivers, the
Orange, the Vaal and the Limpopo, which look so mighty
on the map, are little more than trickles of water or a series
of stagnant pools with long stretches of sand in between.
But during the violent summer rains they run wide and deep,
their waters roaring and tumbling across the landscape.
To tame those waters, to prevent their rape of the soil, to
conserve them for the dry season and to use them for
irrigating the countryside are the objectives of a combined
operation to which South Africans are devoting their wits
and muscles.

4

From the distance of England we are too apt to regard Africa as merely a romantic land, a land where the climate is "always afternoon", a land flowing with milk and honey.

The coastal belt comes nearest to this picture of a land flowing with milk and honey. In the Cape are the vineyards and fruit-farms; in Natal are the sugarcane fields. Numerous streams gush down from the Drakensberg range and through the valleys that run down to the sea. But even in the Cape we are reminded that Africa is part desert and part sown. The Little Karoo and the Great Karoo—those flat, arid plains that I have already described with their stunted, knee-high bushes on which sheep thrive—form a striking contrast to the lush valleys of the Cape Peninsula, to the great forests of Knysna, and the fertile hills of Natal. The good agricultural lands run, as it were, eastwards; the pastoral and desert lands run westwards. The productive lands are nursed by the warm Indian Ocean and the rain-catching Drakensberg range; the desert lands descend in a long, gentle decline to the cold Atlantic Ocean. Namaqualand, in the north-west Cape, is a pastoral wilderness; the Bechuanaland Protectorate, west of the Transvaal, is largely made up of its own "dead heart"—the Kalahari Desert with its sand and sparse grazing and twisted thorn-trees.

Australia has its Dead Heart country and the United States its Dust Bowl, and some fear that the desert lands of South Africa are creeping from the west to the east across the Transvaal and the Orange Free State. Those who fear this say South Africa's rainfall tends to grow less, while its soil erosion is increasing. When the Whiteman came to the Cape from Europe and the Blackman from Equatorial Africa, three hundred years ago, South Africa had no settled population. The Bushmen pigmies, the Hottentot near-pigmies, and the Bantu tribesmen of full stature were nomads, herding their cattle to new pastures. The wild animals of the veld—the teeming antelopes—always left a drought-stricken area for a more favoured district. The Europeans who, a hundred years ago, ventured from the Cape to Natal, to the Orange Free State and to the Transvaal were themselves semi-nomads, exploring the wilderness.

And the wilderness, with its antelopes and virgin soil, easily supported them; but as the numbers of both Europeans and Natives have increased in South Africa, the wilderness has felt the stress and strain of supporting a settled community and their cattle. The nomadic days are over. The sheep and cattle can no longer be driven over unfenced horizons to pastures new; the Natives cannot migrate from one watershed to another; and the Europeans no longer trek as the spirit moves them, with their families and herds of ox-wagons—they must stay on their circumscribed farms, or in their towns or on their mines. Yesterday's wilderness has become patterned with railways and bridges and roads; and these beaten tracks, with their regular and heavy traffic, are, it is said, new causes of soil erosion. As for the settled communities and their cattle, they are using up the grasslands and taking the goodness out of the soil, and thus inviting the desert to advance still further. To combat drought and erosion, the Europeans are planting more and more trees and building more and more dams across the rivers; and they are also filling in dongas down which soil would otherwise be washed away by storm water. All this is not so much man's fight against Nature as man's effort to prevent Nature's delicate balance from being upset by his own disturbing presence in a previously unsettled and virtually unpopulated country.

There is great beauty in the African scene—and great ugliness. The coastal lands and the lands along Africa's backbone are, in the main, extremely lovely; but both, in certain aspects and moods, can be painfully plain. Yet, as I have already pointed out, even those who live in the desert grow to love their flat, dry, grim world—or do they merely get used to it, inured to it? Certainly it is all bright with sunshine; and its sunsets are glorious with brilliant colours. The air is invigorating, and the far distances give a fine sense of freedom to those who live there.

The high plains of South Africa are dotted with boulder-strewn hills or koppies—brown in winter, green in summer; but in the areas of the Drakensberg backbone the scenery is grander and more varied with stately peaks, deep valleys and dancing waterfalls. The whole African scene is sun-filled for the greater part of the year. Even during the rainy season, clouds rarely obscure the sun for long. The rain usually comes in the shape of a storm. It is often heralded by ear-splitting thunderbolts and jagged forked lightning. The rain itself is heavy and violent. It begins in large drops which, as they strike the earth, send up little puffs of dust. Then it pours down in long, crystal-like rods that pierce the soil and beat a deafening tattoo upon the house-tops, which are frequently made of sheets of corrugated-iron—galvanised iron, as it is called, or, popularly, zinc.

At the end of the dry season the winds blow across the veld, causing dust-devils that spiral higher and higher into the sky. And as these dust-devils spiral and expand in the air, they spin on a pointed toe that traces a swift, crazy trail across farms and through villages. Often you can see, in the open expanses of the high-veld, several of these whirl-winds in action simultaneously. Besides the dust, they draw up in to their revolving cone of wind such things as paper, grass and leaves, while heavier articles, such as petrol-cans and jam-tins are sent hurtling along the ground with a great clatter. The bigger dust-devils will even topple over jerry-built shacks and Native huts, and tear the roofs off houses; but as a rule these dust storms are uncomfortable rather than dangerous.

Normally the air is so clear in Africa that you can see for many miles over the veld, for fifty miles and more perhaps from a ridge or koppie—on and on into the far haze that merges with the sky. Afar off you may see clouds gather together, merge, and then let loose their rain; but where you stand the weather is fair and fine, with the sun shining with such blinding light that you dare not look him in the face. The sky, made dazzling by that light, is not a gentle blue, except in certain seasons, but a steel-grey. However, except during a drought, its harshness is relieved by numerous great clouds that float in it with the rhythmic grace of full-rigged windjammers upon the ocean. Flattened by the wind on their under side, these clouds billow upwards into fantastic and astonishing shapes, most pleasing to the eye. At sunset their whiteness is changed into such vivid colours and present so wonderful a sight that they are sometimes not believed in Great Britain when they are shown in the form of an artist's painted canvas.

This glorification of the sky alone divides day from night, for in Africa there is no twilight. The white light of day is quickly succeeded by the darkness of night. The far distances, the scintillating vistas of the veld, are suddenly swallowed up by the blackness left behind by the sun when he plunges out of sight beyond the western rim of the world. But, as a contrast to the darkness on the land, the sky blazes with stars, winking and shining through the clear atmosphere. The Milky Way sweeps through the jewelled heavens like a white veil; while, sometimes high up and sometimes low on the horizon, the Southern Cross sparkles above the deserts and high plains with splendid lustre.

When the moon rides the African night-sky, the blackness disappears from the veld. Again the thorn-trees and the koppies stand clearly in the landscape, as if in the light of an autumn day in England. The whole scene is silvered over and patterned with black, sharp shadows flowing from houses and woods and hills. Sounds, on these moonlight nights, come from long distances—the voices of Natives singing in their kraals or villages, the barking of dogs from a neighbouring farm, the creaking of the wagon wheels of some belated travellers on the road. These nights can be so entrancing and exhilarating that the European settlers in Africa, after a hot day, are reluctant to go to bed. They sit out on their stoeps or verandas, enjoying the moonlit scene as they smoke African tobacco or drink tea or sip a "nightcap" of whisky or brandy. Or they carry baskets of food and drink into the veld and enjoy a "moonlight picnic" beside a river-pool that shows them another moon and star-hung sky.

5

The grass fires can be murderous, flaming like colossal scimitars over plains and hills, burning the dry winter grass, and aiding erosion when the rains fall. And the locusts can be murderous, for in those years when their eggs hatch out in the deserts and they swarm across Africa, they eat up all the crops that lie along their path, thus bringing famine to the Natives. They range over hundreds and, indeed, over thousands of miles; millions of them make up each swarm; and when they fly overhead they can be so numerous that the sun is obscured and the landscape darkened.

For years, first the Natives and then the Europeans waged an unsuccessful war on the locusts in Africa. They fought the locusts in their own individual territories. But the locusts recognised no political boundaries and therefore always won. Now, however, the Pan-African idea is being projected into the anti-locust campaigns. All African territories are co-operating to defeat the winged crop-consumers, the common enemy, and, in consequence, victories are being proclaimed.

Almost as voracious, and more continuous in their eating, are the white ants. After the first rains, the young four-winged ants fly into the sunshine in myriads. It is a beautiful sight, but a terrible one for those who know how they demolish what man builds. The flight of the young ants does not last long. Their wings drop off and they settle far and wide. New queen-ants establish themselves, new anthills rise high and higher, higher than a man, as high as a tree; and, working silently underground, the ants tunnel their way into corn-bins and eat out all the timber of a European's house or a Native's hut. But as the influence of the Whiteman spreads over Africa, as his scientific knowledge is brought to bear on Africa's plagues and pests, the menace of the locusts and white ants, of the mosquitoes and tsetse-flies, is lessened; and as Pan-Africanism is applied in widening circles across the face of Africa, drought and soil erosion and grass fires may begin to lose something of their terror.

Broadly speaking, Africa's past is barbaric and nomadic. Its future is civilisation and settlement. The Europeans in Africa—the British, the South Africans, the Rhodesians, the Kenyans, the Portuguese, the Belgians, the French, the Spaniards, and perhaps the Italians—must together extend their gift of Western civilisation to Africa. That gift to the Africans is at present chiefly apparent in the Whiteman's Africa, that colonised wedge based on the Cape and tapering away in Kenya, all along the high mountain-backbone of Africa.

Ships, railways, and motor-cars have opened up Africa during the past generation or two; and now a new continent-opener is at work—the aeroplane. The aeroplane easily leaps those African distances and mountains which the ox-wagon found so formidable. Nowadays one can travel from one corner of Africa to the other in two or three days. There is an increasing network of air communications over all Africa, and the shadows of many aeroplanes move over desert and jungle and mountain range. Giant planes are carrying passengers from England to South Africa in only thirty-six hours. In this way Africa is coming closer to the rest of the world. More and more aeroplanes flock southwards from Europe, like the cranes and swallows in the winter, and fan out over the whole of Africa—North Coast, West Coast, East Coast, Equatorial Belt, and as far south as the Cape of Good Hope.

For the passing generation, Central Africa was journey's end for slow *safaris* from the north and south, from the east and west coast of the continent. But now, for the men of the air, only days or hours separate all parts of Africa. Stanley required hundreds of porters and months of arduous journeying to reach Livingstone in Central Africa. Now, from Cairo or Mombasa, from Johannesburg or Dakar, the aeroplane effortlessly crosses Africa, dropping down upon airports hacked out of the jungle or set high on the open plateau. As it wings it way low over forest and swamp, the elephants run in fear and the flamingoes scatter like pink clouds.

Brilliant sunshine. Miles and miles of veld. Beehive-shaped Bantu huts. Long-horned antelopes grazing in the wilds. Hippos floating in the rivers. Crocodiles basking on the sandbars. Elephants trampling through the bush. Lions roaring from the dark beyond the camp-fire. Bearded Boers riding their ponies across the landscape. British planters smoking their pipes on the verandas or stoeps of their bungalows. Natives labouring in the farmlands, or herding cattle—Natives whose dark skins glisten and whose teeth flash white in the sunshine.

Such is the romantic form which Africa assumes in the mind of the average person living in England. It cannot be said to be a false picture, for all those people and places, all those animals and scenes go to make up Africa. But there is a lot more to it than that. Besides, there are large towns in Africa apart from Alexandria and Cairo—towns such as Johannesburg, where the gold mines are, or Cape Town, built round the slopes of Table Mountain, or Durban, with its palm-fringed harbour—where the citizens see little of that romantic side of Africa: they are much too busy working in offices and factories, and dodging the street traffic, just as they do in London or New York or Liverpool.

Yet, not far from Cape Town, there are great fruit-farms and vineyards which provide as lovely and romantic a setting for their owners and labourers as one could wish;

and near Durban there are vast sugarcane fields where
Indians and Zulus labour for the European proprietors;
while from the outskirts of Johannesburg, thunderous with
the stamp-batteries crushing gold-shot rock, the veld rolls
on and on to the Drakensberg Mountains and then drops
towards the sea to become the bushveld or lowveld, where
big game still abounds in all its Noah's Ark variety.

The relationship between White and Black is the acutest
and biggest problem confronting present-day Africa. Much
has been done already towards overcoming racial difficulties.
Much more remains to be done to provide increased educa-
tional facilities for the Bantu peoples, to give greater
privileges of free movement throughout the country, to
sweep away many restrictions now limiting their entry into
industry and commerce—not to mention an improved social
adjustment of the "in-between" Coloureds and Asiatics.

There it all is, Africa old and new—Livingstone's
wander-space, Stanley's dark continent, Rhodes's hinterland, Smuts's Pan-African idea.

6

POSTSCRIPT

The restless Boers of the early Cape settlement trekked
into the rising sun. The visitor cannot do better than go
eastwards too. Motor-coaches leave Adderley Street once a
fortnight on the following ten-day tours:

First day: Leaving Cape Town by way of Bellville, the
road passes through beautiful countryside *en route* to Wellington, at the foot of the Drakenstein Mountains. Soon
after traversing the Bain's Kloof Pass, the highway enters
Worcester, set in a fruit and wine producing area. In the
afternoon, the coach passes the farming centre of Robert-
son, and Ashton, site of a canning factory, before reaching
Swellendam on the banks of the Koringlande River in the
Langebergen foothills.

Second day: Leaving Swellendam early in the morning, the coach goes through Tradouw Pass to Ladismith, a village surrounded by very productive farms. After passing through Huis River Pass, and the vineyards of Calitzdorp, the route leads to Oudtshoorn.

Third day: During the morning, an excursion is made to the Cango Caves, with their fantastic stalactites and stalagmites. Their fairy-like effect is heightened by diffused lighting of different hues. In the Oudtshoorn district are numerous ostrich farms. During the afternoon, a trip is made to one of these farms.

Fourth day: Proceeding along the Garden Route via the famous Montagu Pass, a marvel of road and railway engineering, the tour is continued to George, at the base of the Outeniqua Mountains. From here the highway winds through thickly wooded country of rolling hills to the town of Knysna, commanding far views of sea and land.

Fifth day: From Knysna, an all-day excursion is made to Plettenberg Bay, a deep inlet. A boat trip is made up the tree-lined Keurbooms River where lunch is provided. In the afternoon the coach returns to Knysna.

Sixth day: During the morning a visit is made to a stinkwood furniture factory. On the outskirts of Knysna are the indigenous forests from which this stinkwood is obtained. Then a trip is made to the "Heads", huge sandstone cliffs rising to a considerable height and forming the narrow entrance to the almost land-locked harbour. After lunch, the excursion is continued to The Wilderness, a charming seaside resort.

Seventh day: This is a free day, during which the members of the party are at liberty to do as they like. There are numerous recreational facilities, including tennis courts, a golf course, a sandy beach and a lagoon. Fishing rods and boats are available for hire.

Eighth day: After breakfast a trip is made to the well-known "Kaaimansgat", a pool on the Kaaimans River, enlivened by a waterfall. The party returns to The Wilderness for lunch before going on to Mossel Bay.

Ninth day: Mossel Bay grows South Africa's best oysters. It has a beach and many rock-bound coves. During the morning there is sufficient time for a bathe at the "Poort" and a trip by tug around Seal Island. Later in the day the tour is continued as far as Swellendam. Here is the old "Drostdy", built in 1746 as a residence for the Landdrost of the Dutch East India Company and now a national museum containing some 2,000 exhibits.

Tenth day: The return route to Cape Town leads through Caledon, with its health-giving medicinal springs. During September this area is carpeted with multi-coloured wild flowers, including the beautiful Cape heath. Then comes the village of Elgin. The Hottentots Holland Mountains are crossed by way of the Sir Lowry Pass (altitude 1,530 feet), with views of False Bay. Beyond the Pass lies Somerset West, formerly the home of William Adriaan van der Stel, son of Simon. His old homestead, "Vergelegen", is not far from the town. In the late afternoon the coach arrives back in Cape Town.

CHAPTER IV

BARBARIC SPLENDOUR

I

OUT OF Africa's great equatorial belt and down the East Coast came the Bantu, that Hamitic stem of the negroid race. They travelled light and lived on locusts and wild honey, and antelopes slain by the flung assegai or trapped in covered pits, on the milk of driven goats and cows, and on corn planted where they squatted for a season or two. Barefoot and footloose, they swarmed southwards until, about three hundred years ago, the Zulus built their grass huts in the hills of Natal, and organised for themselves a comparatively settled life. But others went on, the Pondos and the Xosas, across the rivers flowing out of the Drakensberg and into the Indian Ocean—the Umkamaas, the Umzimkulu, the Great Kei, the Keiskama, and the Great Fish River. The migration of many became a flight from the marauding impis of the Zulus until the Xosas, the Kafirs, clashed with the Whiteman in the eastern regions of the Cape. Behind them, the short, stabbing assegai of Shaka prevented any retreat at the beginning of the nineteenth century; before them the Whiteman with his musket stopped any further advance.

From all these migrations, and the Whiteman's migrations through the Drakensberg and into the interior that continued throughout that century, has developed the racial mosaic of South Africa. And that mosaic, developing with the startling swiftness of a shaken and re-shaken kaleidoscope, evolving and changing direction as diamonds and gold and factories have turned farmers and tribesmen into town dwellers, has left little of that barbaric splendour which, of yore, held the sometimes horrified and sometimes

delighted gaze of European travellers. The little that is
left—where is it? In Zululand? Most people in England,
and even most people in South Africa, would say, "Yes—
Zululand, surely, is still splendidly barbaric!" I would
have said so myself before my recent visit to it, across the
Tugela River, into the hill country where the Zulu kraals
scatter across the far-seen landscapes, and to Nongoma,
the royal capital, where those who inherit the kingship of
Shaka still seek to rule. But, as I shall show later, the
shining splendour that hid the inner cruelty of Shaka's
Zulus is now tarnished at the centre, and the cruelty has
been replaced by strange sects of Christianity. There *is*
still barbaric splendour in Zululand—but it is found only
in remote areas or on specially organised occasions.

In the hot, low-lying valleys of the Northern Transvaal,
where Rider Haggard's *She-who-must-be-obeyed* still weaves
her spells for the heavenly blessing of rain—there, among
Mujaji's people or the people of Vendaland, might there
not still linger this barbaric splendour? But my answer,
given after a sojourn in that awe-inspiring land of the Rain
Queen, is again, "No". Mystery, secrecy, tribal custom,
curious ritual: yes, all that still goes on in the fascinating
and comparatively unknown Northern Transvaal, whose
malarial mosquitoes and cattle-killing tsetse flies delayed the
advance of the Whiteman for two generations; but not
barbaric splendour. Perhaps it was never there, for it needs
the terrible touch of the savage warrior, the Zulu with his
ox-hide shields and death-dealing assegais, to satisfy the
eager gaze of your civilised European.

Where then? The answer I give is, "Among the Swazis".
Least affected by the march of the Whiteman across the
sub-continent, separate from the Union and the main
stream of his progress, isolated by mountains and fever
belts, free of all railways, the Swazis not only retain the
customs of their ancestors but also that brave show of
barbaric finery and pomp, of tribal dancing, singing, shouting, and assegai-brandishing for which, at this moment,

we are searching; treasure tombs, too, for the Swazis, despite the work of many missionaries, still cling tenaciously to their ancient ways, as may be judged from the rites that their witch-doctors still perform; and it is not difficult to understand why they bury their big chiefs today as they did in the obscure dawn of their history. Not in the public eye, but—as it were—behind the backs of the people are the mighty put to rest in a sitting posture. It is said by some that the dead are hidden away in this manner to frustrate any efforts made by witch-doctors to secure portions of the body for their strong medicines. And, in order more completely to hoodwink them, a bogus grave is dug with much fuss in a place obvious to all. To a chosen few is given the important task of carrying the body to its real resting-place, unknown to all the rest.

"When the king dies, his corpse is treated with reverent care and unique ritual", according to the latest authority[1] on the esoteric life of the Swazi tribe. "His death is kept secret until his heir is installed. Only the queen mother, governors of the royal village, *tinsila* (blood-brothers), specialists in the death ritual, and a couple of intimate attendants know the truth. Day and night the body is guarded. People are told 'The king is ill' or 'The king is busy'. Swazi believe that if the king's death were known before his successor was appointed, the country would be 'light'—weak and vulnerable to an attack from enemies. Though the people may suspect that he is dead, they will not dare to speak, lest they be accused of 'wishing to kill the country'. Secretly, in the darkness of night, he is moved to the ritual hut in the harem where he celebrated his marriage with his first ritual queen.

"For the king, and the king alone, a primitive method of embalming is practised. The specialist . . . 'squeezes the juices' from the body to prevent too rapid decay; and informants insist that as a result of this treatment the body

[1] Hilda Kuper in *An African Aristocracy* (Oxford University Press for the International African Institute, 1947).

does not putrefy. This practice is another indication of the
symbolic value of the king who is not permitted to suffer
the usual physical decomposition. Over the body are rubbed
medicines pleasant to the ancestral spirits, and round the
body is wrapped the flexible hide of a pitch-black ox. On
the head, which is left exposed, the magicians place a
covering of fatty membrane and over the forehead is stuck
the inflated bladder of a black goat and a sprig of wild
asparagus. Diviners in their period of training use similar
medicines to break down the barrier between this world
and the world of the dead. The dead king's fists are closed
over twigs of the powerful *masweti*, imbued with the
sanctity of national rituals. The body, until burial, lies on
a shelf cut from the same wood that supports the national
shrine hut. Cattle are slaughtered and roasted 'to keep off
the smell of death' and 'to rejoice the dead'. The ancestors
must be placated and prepared to accept the newly dead,
who becomes the most important link between the two
worlds.

"The corpse is buried when the heir is announced. Chiefs
and subjects from the entire country are summoned, and on
a night 'when the moon is black' (when no moon is visible)
they carry the corpse on a bier of special wood to the royal
caves. The mourners keen the song that marked his marriage
to his queen. As dawn breaks, the men leave the cave. He
has been settled among the dead with a live black goat and
other personal articles for his comforts. Then the men of
the nation return and fold their hands behind their backs
and sling lion skins as cowls over their shoulders; women,
especially those connected with the dead by blood or
marriage, cut their hair and wear mourning robes. But
mourning may not go on indefinitely: the new heir is
alive, and through him the nation will again be strong. . . .

"The royal groves are said to be very fearful. Graves
of ordinary people become part of the homestead where
they died, beacons by which claims can be staked in land,
but kings are buried in caves far from their villages. Round

Thatched *rondavels* for holiday-makers in the dense vegetation of the Wilderness, a seaside resort on the edge of primeval forest.

Young Swazi wives in screened-off beauty parlour prepare themselves for the annual dance of the First Fruits at the Royal Kraal.

Son of a chief, the Keeper of the Shields waits for the Swazi warriors of the *incwala* ceremony.

the caves are dense forests with impenetrable undergrowth broken by narrow footpaths. The air is full of noises. The royal command 'With all power' comes from invisible beings. Huge snakes glide through the trees and are praised as kings. The groves can only be entered with safety with the assistance of keepers, trusted men appointed as chiefs over the surrounding locality. There are three royal groves, two in the south and one in the central area, and each has its own guardian. Woe betide the man who stumbles unaware into the grove, for he will not be able to get out unless the keeper hears his call and releases him with the sacrifice of a beast to the powerful captors."

Out of this custom has arisen an interesting story of treasure tombs in the fastnesses of the mountains between Mbabane and Bremersdorp. There, in places unfrequented by the Whiteman and too barren to invite the hoe of the Swazi, is supposed to exist the burying ground of chiefs. They were buried there with a live goat for company, and the cave entrance was sealed up with stones. Even if a chief died far from home, he was carried by his warriors for days and nights until he could be fittingly secreted with his fathers.

Picturesque in the extreme those funeral processions from foreign soil to the home kraal are said to be. By night the warriors light great fires and feast on slaughtered cattle. Thrilling singing is heard in the stretches of veld through which they pass, their triumphant voices overcoming evil spirits lurking in the bush.

Those who live in Swaziland will tell you that heaps of ivory tusks and even vessels filled with gold were buried with the great ones of long ago. So that the walled-up caves have a double secret to keep. But they do not have to keep it unassisted, for scattered about those rocky fastnesses are lonely huts whose occupants guard the approaches to the treasure tombs by day and night—silent and trusty sentinels of the nation's kings.

Once an enterprising speculator journeyed to Swaziland

F

with the special object of obtaining a concession over those sacred mountains. He wanted to open up the tombs and mine them for their hoarded wealth. His idea was to float a joint-stock company and allow the living to enjoy the riches scattered about the dust and bones of their sleeping owners. Not a bad idea in a way; but it was not the sort of bright idea to please Sobhuza, the Chief, or find favour with his councillors or people. The scheme to filch the tombs of the nation's rulers did not kindle enthusiasm in the hearts of the Swazis, and the disappointed financier had to return to the haunts of civilisation with empty hands.

What is the truth of the story of the treasure tombs of the Swazi nation? Who can say? Such things are not to be found out by questioning, for about them the Swazi keeps a seal upon his lips. Nor by searching, for the sentinels on the barren ridges send all wanderers back to the beaten trail. And certainly wondering only ends in wondering. I wonder!

2

And that black ox being trampled to death by the Swazi youths—what does it mean? It takes place each January when the Swazi nation gives itself up to the annual *incwala* ceremonies. On several occasions I have gone to witness those ceremonies. Once, when I arrived at Mbabane, the administrative capital of Swaziland, they told me that old Vanyane, then Hereditary Master of Tribal Ceremonies,[1] had returned to the royal kraal with his escort after a long walk to Mozambique to fetch seawater. He carried the water in a calabash which was filled before sunrise to the accompaniment of sacred songs. Others had fetched water from three rivers. Vanyane's return signalised the beginning of Swaziland's Feast of the First Fruits at the season of the harvest moon. Covered by the skin and gall-bladder of a black beast specially sacrificed for this purpose,

---

[1] On his death Vanyane was succeeded in this office by his son, Mgwedjeza.

the calabashes of sea and river water for the rain-medicines were placed in a hut in a large cattle kraal in which secret rites were performed preparatory to the public ceremonies in which the whole Swazi nation was to participate, directly or indirectly.

Chief Sobhuza and his mother, in whose village tradition demands that this festival shall be held, made elaborate preparations for this great occasion, and thousands of Swazi warriors dressed in all their savage finery and girls from far-flung villages were encamped on the hillside as both spectators and participants in the various ceremonies of song and dance.

When I got to the Queen Mother's village, the secret hut was being built by unmarried men who had just returned from the lowveld, where they had collected branches of the *lusekwane* tree, a kind of acacia. Streaming back by the light of the moon, they rushed to the royal cattle kraal at sunrise, and, dumping their branches in a heap, they performed a dance and sang lustily, Sobhuza, now a king indeed, joining in joyously. Thereafter piccanins scoured the surrounding countryside for leaves with which they filled in all gaps in the secret hut built of the *lusekwane* branches. The king and his medicine man, Vanyane, then entered the hut to go through an inherited ritual with the seawater, special herbs, mealies and gourds.

These ceremonies, which take place as the old moon dies and the new moon is born, constitute one of the greatest spectacles savage Africa nowadays stages. They are not in the slightest detail influenced by ideas imparted with European religion and culture, but remain intact, with all their superstitions and barbaric grandeur.

On the third day the festival reached a dramatic climax at sunset, when a black ox suffered one of the strangest ceremonial deaths in the world. To a chorus of dancing regiments, uniformed in leopard skins and *sakabula* feathers, the feathers of the widow-bird, about two hundred striplings, naked and unarmed, hurled themselves on a black ox and trampled out its life as they chanted to their king. This so-called bullfight took place in the mire of the cattle kraal and the whole day's activity was a preparation for this moment. Singing and dancing went on intermittently throughout the day. More and more branches were brandished high by teams of boys coming in from the surrounding bush, and entwined by the old men into the secret hut erected within the cattle kraal. Long lines of women bearing bed mats and wooden pillows on their heads marched in from all points of the compass to swell the already great crowd gathered to witness the show.

All this bewildering movement went on even throughout the hot hours of midday and the rainy hours of the afternoon, when everybody remained cheerful though drenched. A dozen heifers were speared in the cattle kraal at noon, cut up and rationed out to the warriors. Then as the sun neared the western hills several beasts were herded to the secret hut, bright green with its covering of fresh leaves, and one of their number, a black ox, was goaded through its doorway.

Chief Sobhuza, after showing himself to his people adorned with a necklace and draped in a blue bordered cloak of figured silk, went into the secret hut with Vanyane, the medicine man, who had collected about him all the requisite herbs and the calabash of seawater required for the ritual, which was not for the eyes of the mob. From the hut came the sound of sharp blows being administered to the ox, which then came charging out. The striplings, on their tiptoes for this moment in a gapless circle, fell upon the ox, which moaned thrice and was then beyond complaining. The carcass was dragged back into the hut, where Vanyane was ready with his knife to cut out those portions of it required for his ritual.

The gall-bladder he emptied and hung on the king's breast. Then the waiting youths, still singing their monotonous chant to "the child who is growing up", that is to say the king, were given the carcass not for their own eating but for an orgy of meat-eating among the children. Thus by

symbols not obvious to the European and even vague to
the Swazi, the authority of the king was once more proved,
the valour of the rising generation established, and the
end of another year fittingly marked.

3

On the fourth day, the Great Day, the Queen Mother's
village became a large and intensely busy beauty parlour
as the *incwala* ceremonies of the afternoon demanded full
war attire for the men and an elaborate toilet for the women.
At sunrise (while the chief was being washed by his blood-
brothers) the warriors bathed in the river which rushes
through the valley below the village, which is built on
rising ground in the midst of stone-crested hills. They
returned to catch a glimpse of their king walking naked and
unashamed. From then till the early afternoon they were
engaged in cleaning and curling the feathers of their headgear, combing their mantles of white oxtails, washing and
smoothing out their kilts of coloured cloth and leopard
skins.

In separate kraals consisting of new beehive huts parti-
tioned by high reed fences into family suites complete with
kitchen, the Swazi women indulged in beauty culture for
a period of eight hours. Lying and kneeling on mats, they
massaged their faces with green vegetable pulp, trimmed
and polished their long, well-shaped fingernails, washed
and repacked their foot-high towers of hair, and draped
themselves from shoulder to ankle in loose, gaily coloured
wraps.

With mirror in hand, both men and women put the
finishing touches to their adornment, the men carefully
sticking small red and blue feathers on their foreheads and
into their hair, while the women arranged beaded hairpins
about their ears at carefully calculated angles and put on
brilliant necklaces and earrings. Everywhere in the scat-

tered village the mirrors, as they were turned anxiously first this way and then that, flashed like helios in the sun. And from all points of this vast and busy beauty parlour a tumult of gossip and laughter went up.

At last the sound of horns summoned the warriors into the large cattle kraal, where they formed in long lines and began chanting special songs which must not be heard on any other occasion, dancing to and fro and brandishing their fighting sticks in the air. With their oxhide shields, their leopard kilts and their massive headgear of ostrich and *sakabula* feathers, they presented, indeed, a spectacle of barbaric splendour.

After an hour had passed the wives of Sobhuza filed from the large huts of their royal mother-in-law, who disciplines them to a set of rigid rules. Thirty in number, these wives were attractively clad in black ox-skins rubbed to the softness of kid, and each carried a long thin white wand in her right hand. Between the secret hut of green leaves in which Vanyane, the medicine man, was busy, and the line of prancing warriors, they advanced and retreated, swaying rhythmically, singing, and with a jerk of the wrist making their long wands tremble above their heads. Gradually the Swazi spectators packed themselves into the cattle kraal, which is surrounded by an unusually high palisade of roughly trimmed trees. All the colours of the rainbow flowed in the oval-shaped arena and several thousand reeds and rods were raised aloft by the massed women who jerked them into a tremble timed to the tremble of the wands waved by the king's wives.

This quivering scene was suddenly disturbed by a sound like whistling rockets. The warriors had caught sight of Sobhuza and this was their salute to him. He was dressed elaborately like his men, only his mantle was composed of black ox-tails and a long scarlet feather was stuck into his wind-tossed *sakabula* headgear. Lifting his shield fashioned from a black and white ox-hide, the chief, an impressive figure, slowly began to dance. The chanting at once took on a new note of enthusiasm and knobkerries and wands were flourished with greater emphasis.

In the late afternoon jagged lightning flashed, thunder pealed and rain poured down, but the weather in no way interfered with the proceedings. Sobhuza went into his secret hut to strip and be anointed by Vanyane with the seawater he had fetched from Mozambique and to eat the first fruits. Having tasted from a gourd, he danced out into the open, now clad in river rushes and with his face hidden behind a mask of feathers. The warriors massed about him and he tossed the gourd among them. Three times he danced out in this way from the secret hut into the kraal to distribute the tasted first fruits and thus signify that the new season's crops might now be partaken of by the tribe.

On the fifth day noisy rejoicing was replaced by silence in the village of the Cow Elephant, for the warrior guests and their womenfolk scattered themselves in the royal farm-lands and occupied themselves in weeding. In the village itself a curious quiet prevailed while Chief Sobhuza and his Master of Ceremonies, Vanyane, were restricted to the huts of chosen wives.

On the sixth day the festival came to an end. For the grand finale the cattle kraal at the Queen Mother's village was packed densely with a rejoicing throng of men, women and children, who surged from palisade to palisade in a ceaseless dance. The final series of songs, which included the Swazi national anthem, went on all day. The main interest was focused on the bones of the black ox which had been sacrificed. These, together with a portion of the gourd which Chief Sobhuza had flung to his regiments, were heaped among the embers of a fire lit by the indunas in the centre of the cattle kraal. A white column of sacrificial smoke rose slowly into the sky of Swaziland's gods, while Chief Sobhuza, dressed again in his skins and feathers, danced on the churned-up mud in the midst of his people. And, as it was supposed to, rain fell obediently!

4

As I motored back to the Transvaal during the next day
the warriors could be seen marching home along a hundred
and one footpaths which link up Swaziland's scattered
villages. With them went their women contentedly carrying
food and bed mats while their lords and masters gesticulated
with their fighting sticks, as they told of the important part
they had played in the week's festival.

This week of barbaric splendour when Sobhuza, in the
savage finery of his forebears, sings and dances with his
warriors, is mainly remarkable for its absence of anything
hinting of the Whiteman's influence; and yet there are
signs, slight it is true, and for the most part negative,
which tell a new story to those with a long and intimate
knowledge of Swazi ways. This new story marks a slight
slackening off, more especially among the rising generation,
of tribal interest in this annual Feast of the First Fruits.

In some ways this is a great pity; in other ways, it is
regarded as a good thing by intelligent opinion, both Swazi
and European. While it is very pleasing to see the Swazis
in their skins and feathers and hear them chanting ancient
songs of war and feasting, it is disconcerting for those
responsible for guiding this picturesque nation from
savagery and black magic towards civilisation and Christianity to recognise in their esoteric ritual a perpetuation of
the superstitions of darkest Africa. It is not an edifying
spectacle, for instance, that trampling to death of the black
ox by the feet of young men; but, worse still, it is in the
minds of some a disconcerting symbol making it probable
that human sacrifice will flourish in private as long as this
animal sacrifice is practised in public.

Not that there is any direct connection between the
incwala ceremonies and ritual murder. That much, at any
rate, authoritative information has established quite definitely. Those who are in the closest possible contact with

Swazi. A few years ago a traveller took a few photographs of one of the ceremonies performed in the cattle kraal at the Queen Mother's village. The fact was reported to Sobhuza by several Swazis, who had seen the camera being used. He at once protested to the Resident Commissioner, who had the precious films of the traveller destroyed. Since then, with royal permission, several photographs have been taken of the ceremonies; but certain of them are still barred to the camera's lens and even to the European eye.

Then, as a very special favour, American newsreel representatives, taking moving pictures with sound, were allowed to take shots of certain parts of the ceremonies; but the *incwala* songs were very emphatically denied to the microphone, Sobhuza saying that those songs were not meant to be heard on any other occasion.

5

Thus, by venerating his ancestral spirits and honouring ancient tribal customs, Sobhuza seeks both to keep the Swazis in Swaziland and to retain Swaziland for the Swazis. To the Whiteman he pays diplomatic homage in accordance with the prudent policy laid down in the days of the Voortrekkers by Sobhuza I. That death-dealing tyrant of the Shaka pattern believed, as Shaka believed, that friendship with the Whiteman, all-wise, all-powerful, was the safest policy. And so he "dreamed[1] that people of a strange species entered his country. They were the colour of the red mealies; their hair resembled the tails of cattle; their houses were built on platforms and dragged by oxen; they spoke an unknown tongue and they knew not the courtesies of humanity. The men carried weapons of terrible destruction. This dream was interpreted as a warning from the ancestors never to fight the white people, 'and see,' the story-teller added, 'we have obeyed'. Before the Europeans penetrated

[1] *An African Aristocracy* (Oxford University Press).

Swaziland, before there was any direct contact, the Swazi acknowledged their difference and the white man's military strength. . . . The European advance guard arrived in the country and was received in peace. Farmers drifted through on their way to the coast, traders bartered their wares for ivory and skins, hunters shot the wild game teeming in the low and middle veld, and a missionary settled for a while in the south. . . .

"The discovery of gold in the north-west in 1882 lured European fortune-hunters to Swaziland. Adventurers with their worldly wealth slung in knapsacks over their shoulders trudged along the native footpaths; the more fortunate travelled in wagons that laboriously carved tracks over hills and valleys. . . . Companies were floated, largely with capital from overseas, and the possibilities of a harbour and a railway were investigated. The men bribed their way past the councillors to obtain personal interviews with the king. They brought him cash, blankets, dogs, horses, liquor, and other products of the 'civilised world'; in return, he was merely requested to make crosses on the document that they placed before him."

But many of these crossings were cancelled out by double-crossings as Boer, Briton and Bantu went waltzing and fighting with one another in fits and starts; and the Swazis held on to the hill country of their ancestors while the Europeans, sometimes described as red ants, turned away to burrow for diamonds in Kimberley and for gold in Johannesburg. With the process of detribalisation going on in all parts of South Africa as the Bantu pastoralists become labourers in the Whiteman's mines and factories, Sobhuza zealously makes medicine and dances before his people in order to keep the Swazis together. He has even told his learned European friends that anthropology is the antidote to the social disease of detribalisation.

"Anthropology", runs his argument,[1] "makes possible comparison and selection of lines of further development.

[1] New Education Conference, Witwatersrand University, 1934.

European culture is not all good; ours is often better. We must be able to choose how to live, and for that we must see how others live. I do not want my people to be imitation Europeans, but to be respected for their own laws and customs."

Other Bantu leaders take the opposite view, saying that the sentimental anthropologist would bind them and their fellow-tribesmen to their witchbound, barbaric past, preventing their release into the enlightened world of European culture; nevertheless, they are brave words, these of Sobhuza who himself dexterously manages to be a man of two worlds. When he visited England on a diplomatic mission in the years between the two World Wars, he was described by Fleet Street gossip-writers as the best-dressed man in London. And it certainly seemed to me that he wore his European clothes extremely well when he went to Pretoria in 1934 to pay his respects to the Prince George, the late Duke of Kent, and present him with a beautifully carved set of Swazi eating dishes. But by 1947, when I was playing the part of Government Press Officer to the Royal Visit, his sartorial taste, I regret to say, had gone the fanciful way of most African chiefs, who, for State occasions of unusual importance, believe profoundly in the efficacy of the wildly extravagant uniforms of comic opera.

To welcome the British King and Queen and the two Princesses, Sobhuza, according to the correspondent of *The Times*,[1] was clad in "a uniform in the height of the military fashion of the Second Empire. It included a tunic of armorial azure, trousers of blazing scarlet, gold epaulettes, and a lemon-coloured sash crossing diagonally from the shoulder to the waist." So much by way of tribute to the European world, to European culture. But "in contrast to this polychromatic figure, the Queen Mother, who stood beside him, was barefooted and clothed in a costume entirely of skins, which it was easy to believe had not been changed for many years. The lady . . . exercises magical

[1] Dermot Morrah in *The Royal Family in Africa* (Hutchinson, 1947).

powers over the rainfall, and if she changed her clothes the
effects on the crops would be disastrous. There was, in fact,
a light rain falling while the party waited for the arrival of
the royal procession; but the Queen Mother blandly explained that she had herself arranged for this, in order to
lay the dust during His Majesty's long journey. . . . The
weather, she said, would clear in time for the ceremonies
of the day; and so it did. Bizarre as both the two Natives
appeared to European eyes, when they took their places in
the *indaba* . . . they performed their allotted parts with a
measured dignity that was truly impressive.

"The proceedings at the *indaba* showed the double aspect
of the life of the Swazis, who within their own boundaries
preserve much of their tribal system and ancestral traditions,
and yet have made their mark in another continent. The
latter aspect was typified in the march past of the Swazi
Pioneer Corps, who strode along in British khaki uniform
at a swinging pace that seemed to declare their pride in the
battle honours they had won so far away as the beaches of
Anzio. But they were succeeded in the arena by a phalanx
of warriors of an older fashion, perhaps a thousand in
number, who surged forward towards the royal platform in
the slow rhythm of the 'dance of impenetrable mystery',
which is the ancient salute accorded to visitors of the highest
degree. . . .

"The men, all in leopard-skin girdles, with gleaming
black skins, and their towering headdresses looking like a
thicket of feathers, carried their assegais and knobkerries
with a suggestion of menace that gave a very real idea of
how formidable must have been the *impis* of the ancient
wars. They swung their big ox-hide shields out and down in
homage, and they hailed the King with an eerie whistle
between clenched teeth, which is the Swazi form of the
royal salute. There was no suggestion of fancy dress in their
display; it was impossible to doubt that this stately dance
came out of the living customs of the country."

Yes, the *sartor resartus* of Sobhuza symbolises the double

life forced upon him by the collision of the white world
with the black world. No such quick-change artistry is
required of the Queen Mother. As the Swazi rain-giver,
she greets the British Royal Family; and a little later she is
again sitting "on the mat in her yard, discussing cases,
hearing gossip, organising work, plaiting rope, or performing other duties associated with women. She is dressed in
skins similar to those of any other conservative woman.
But on her hair is a crown of wooden pegs topped by a
jaunty red flamingo feather set between lucky beans; round
her ankles and wrists are tied small pouches of potent
medicines."[1]

But Sobhuza, after bowing farewell to Their Majesties
and the two Princesses, must divest himself of the sartorial
glory that was the Second Empire in order to visit the Great
Abode of Swazi chieftainship and ritual. Such a uniform
would not be appropriate to the national shrine, the hut
always honoured with the royal salute, *Bayete!*—the hut
whose weave is sanctified and fortified with ceremonial
mats and ropes, and in which, hidden behind a red screen,
are sacred calabashes, grain of a kind no longer sown, and
offerings of beer.

"The supports of the hut", we are told,[1] "are strongly
doctored, and above the door are two tiny holes in the inner
layers of the thatching through which the King spits on
certain occasions, thereby radiating his power over the
nation. Over the doorway, on the outside, are skulls of
sacrificial cattle. . . . Here the King and the Queen Mother
speak to the ancestral spirits on behalf of their subjects,
and perform rites to bring rain. . . . No one impure, no
one who has recently had sexual relations, no menstruating
women, no one with ropes of mourning may enter."

And on the Great Day of the *incwala* mysteries, Sobhuza
is stripped even of his barbaric finery—his kilt of leopard
skin, his mantle of flowing ox-tails, his headdress of waving
black plumes. After being bathed by his blood-brothers,

[1] *An African Aristocracy* (Oxford University Press).

Sobhuza, in the full light of day walks naked among his Swazi people: "naked but for a glowing white penis-cap of ivory". *Sartor resartus*, Swazi-fashion.

6

POSTSCRIPT

There is no railway in Swaziland; and in January, the time of the First Fruits Ceremony, the unbridged rivers are often swollen with seasonal rains. This makes motoring uncertain and sometimes impossible. From Breyton, in the Eastern Transvaal, railway buses run to Mbabane, the Swaziland capital, Bremersdorp and Stegi; from Piet Retief, also in the Eastern Transvaal, there is a bus service to Hlatikulu and Hluti; and from Gollel, in Northern Natal, buses go to Bremersdorp.

From the Transvaal the main road to Mbabane goes on through Swaziland to Lourenço Marques in the Portuguese colony of Mozambique—South Africans frequently make this journey; but for the average visitor it would be going off at a tangent from the South African circle of his journeyings. Swaziland is one of the three British Protectorates outside the Union politically, but inside or alongside the Union geographically.

Basutoland, another of the Protectorates, is right in the middle of the Union. Its one mile of railway track—to Maseru, the capital—is a branch line of the South African Railways. Also, its postal system is run by the South African Posts and Telegraphs, and, in Lionel Curtis's words, "socially and economically the Union and the Protectorates are integral parts of a single system". On an average, anything between 50 and 70 per cent of Basutoland's able-bodied manpower (total population is about 600,000) goes to the gold mines of the Witwatersrand every year to work on contract.

Thousands more are recruited in Swaziland and Bechuanaland, the third British Protectorate, which forms the

Members of a Swazi impi fording a river on their march to the Queen Mother's kraal to share in the mystery of Chief Sobhuza's rain-making.

In the Transkei, while their blanketed elders look on, the boys are initiated into manhood by rustling their ceremonial reed kilts to the rhythm of drums beaten by women.

western boundary of the Transvaal. A railroad runs from Mafeking in the Cape right through the Bechuanaland Protectorate, paralleling the eastern border of the Transvaal and linking up with the Southern Rhodesian Railways. The veld it traverses is semi-desert, hot and dusty.

Many hundreds of the Natives trek into the Union on their own account in search of higher wages and a livelier town life. The mines and factories of South Africa attract Native labour from very much farther afield than the Protectorates. From Nyasaland, from Northern and Southern Rhodesia, and from Uganda, Natives trek southward, saying, "*Mina funa sebenza, baas!*" ("I want work, master!")

Of the three Protectorates only Basutoland has ever claimed to be self-supporting. Like the other two it has, of late years, tackled its growing agricultural difficulties with zest, on the urgent advice of the Europeans and with the direction of their Chiefs. High-lying Basutoland is the watershed of South Africa, which therefore has an interest in its fight against soil erosion. In a speech during the 1945 session of the Union Parliament, General Smuts, then Prime Minister, spoke of the Protectorates as "anomalies" on the map of Southern Africa which, in time, would need to be adjusted within the framework of a greater South Africa. This expansion is visualised in a clause contained in the Act of Union of 1910. The schedule in which this point is made specifies guarantees to the Natives regarding their lands, their tribal institutions and the liquor traffic, and the assurance that their wishes will be consulted whenever such amalgamation is contemplated.

G

CHAPTER V

IN SAVAGE SURROUNDINGS

I

THE ASTONISHING thing about South Africa is the way the Blackman has thriven in the company of the Whiteman. For it is not only the Swazis who have survived the advance of the long-haired, red-faced, wagon-driving musket-bearers—all the other tribes have survived, too, and multiplied exceedingly: the Xosas, the Pondos, the Tembus, the Basutos, the Bechuanas, the Zulus, and all the tribes of the Northern Transvaal clustering about the mist-enshrouded hills of the Rain Queen, of whom Rider Haggard's *She* is the prototype.

The greatest historical fact in South Africa's three hundred years of European occupation is the rise of the Bantu. Here and there, their assegai-wielding warriors were beaten in battle by the gun-firing Europeans; but these sporadic, brief encounters caused fewer casualties than the hand-to-hand slaughters of habitual, inter-tribal warfare. In Darkest Africa, famines, epidemics and infant mortality took enormous toll of the Bantu: but in the presence of the Whiteman, with his transport and medicine and science, these acts of God ceased. The *Pax Britannica* has given to Africa only a sprinkling of Europeans but teeming millions of Bantu, rescued from slave-dealers, from their own bloodthirsty warlords, from starvation and from disease.

The South Africans, advancing and settling, *laager* by *laager*,[1] in the comparatively empty, war-wasted lands of the high plateau above the Drakensberg, turned the savages into gun-bearers, drivers and herders of cattle, farm labourers and domestic servants; and now, looking about them,

[1] Afrikaans for leaguer.

they see that the sons of Ham have become as numerous as the grass, while, gazing into the equatorial heart of Africa, they realise that their neighbours, and their neighbours' neighbours, are savages—savages beyond computation. The first tidy pattern of conquerors with gun and bible—a pattern traced lightly across a veld pleasantly abounding in game for the pot and simple Kafirs for the chores—has been shaken askew in the world-wide shatterings of two Great Wars waged by Germany against her own world—Western Europe. With Europe desperately wounded, the Whiteman's colonial writ no longer runs so surely and his sanctions are now questioned by the lesser tribes without the law.

And, Sobhuza's anthropological discourse notwithstanding, so many of Africa's tribes are still without the law. In Swaziland the *incwala* may pass for barbaric splendour as the shining dancers screen superstition by the beauty and vigour of their physical energy; but what goes on in the brooding valleys of Zululand or in the incestuous shrines of the Transvaal lowveld where *She-who-never-dies* ritualistically immolates herself to rise again with youth renewed? The sons and daughters of these broods, drawn as workers to mine and factory and office, now surround not merely the ox-wagons, linked into a *laager*, but the Whiteman's towns, where his little nation dwells, and indeed invades his way of life.

Much more efficiently and vividly than formerly, South African newspapers record this drama of the Dark Continent. Its millions are stirring like a giant—perhaps, from the Whiteman's point of view, like a Frankenstein largely of his own creation: a Frankenstein *ex machina*, from the *Pax Britannica* no less. The racial story, as he cannot help recalling with a certain fretfulness, was so much easier in Australia, where the Blackfellows died without fuss on smelling brandy, or in North America, where the Red Indians despairingly turned up their toes at the tricks of the Palefaces, or in the South Sea Islands, where the

Polynesians found Western commerce in goods and bodies more than they could endure. But the Bantu, like the Negro, has taken all that Europe offered him or forced upon him, and now he is clamouring for more. Yet still, from Equatoria, whose denizens now tend to press southwards, come stories that make the flesh creep—stories of the Leopard-men, the Alligator-men, and the Lion-men.

From the reeds of a West African river an Alligator-man, dressed for the part, rises up to seize an unwanted tribesman whom he carries off, not into the water, but into the bush, where fellow members of the Alligator Society are waiting to disembowel their victim. Or an Alligator-man, breathing in a "diving bell" fixed under a large canoe, drags under a bathing child and carries it downstream to the place of dissection.

In the thorn-forests of Tanganyika mass murders are traced to the Lions who practise ritual killing, black magic and witchcraft. The Lions, garbed in long, loose hides, and wearing a grotesque mask, are powerfully built men who lift up their victims and carry them deep into the bush. Small knife cuts, it is said,[1] and punctures, as if from spike-like instruments, are always noticed on the neck, shoulders and chests of the murdered natives. Long strips of flesh are invariably cut from the thighs to heighten the illusion that the natives were victims of prowling man-eating lions. When the ground is soft or sandy, artificial lion spoors are detected at the scene of the killing.

The Leopard-men, of whom there are century-old accounts, are called to meetings by messengers who show a hip bearing a longitudinal cicatrix: the sign. The tribal calabash containing strong medicine of human ingredients needs replenishing, so a victim is named. Then, "at the appointed hour,[2] when it is quite dark, a strange flute-like whistling ... produced by blowing over short lengths of bamboo, is heard in the bush which comes right up to the outermost

[1] *The Imperial Review*, July 1947.
[2] *The Human Leopard Society of Sierra Leone*, by Dr. D. Burrows in the January 1914 number of *The Journal of the African Society*.

houses. . . . At the dread sound there is a scurrying into the houses, and doors are closed securely. The hapless victim is sent on some fictitious errand, and is pounced on by the leopard-men, who first lacerate the throat with the sharp claw-knives, sometimes severing all the vital structures; and they then return into the bush growling and roaring like leopards the while, and this noise is continued until the victim is carried safely into the sacred bush. The villagers are afraid to venture out—some, the uninitiated, imagining there are real leopards about . . . are not these marks of the leopard's feet?'' In the bush, the victim is cut up, the omens interpreted, the ingredients for the magic calabash carefully set aside, and the flesh, rationed into small pieces, is wrapped in banana leaves and delivered by runners to the scattered members of the various lodges of the society.

Of course, Africa can no more be judged by its Leopard-men than Chicago by its gunmen, or Sydney by its razor-gangsters, or London by its spivs. But the Leopard-men, like the Alligator-men and the Lion-men, are part of a society surrounding the Whiteman as he seeks to establish Western, Christian civilisation among the Bantu. First in the days of Rhodes and Kruger, and then in the days of Botha and Smuts—for half a century up to the second World War—it looked a feasible proposition; but with the collapse of the West and the emergence of the East, with the power politics of the disunited United Nations, with the stretching of the Blackman's limbs and the half-awakening of his mind, with the increased hold of Africa's East Coast by the Indians, and with a new scramble for Africa quietly going on, the Whiteman's South Africa, as pictured by the optimistic generation now passing away, looks a much less likely proposition.

The southward drag of Equatoria goes on, as it has for over three hundred years; and in the Cape itself, no less than in Swaziland, or Zululand, or Vendaland, the tribal customs of Darkest Africa are still practised, if in modified forms. Even among the urban Bantu, the workers who en-

circle the South African towns, voodooism is practised—
without the larger corrective of tribal family life and the
patriarchal sanctions of the chief—and gangs, such as the
amalaitas of Johannesburg, exist for Bantu *esprit-de-corps*
and for all the crimes known to man.

2

Although, generally speaking, Africa's old order has
gone, Africa's new order has not yet taken shape. The
Whiteman, especially in the south, is trying, with a sort of
feverish anxiety, to give it shape; but recently released
forces in Africa itself, in India and in Europe are inter-
fering with his original, long-range plan. The world's
accelerated tempo is playing against Africa's slow rhythm
and disturbing its equilibrium. The puzzled Whiteman asks
himself, "What is the music of the future?" and takes
stock of his surroundings.

South Africa's traditional warrior-kings, who worked to
the law of kill or be killed, are one with yesterday. The
Whiteman saw to that. They have been succeeded by chiefs
who, with the advice of European commissioners and
magistrates, rule their tribes according to their many
ancient customs—except where those customs are so bar-
barous that they conflict too sharply with the higher law
of the Whiteman. When this happens the commissioners
and magistrates gently turn the face of the chiefs towards
the light. If the chiefs obstinately refuse to look towards the
light, *force majeure* compels them to do so.

But the chiefs are not allowed to sit in judgment on
Europeans—there are not many of them—living in their
tribal area. That is understood not only in the Native
territories within the Union such as Zululand, the Transkei,
Pondoland and Vendaland, but also in the Protectorates
which are ruled not from Pretoria but from Downing Street
—the Protectorates of Swaziland, Basutoland and Bechuana-

land. This interesting division of authority is perhaps best
explained by citing the particular case of Regent Tshekedi,
the youngest son of the late King Khama, one of the Queen
Victoria's so-called treaty chiefs. The incident began when
two Europeans "went native" in Serowe, royal capital of
the Bamangwato—the most numerous and influential tribe
in Bechuanaland. Not only that: their huts, it was said,
were often noisy with Kafir-beer carousals which ended in
Native girls being taken into the bush. Tshekedi, claiming
that he had first done his best to persuade the European
authorities to put an end to the scandal, then brought things
to a head by summoning one of the "White Kafirs" to
his *khotla*, his place of council and justice, on a charge of
assaulting a Native youth who had been talking to a Native
girl with whom the accused was said to be in love. The
"White Kafir" was found guilty and punished with
lashes.

In doing this, Tshekedi was exceeding his authority as
chief, despite the fact that, as the acting successor of Khama,
a "treaty chief", he claimed to have inherited powers greater
than those exercised by a conquered chief. The Administration officials may have been lax in not themselves taking
action against the turbulent "White Kafirs", though it
must be emphasised that miscegenation[1] is not a crime in the
Protectorate as it is in the Union, while no complaint had

[1] An important instance of the "colour bar" being applied by Black against White
occurred in 1948 when Seretse Khama, the Chief-Designate for whom Tshekedi is
Regent, married Miss Ruth Williams, an English girl, in London, where he was
studying law. On hearing the news, Tshekedi, after a council meeting, at once
summoned Seretse to Serowe, the Bamangwato capital in the Bechuanaland Protectorate. There he had to face a conference of 3,000 tribesmen, only seven of whom
supported his plea to be allowed to assume the chieftainship in due course with his
European wife by his side. He returned to London with the tribal judgment that,
after his final law examinations towards the end of 1949, he must either give up
his English wife and return to Serowe to rule the Bamangwato, or he must renounce
his right to the chieftainship. Seretse is the eldest son of the late Sekgoma who was
the eldest son of the late Khama. When Sekgoma died in 1926 Seretse was four years
old. His uncle, Tshekedi, then studying at Lovedale College, was recalled to Serowe
and installed as Regent. "The case of Seretse Khama", comments the *African
World* in its February 1949 issue "is of interest to all Africa", and adds, "He was
left in no doubt that the tribe were solidly opposed to his marriage to a European.
It was made plain that in no circumstances would his wife be recognised as the wife
of the chief and that no son of the marriage could possibly succeed to the chieftainship."

been lodged about this particular case of common assault. But one thing was perfectly clear in the law of the land— Tshekedi's high-handed action in lashing a European could not be tolerated, even though that European might say, as he did at the subsequent inquiry, "I am satisfied with the chief's judgment".

At this little moment in history between the two Great Wars, Admiral Evans—Evans of the *Broke*—was both the Commander-in-Chief of the Royal Navy's Africa Station at Simonstown and His Majesty's Acting High Commissioner; and he at once rushed two hundred of his blue-jackets and marines with two howitzers to Serowe, ordered an inquiry, arrived on the scene himself by aeroplane, received a salute of nineteen shots, banished the "White Kafirs", and suspended Tshekedi from the chieftainship.

The defenders of Tshekedi then made themselves heard both in South Africa and England, gaining for him a great deal of sympathy. "White Kafirs" are beyond the pale, and on their heads their fellow Europeans are always ready to heap hatred and scorn. Was a son of the great Khama, to whose name are attached many sentiments born of his long association with British endeavour in Bechuanaland, the Transvaal and Rhodesia—endeavour political, military and missionary—to be deposed because, exasperated by the inactivity of the Administration officials, he lashed a "White Kafir", one who had lost caste? And all good mothers wept, as the cynical journalist who published the letter said they would, when Semane, Queen Mother of the Bamangwato, wrote to King George V in the following strain:

"I send my weeping to you, my King, I who am the widow of Khama; and I pray let my weeping reach your ears because you are the refuge pointed to me by my master Khama. When he died, he left me in your power.

"My life, I know, subsists in you, although I am in bitter weeping because of the castigation which you have given me. I am unable to flee anywhere except to you. Pity me, because you are my refuge and the life of your tribe.

Let the great Lion, when he kills, spare a few bones: a man is the property of his King.

"This is the cry of the widow of your servant Khama. This is our law, O King! Should the ruling chiefs decide to beat a person, or do something to him very painful when he transgresses one of the laws, they are unable to harm him any longer if he runs away to me, for they remember the name of Khama. And I say, O King, I run to you because this law is yours, and I continue to weep while running to you.

"O King, release for me the boy. I am undone and the tribe is undone. This is my weeping, my Master. O let it be regarded! I am the widow of Khama, Semane."

This appeal, however, did not melt the hearts of those in Downing Street occupying places of ultimate authority. So Tshekedi, from his place of exile on the Bamangwatoland border, apologised for what he had done and promised not to do it again. Ah, that was different! Admiral Evans, on this, at once recommended to the Colonial Secretary that His Majesty should be advised to terminate forthwith the period of Tshekedi's suspension; and this His Majesty was graciously pleased to do. So that was that, and Admiral Evans, to the sound of more gunfire, reinstated Tshekedi while uttering this airy aphorism: "It can never be for the good of the people that a chief should break the law."

Whatever the rights and wrongs of that unhappy series of petty incidents may have been, the reassuring fact emerges that it transformed a desert of negative politics into a garden of administrative loveliness. British officialdom awoke from its prolonged coma like a giant refreshed, and began carrying out a positive policy with vigour and enthusiasm. And the Native chiefs, who had been sulking in their huts, suddenly came forward with hands outstretched to help and to be helped by the commissioners and magistrates. The Tshekedi incident, small and ridiculous though it may have been, had the same health-restoring effect on the body corporate of the Protectorate as the lancing of a boil on a sick man's neck.

3

The Whiteman's discovery of the "fairest Cape", his journeyings into the death-dealing wilds, his encounters with the fierce beasts of the veld, his wars with the blood-thirsty Kafirs, his stumbling upon the world's greatest stores of diamonds and gold, his taming of the jungle, his building of new cities for a new nation—all these events make South Africa's history a stirring thing and enrich its literature. There were Bantu giants in this land—Shaka, Dingaan, Mziligazi, Moshesh, Lobengula, Khama; and from the ranks of the Dutch and British stepped out giants of equal stature to measure strength with strength and wisdom with wisdom—Pieter Retief, Andries Pretorius, Sir Harry Smith, Paul Kruger, Robert Moffat, David Livingstone, Cecil Rhodes, Starr Jameson, Louis Botha, Jan Smuts; and Jan Smuts is the very last of that race of giants. But in spite of the Whiteman's long saga of exploration and conquest, the Blackman is still in possession of his country, the country that lies hidden between the towns; and there the hills echo with his laughter and the valleys vibrate with his dancing.

There is the *bula* dance which, although nowadays against the country's penal code, is still performed, deep in the heart of Zululand. With perfect secrecy, arrangements for this death-dance are made by local *indunas* and headmen, whose trusted messengers, by signs and passwords, command the clan to gather on a given day and at some remote spot guarded by watchmen. Here the most terrible of all tribal ordeals is carried out precisely as in the old days of Shaka and Dingaan or, during the nineties, of Lobengula in Matabeleland: it is the ordeal by smelling-out, the ordeal in which a frenzied witch-doctor, having reduced the super-stitious clan to a state of terror, smells out the victim or victims, whom he thus condemns of causing the evil that is abroad—the sickness among the cattle, the ineffectiveness of the rain-making, or deaths in the chief's kraal. Such inspired detection is also a verdict of guilty and a pronouncement of the death penalty; and there is no appeal against the witch-doctor's smelling-out. At the *bula* dance, death strikes by the highest sanction of tribal custom; and from the corpse or corpses, strong medicine is made to rid the land of the evil wished upon it.

No smelling-out ceremony is necessary when the witch-doctor needs the bodies of babies for his charms and *muti*: the babies disappear from their kraals—that is all. That still goes on, according to an American investigator,[1] who admits, however, that the South African criminal code tends to curb the activities of the Zulu witch-doctors. Nevertheless, when a witch-doctor must have a human heart or liver, a baby vanishes. The mother, often with more faith in witchcraft than in the Whiteman's law, does not report the disappearance of her baby to the police—she simply forgets all about it. "The South African witch-doctor is neither played out nor finished," says this American investigator. "He is not even in decline, but on the contrary has as much power today as he had a couple of centuries ago. The witch-doctor's craft is one of the most lucrative in South Africa, and he might well be the envy of many medical practitioners. The craft is jealously guarded, and while the oath of Hippocrates does not apply to the native witch-doctor, he stands under rules which are equally as rigid. Among his own people the native witch-doctor in South Africa is highly respected and honoured. He holds a position which only an eminent specialist in our medical world might hope to hold."

Witch-doctors, however, who deal in black magic and who employ evil powers to defeat evil, must not be confused with medicine-men, whose great knowledge of herbs is skilfully applied to cases of ordinary sickness. At their best, they are true physicians; at their worst, they are false to their profession by resorting to mild forms of magic as a

[1] Dr. C. G. Mason, of Washington, representing the Geographical Society, in an interview published by the *Sunday Times*, Johannesburg, on 19 January 1947.

quick way to fame and fortune. Harley Street specialists themselves are not unacquainted with that temptation.

As superstition has not yet been wholly rooted out in Europe, we cannot expect an Act of Parliament to abolish it in Africa. Long-pig, that former delicacy of the South Sea Islanders, is still eaten as a ritual by the members of Africa's secret societies, such as the Society of the Leopard-men; it is said to give them dark powers and to band them together in a brotherhood of silence.

"Few people realise", writes a South African journalist,[1] "that cannibalism once flourished within South Africa to a greater extent than ever it did on any South Sea Island paradise. Indeed one early missionary, Arbousset, computed that no fewer than 300,000 victims vanished down the hungry gullets of Basutoland's man-eaters alone, between the years 1822 and 1828. This figure appears to be some-what exaggerated but the first half of the nineteenth century, the heyday of South Africa's cannibals, was a troubled period in the Bantu world when entire clans disappeared in the chaos of inter-tribal warfare and survivors fell a ready prey to the bloodthirsty monsters who flourished on their fellows' misery. . . .

"The wild orgies of the cannibals became notorious. They appear to have lived in an evil world of their own, with peculiar dances and customs. One of their songs has been preserved and a translation makes strange reading. It was sung by the men whilst their womenfolk, delightful creatures, clapped hands in accompaniment and eyed the victim appraisingly.

> We are cannibals, we eat people,
> We eat thee, we eat people;
> We eat the brain of a dog,
> And that of a little child.
> We eat the fingers of people,
> We eat the fat of mankind.

[1]. T. V. Bulpin under the heading *The Cannibals of South Africa*, in *The Cape Times Week-end Magazine* of 25 May 1946.

Thou toy of the man-eaters,
Thou delicious morsel.
Strike! Strike him down!
My comrades!

"One of the principal cannibal areas was in the Eastern Transvaal. . . . Entire clans turned cannibal and life became exceedingly difficult for the unfortunate peasants already reduced by the Matabele to possession of little more than their lives. . . . One of the most celebrated of the Natal cannibals was a certain Mahlapalapa who had his stronghold on Job's Kop, near modern Ladysmith. He waxed so prosperous on the troubled times that he grew overfat and, his followers over-tempted, they ate him!"

I do not know whether cannibalism was encouraged by the mass cattle-killing by the Xosas of Kaffraria in 1857; but it seems likely, for its sequel was widespread famine. Nongquase, a sort of Joan of Arc, while fetching water from a stream near her kraal, was told by spirits that the hour of deliverance was at hand: the souls of the mighty were ready to descend from the clouds, to sweep the Whiteman into the sea, and to restore to Kaffraria corn in plenty, cattle fat and sleek, and milk of the purest kind. So "hundreds and thousands of splendid cattle were slaughtered, madly, indiscriminately, stupidly. Fields of corn were laid waste. . . . While the killing went on the tribes built vast new kraals for the cattle that were to rise like stars in their multitude. They built enormous vats to store the milk that was to rain from heaven. They cleared the bush for the fields of corn that the gods were to raise and tend."[1]

But the girl's prophecy failed. The story of the terrible sequel was secured by George McCall Theal, South Africa's great historian, from eye-witnesses. Brother fought with brother, father with son, for scraps and shreds from those great milk vats so carefully made in the days when hope was high. The aged and sick and feeble were abandoned by the

[1] Version by Ross Bresler under the heading *Prophetess of a Nation's Doom*, in the *Sunday Times*, Johannesburg, on 11 May 1947.

young and vigorous. Some struggled to the sea-shore and fought for bits of fish that littered the waterside. Unused to this diet, they were attacked by dysentery which rounded off the work of famine. Whole families sat down and died together. From fifteen to twenty skeletons were frequently found under a single tree.

The official census returns of British Kaffraria show a decrease in the Bantu population between 1 January and 31 July of that fatal year of 1857 from 104,721 to 37,229 of both sexes and all ages. Beyond the Kei River the death roll, say some, was 25,000, others say 50,000.

4

The Bantu were shaken from the tropics into the south-east. Were the Bushmen shaken from the tropics into the south-west?

The Whiteman has sited his main *laager* on the high plateau. In the low-lying, sub-tropical regions to the east are the Swazis and the Zulus; and in the sandy wastes to the falling west, in the Kalahari and its far, undefined extensions, are the desert folk of the Bechuana breed and the Bushmen. The Bushmen are, in the words of a South African politician and author,[1] "a yellow-skinned pygmy race standing about four-foot six, and they have tremendously developed hind-quarters which serve them like the camel's hump from which to draw on in lean periods." A South-West African policeman "told me that shortly before, while out on patrol, he had come on a bushwoman lying in a small hollow she had scooped in the ground, and she was in the very act of parturition. As he approached, the child made its appearance and the mother, seeing him ride up, hastily scrabbled the new-born infant in the sand to dry it, and holding it close to her body she fled into the bush like any wild animal. He said he had been present when . . . the magistrate was

[1] The late Deneys Reitz in *No Outspan* (Faber, 1943).

killed the year before. They saw a bushman running through
the trees. . . . When brought to bay he pulled out one of
the tiny bows they carry and shot his captor with a poisoned
dart at a range of a few feet. The magistrate died in great
agony in less than half an hour and by next morning the
body was so decomposed that it fell to pieces when they
tried to handle it. These little bows are about two inches
long, beautifully fashioned from what appears to be rhino
horn. The arrows are the size of a safety match, of heavy
wood, the points covered with a deadly poison brewed from
some vegetable toxin or from putrid caterpillars. . . . The
arrows are carried in a tiny leathern quiver and each has its
point sheathed in grass to prevent accidental contact. The
bushman also carries his ordinary hunting bow and he uses
the smaller weapon in the same way as a gangster might
carry an automatic pistol in addition to a larger gun."

Nomadic hunters, the Bushmen bivouac in nests on the
ground made of grass flung loosely over a few branches
propped against one another. In the Great Thirstland, the
Kalahari, they survive during times of drought by digging
up the ostrich eggs they had filled with water and buried
when the rains were good. To be free of the Whiteman's
law and complicated conventions, they live where nobody
else wants to live, in the blistering, unfertile sands; but they
are cheerful folk, unshackled to any past and not toiling towards any future. They belong to the present only. And when
the day's hunting and eating is over, they sing and dance.

"The unmarried girls", records an eye-witness[1] of their
revels, "were led by a girl of fourteen. She was beautiful
according to Bushmen standards, a dancer and natural
actress who would have delighted audiences in Europe.
She led her little family troupe with all the skill of a ballet
mistress, bringing into the dance a wonderful grace of
movement. . . . The girls had decorated their faces with
gemsbok blood; they wore springbok skins round their
waists and beads of ostrich shell. Each girl carried her make-

[1] Lawrence G. Green in *Where Men Still Dream* (Timm ins, Cape Town, 1945).

up of powdered roots in the shell of a tiny tortoise fastened
to her ankle. . . . Later that night all the Bushmen of the
camp danced. . . . Under a moon that was almost full, and
with naked limbs reddened in the firelight, the men
stamped out a circle in the sand with feet thudding, cocoon
anklets rattling and the women clapping and singing in
barbaric cadence."

Their brothers in the north, the Congo pigmies, also
live beyond the effective reach of the law and the stifling
routines of the Whiteman's daily round. But instead of the
desert, the deep, dark forest protects them from advancing
civilisation and provides them with edible roots and meat.

"These tiny creatures", says a scientist[1] who lived among
them for a while, "are among the most independent of all
the natives in Africa. No one has ever succeeded in making
them pay taxes or work as carriers or on road labour like
the rest of the natives in the Colonies. Their happiness lies
in their complete freedom from wealth or possessions. Their
huts are built with a few branches, thrown together care-
lessly. The forest supplies them with all the food they desire
—wild beans and bananas and the same *miondo*[2] which the
gorilla eats. The forest gives them also wood for their fires
and iron-wood for their spears and arrows, the points of
which, as well as the semi-lunar blades of their machetes,
are prepared by their witch-doctors who are workers in
iron. Some little animal provides meat and pieces of skin
more than adequate for the very meagre attire they wear.
They do not require wealth to buy wives, for it is their
custom to take them without payment, and these diminu-
tive women make no pretension to ornaments, or to anything else. Therefore, why work? And if they never work
and earn no money, how can they be expected to pay taxes?
. . . As they are the only ones who can guide the few Whites
who go now and then to the forest, and are very trustworthy
in this function, the authorities finally closed their eyes and
left them in peace. So the pygmies continue their life of

---

[1] Attilio Gatti in *Hidden Africa* (Hutchinson, 1933).   [2] Wild celery.

poverty and happy carelessness, maintaining all their traditions, independence and pride. . . . These wretched little men, whom a handful of salt or an old cigar butt could make happy, would not lower their dignity to be carriers, and had no interest in the francs I offered them in payment. But as guides and hunting companions they were priceless; intelligent, affectionate, faithful; always ready to free the way of the Whiteman from a snake or a bramble; always intent to do something useful and kind, and with a courage beyond belief."

When the scientist shot a gorilla for a museum, the pigmies "came running to the scene a moment after, and began at once a dance of joy around me and the huge body lying prone on the ground. . . . Their wrinkled gnome-like little faces wreathed in ecstatic smiles, their eyes gleaming greedily at the thought of the prospective banquet, they jumped to hack down small trees, cut strips of fibre with which to bind them together, and in a few minutes they had prepared a rough stretcher. Upon this the gorilla was stretched upon its back . . ." The march through the forest over, the chief of the pigmies settled down to divide the gorilla-meat, which is pink like veal. "Under the staring eyes of the hunters squatted on the ground, and of all the others, men, women and children, who formed a great circle around him, he distributed the flesh, bit by bit, with the concentration and solemnity of some mighty banker dividing a colossal fortune. Each piece had . . . its special value, and it was certainly no easy task to divide the meat with true justice so that all men could be satisfied. Gravely weighing each bit in the palm of his hand", the chief "looked with his keen eyes all around him; estimated the value of the little mounds of meat piling up before every participator; made the gesture of adding it to one pile; regretted his decision and snatched back the bit; looked again carefully at it and finally with as lacerating a sigh as if he were parting from a piece of his own flesh, dropped it upon a different pile. If, however, it were a really luscious morsel, after all that comedy of weighing and hesitating,

H

he would put it on one of the two piles belonging to himself, one for his services as hunter, and one for his rank as chief."

These pigmies of desert and forest are Africa's ultimate social minority; and one of these fine days UNO must offer them a voice in the affairs of the human race. They are even less likely to understand or desire the vote than they do money or a settled habitation and a home. Over the burning Kalahari sands the Bushman hunter runs, for hour after hour if need be, to overtake his wounded gemsbok; across a Congo river, at the end of a long liana or monkey-rope, swings the pigmy, from tree to tree; and somewhere else, though neither knows it, Time marches on.

5

These are some of the peoples and places which surround the Whiteman in Africa. There are also the Barotse canoe-folk, who live in the swamps of the upper Zambesi. Barotse-land remains one of the unknown sockets of Africa, for it is difficult of access. Sir Ronald Storrs, now retired, was the first Governor of Northern Rhodesia to visit its Paramount Chief after the Imperial Government had taken over his Protectorate from the Chartered Company. The expedition managed to get to Lealui, the capital, in the dry season of the year.

"The general topography of the country", telegraphed a special correspondent who accompanied that expedition,[1] "is that of an ancient lake bed, bounded by hills modest in height. Rivers seep into it from all directions, and large areas are too unstable to carry buildings of any weight. Like Central Egypt, the heart of Barotseland is annually inundated, with the difference that the floods occur in the local rainy season and are due to the incapacity of the Zambesi to carry off the water as fast as it accumulates. . . . Yeta met us at the entrance enclosure of his well-laid-out residence,

---

[1] *The Star*, Johannesburg, 25 August 1933.

wearing a light silk suit, suede shoes and a fashionable hat.
He is a tall, handsome man, dignified but homely. We
enjoyed tea from delicate chinaware, and spoke through an
interpreter for an hour. Yeta has won great esteem for the
sagacity and discretion with which he has steadily co-
operated with the white Administration to raise his subjects
in the scale of civilisation. His life story, and that of his
land and race, is rich in romance. It has also a spell of
mystery, for his country is . . . less familiar to white travellers
and readers than almost any other African territory. . . .
Wild bird life abounds, crocodiles slide off sandbanks as
we approach in a forty-foot barge propelled by sixteen
paddlers, and hippos boom and hyenas call by night."

Yeta, with short white beard and dignified mien, abdicated
in 1945. He handed over to his brother, Imwiko, not only
the chief's authority inherited from his famous grandfather,
Lewanika, who secured the protection of Queen Victoria,
but also the dark-green, frockcoated uniform, richly gold-
braided, and the cocked hat that goes with it. Ever since
Lewanika wore it at the coronation of Edward VII, it has
served successive chiefs for those occasions when honour is
done to the Kings and Queens of England.

Beyond the Barotse swamps are the forests and plains of
Angola and the Congo. It seemed to me, in my journeyings,
that, whenever there were clouds about, the Congo
night fell on me like a thick blanket. From the train absolutely nothing was visible. Blackness was everywhere and
into it merged the anthills and the twisted trees, the savannas
and the straight rivers. With the stars screened off, there was
no horizon, no sky distinct from the earth: blackness lay
heavy on the land and filled the heavens, so that blackness
became my world and through it the train sped, a glimmer
of yellow light, a great glow-worm in a racing mood. There
was something of impertinence in this lighted train which
streaked on through hundreds of miles of untamed Africa;
and when the engine emitted its heartrending bleat of pain,
warning an uncomplaining Congo to beware of its swiftness,

I held my breath, half expecting the denizens of the forest, the animals and reptiles and even the patient Natives, to rise screaming from their outer darkness and scorch the man-carrying train with the hot, mad breath of ancient Africa, to trample it beneath the long-suffering slave-feet of the Congo, to smite it and me dead with claw and cannibal-tooth. But I was spared such an unhappy end to my journey; and, indeed, peering into mile after monotonous mile of darkness, unrelieved by the gleaming eyes of wild beasts or the kraal fires of natives, I wondered whether anything, apart from the trees, breathed in that invisible wilderness. Empty, voiceless, vast, it was the answer to the puzzled child's demand for a description of the space above the stars, the world beyond the universe, the wall or width at the end of the very end of things.

The dense forests had thinned out by the time I crossed into Angola over the running waters of the Luao River, with the Belgian flag fluttering on the one bank and the Portuguese flag on the other. But timber was still plentiful, and great piles of chopped wood lay here and there beside the line, ready to feed the engines which do pretty well on it with a proportion of coke bricks. The sawmill and the axe are making great scars in the forests that sweep from the line and one dreads to think of the number of young *tacula* trees that have been fed to the boiler fires—those trees which, in full maturity, are of gigantic size, providing a beautiful wood, blood-red in colour.

Over Angola's high plateau the train raced, savannas, flat and grass-covered, taking the place of the forests from time to time. The genuine long grass became a frequent feature of the landscape, and through it occasionally peeped a piccanin, with his father or his mother, reminding one of the slave days when the captured blacks were marched to the coast through this same long grass, whose dew falls upon the body like a drenching rain.

Near the coast, oil-palms patterned the sky picturesquely, and rubber vines and trees whose roots yield rubber were conspicuous in the woods. When the actual traffic in slaves had been largely stamped out, trade in palm-oil and rubber caused a new form of slavery as porters were needed to transport these raw products to the coast after they had been won from the jungle. Again the long lines of blacks, winding towards the sea, became a feature of the Angola scene and from it developed that system of indentured labour whose abuses were finally exposed at the beginning of the century by a British journalist.[1]

Remembering these evil days, particular interest was given to Benguella, a native town by the sea, to which I came soon after the train had slid down the mountains by way of three miles of rack-line. The rectangular huts, thatched and fenced about with reeds or palings, pack closely about the few Portuguese buildings, pale pink and blue, where government officials rest and rule—and then the huts scatter formlessly over a wide area. Here it was that the slaves of yesterday were herded and the rubber porters concentrated. Today the Benguella blacks push seaward in their fishing boats and find work and wages on the vast sugarcane fields that run, mile after mile, along the irrigated littoral to Lobito.

Southwards, through the dense bush of Angola, lies the wilderness of the Kaokoveld and the sands of the Kalahari. Thus we have come full circle, ranging in a generous sweep round the Whiteman's *laager*, watchful on the high plains of Africa's backbone.

6

POSTSCRIPT

At the end of the Garden Route from Cape Town is Port Elizabeth, with its high Campanile commemorating the landing of the 1820 Settlers and its sunken Snake Park. Close to the town, at Humewood, is a magnificent beach. A splendid harbour and a pastoral hinterland give Port

[1] H. W. Nevinson in *A Modern Slavery* (Harpers).

Elizabeth a healthy commerce in wool, mohair, and ostrich feathers; also it has developed industrially, with its assembly plants for motor-cars and its wide range of factories.

The Addo Elephant National Park, in the Cape Midlands, is near Zuurberg in the neighbourhood of Port Elizabeth. Among its 17,000 acres of evergreen indigenous bush roam the elephants, smaller in stature and tusk than the equatorial giants, but identical in other respects. From observation posts visitors may watch them drinking and wallowing and roaming through the bush with their calves. Near Port Elizabeth are the Sundays River orange groves, on the one hand, and on the other hand, Grahamstown, "the City of Saints", with its church spires, its first-rate schools and Rhodes University College.

Farther north along the coast is the neighbouring river-port of East London, more leisurely but also important commercially and industrially to the Eastern Province, whose landscape breaks into mountains, streams and valleys that run into the great Native Reserves of the Ciskei and the Transkei. A few miles inland is King-williamstown on the Buffalo River—"King" as it is called; and then Queenstown—"Queen of the Border". This whole area is both delightful and interesting as it merges and becomes one with the Native Reserves by way of Umtata, Amabele, Idutywa, Komgha, Cala, and Lusikisiki: names that make music.

Five main tribes inhabit the Transkei—the Xosa, Tembu, Baca, Pondo and Fingo. They occupy an area roughly the size of Switzerland and total, according to the 1946 census, 1,300,000. The only Europeans living in this huge and fertile zone are magistrates and other officials, traders and missionaries. Umtata, the administrative centre, is a small town set around a square large enough for many ox-wagons to "outspan". It has its shops and cinemas, but everywhere in the streets you meet the red- and white-blanketed tribes-folk, the men smoking their long-stemmed, wild olive-wood pipes. Their favourite place for congregating is outside the magistrate's court which adjourns the white, cupola-topped block of the Bunga or Native Parliament.

Some Councillors jog into Umtata on wiry ponies.

Others use motor-cars. Xosa, Tembu, Baca, Pondo—
whatever their tribe, the Councillors all enjoy the opportunity of addressing the Bunga. Mostly the talk is in Xosa,
a Bantu language with close affinities to Zulu. Each side of
the assembly has its interpreter: a third is attached to the
presiding Chief Magistrate. The Bunga always opens with
the Lord's Prayer recited in Xosa.

CHAPTER VI

THE CITY BUILT ON GOLD

I

PLUMB IN the middle of the Whiteman's *laager* is his city built on gold—Johannesburg. It is his answer to the Black-man's city built on rock—Zimbabwe. Nothing in all Southern Africa has caused as much controversy as Zimbabwe, jungle-conquered, deserted in the Rhodesian wilds; and experts still brood over its walls and towers seeking to probe the secret of its origin. Among those who visit it nowadays are an increasing number of Natives from all parts of Southern Africa: they stare and ejaculate words of amazement. The European visitors argue over the many guesses and theories which seek to answer the riddle of Zimbabwe.

Romance dies hard and fascinating explanations linking Zimbabwe with King Solomon and the Queen of Sheba are still discussed at the magic hour of sundown. But the public is gradually, reluctantly relinquishing these romantic names and with them the Arabs, Persians, Chinese, Phœni-cians, and Zoroastrians, all of whom have been credited with building Zimbabwe. Rider Haggard's novels are working themselves out of the present generation's blood, and credence is at last being given to the solution twice offered by archæologists of the British Association who, after carrying out investigations of the ruins, attributed them to a high Bantu culture which formerly flourished.

Even Rhodesia's publicity agents, who for years frowned at the mere mention of a Bantu explanation and wrote still more colourfully and picturesquely of the source of the gold of Ophir, are now beginning to view the archæology of

Randall MacIver and Miss Caton Thompson more toler-
antly, and in their new brochures they emphasise the fact
that the ruins are rendered more interesting now that they
indicate a former Bantu civilisation of a high order. In the
stone walls and towers, they say happily, are contained
more mysteries than ever.

When I was there, I explored the Zimbabwe ruins with
zest and energetically clambered through broken walls
and up winding steps—all shaped from the surrounding
rocks and packed without mortar. At the summit of the
acropolis, I sat down for a spell to enjoy the rocky view,
once the setting for great human toil and striving, for the
practice of phallic worship and commerce in untamed
Africa. The functional outcome of it all was Zimbabwe,
which was then deserted as mysteriously as it had been built
and occupied. The temple with its conical tower remains to
remind us of African sanctions and disciplines that have
gone like those later exercised by Shaka in the hills of
Zululand. I have heard it seriously argued that one day
Johannesburg, when all the gold has been dug up or is no
longer wanted by bankers, will end like Zimbabwe. Then
the wind-blown dust of the mine-dumps will settle thickly
in the deserted offices and monkeys will play with the
paralysed hands of the post-office clock.

I have seen Johannesburg in many moods and shared its
anger and joy; but, in its normal aspects, I think it is from
five o'clock in the afternoon that the city best reveals itself
as a spectacle. I do not mean an architectural spectacle,
although then its new and newer buildings glow and glitter
in the horizontal light and grow mysterious in the eastern
shade; but I mean a spectacle of human life, swiftly,
turbulently tumbling along and across its bickering streets.

In Rissik Street, as the old post-office clock, unperturbed
by prophecies about monkeys, is marking the hour with its
familiar chimes, typists cover up their machines, dab powder
and lipstick on their faces, pull on their hats and gladly
sink to the ground floor in the droning lift. The noble army

of clerks wipe their pens on the left sleeves of their ink-stained office jackets, change into their clean coats, and hurry into the street to join the evening rush for newspapers, thirst-quenchers and home.

But the shopkeepers do not hurry from their counters. They remain faithfully on guard for that last round of intense trade when dutiful husbands and daughters make those small household purchases for which forgetful wives and mothers have telephoned frantically earlier in the afternoon. On the chiming of the half-hour, however, they put up their shutters and the new rush begins. Mannequins, cashiers and saleswomen stream on to the pavement and weave their high-heeled way into the moving maze. Shop-walkers, managers, proprietors clang the safes, lock their doors and lose their dignified identity in the jostling crowd.

This city of swift moods is joyous in its home-going. Having worked at high pressure during the day, its slaves laugh in their sudden freedom and prepare to play the night merrily to its bed-time. The highbrows often bitterly complain that Johannesburg is a city without a soul, but for those who work and play hard it is undoubtedly a city with an exhilarating spirit. Just to live in Johannesburg—to suffer its growing pains, to respond to its youthful enthusiasms, to feel oneself part of its fascinating microcosm—is an adventure.

Dusk falls with the coming of the shopkeepers. White lights begin to blaze along Eloff Street, and the brilliant colours of its sky-signs blink and black out in their repeating patterns. The trams are still overcrowded, and the motor-cars are numerically terrible. Traffic and pedestrians swerve and eddy about the poor pointsman, flow past him, pile up against his uplifted hand. The automatic controls inexorably show green and red, and the vortex of omnibuses, horse lorries, cars, bicycles and pedestrians rages marvellously, and escapes with a devilish din this way and that in bewildering tangles. The lights grow stronger as the dusk deepens: the display windows of shops blaze gloriously like

the noonday sun and make the faces of the passers-by glow
pleasantly; high up against the blackening sky innumerable
squares of yellow show where the city's offices are being
swept and dusted by the Native cleaners. It is night; the
daily rush for home is over. Almost magically, it seems, the
pavements and streets have freed themselves of their over-
burden of feet and wheels.

More leisurely is the lunch-hour when Johannesburg is
a parade ground. Girls and young men, while digesting
their too-easily-swallowed sandwiches, wander up and down
Pritchard Street. Smart, most of them are; alert and healthy.
Friends hail one another and gather in little groups to
exchange the latest gossip and make appointments. And
wherever building is being done, spectators eagerly line the
kerb opposite, throw back their heads and gaze at the steel
girders being swung into position and at the men perched
in perilous places on brick and stone and scaffolding.

As for Johannesburg on a Saturday night, its hurly-burly
is intensified by street instrumentalists, singers and showmen. They take up their position along the kerb, or in the
gutter, near the cinemas and theatres, and battle for a
hearing against the laughter and shouts of the surging
throng and the ear-splitting din of motor-car sirens. Some
of these singers and showmen look jolly; some of them look
sad; and some of them have the expressionless look of the
damned. But all of them perform with hopeful energy,
whether skilfully or clumsily, intent on making up the rent
money. They struggle bravely enough for a mere bellyful
in this bright street of mixed humanity—humanity which,
after the week's toil in mine, factory, office and home, is
searching, in rather an hysterical mood, for a few hours of
delight.

The people press eagerly along the pavement—restless,
feverish, excited. Their incessant chatter unites into a great
murmur, which rises over the buildings and is lost in the
calm, star-scattered vastness of the night. They wear their
gayest clothes and most carefree manner. The street pulsates

with life. Merry cries go up, eyes light with laughter, feet hurry along.

Divers instruments, from harps to concertinas, give out their notes. A woman and two girls valiantly endeavour to attract an audience from the crowd which remorselessly moves past them. The woman is seated on a stool at a harmonium, which she deftly pedals and plays while singing in a splendidly strong and clear voice. The voice overcomes the surrounding cacophony and its crescendo emerges— irresistible, triumphant. Not for nothing have those lungs been strengthened in the open air. The girl by her side sweeps decisive fingers across a guitar, while the other takes her stand among the passing people, trusting to the generous hand for reward, and to Providence not to be swept off her feet by the human stream.

The spasmodic strains of an asthmatic concertina, between the hands of a down-at-heel but picturesque vagabond, come from a corner from which towers a store of seventeen storeys. A less pretentious concertina is quietly played near a busy restaurant by a woman sitting on a chair. Her programme consists of Moody and Sankey hymns; and such coins as they move the compassionate to part with are gratefully deposited by her daughter in a small money-box. On a placard the words, "Blind woman with four children", tell the tale.

Immobile, silent, with neither voice nor instrument to kill the slow hours and advertise his presence, there sits against the wall in a gloomy portion of the pavement an old Malay. He also is blind. His head is sunk forward on his chest, where his beard, streaked with grey, straggles, unkempt, on his shabby coat. Beside him the small figure of a boy, fast asleep, huddles on the cement. When the crowd thins the old man wakes him, and, holding the small hand, is led slowly away.

Between the garish fronts of rival cinemas stands a formidable barrel-organ. It is so insistent that youths, a cigarette hanging from the lip and a girl from the arm, hesitate on their way to the box-office, balance first on one foot, then on the other. The woman sturdily grinds the handle and familiar tunes fill the air. Further on, a banjo player expertly twangs out popular tunes, while at his elbow a granite-faced man, who looks like a well-used prizefighter, throws back his head and sings in an almost masterly way. A badly driven motor-car, loaded with sprawling men and women, blatant in their drunkenness, swerves past. The women call out so that the banjo and the voice of the granite-faced singer are momentarily silenced; but as soon as the car-load has passed, the voice comes back in all its rugged vigour with the twanging accompaniment as cocksure as ever.

The instrumentalists, singers and showmen fade away. Some of them return to practise their art in front of the theatres during the intervals; and then they finally pack up. Gradually the hubbub of Saturday night dies down to the quiet of Sunday morning.

In the lunch hour, Johannesburg strolls lazily; from five o'clock in the afternoon till dark it rushes gladly, madly; and on Saturday night it plays and dances and sings.

2

Bearded and wrinkled they may be, and some doubtless have elbow-lifting propensities: but the astonishing truth remains that there is a fairy-like quality about Johannesburg's pioneers. They do not wield a magic wand, of course; yet by a few yarns between drinks they can change the heaped-up debris of the Rand's rich mines back into the pristine flatness of the veld, and shrivel up the present-day magnificence of the Golden City to its initial ugliness of tin and tent.

Without the evidence of these diehards I would doubt the fact of Eloff Street's extreme youth—the Eloff Street of splendid buildings. Yet they can recall its early days

when the nimble duiker nibbled the sweet grass where now
is only macadam, and the then unsymbolical springbok,
untroubled by tramcars, buildings and telegraph poles
sprang unconcernedly about the Witwatersrand. On the
now fabulously precious site where some grey structure
uprises to blot out a fair proportion of the sky, there passed
on his way the carefree Kafir. His lusty shouts were the
only human sounds in that bare stretch of wilderness which
spread in all directions to an uninterfered-with horizon.

And then, all in a bewildering moment, something hit
this peaceful Rand of white-stone outcroppings—the prospector, the speculator, the pioneer: the gold-rush; in a
word, the Whiteman. Heavy boots tramped upon the shrill
green grass blades (for it was summer—the summer of
1886) and solemnly declared: "This shall be Eloff Street."
And it was so.

The history of Eloff Street in the long, long centuries
before it was named can be written in one syllable: veld;
the brief chapter of restlessness which followed takes three:
tin shanties; and thereafter, each succeeding year requires
more and more words until today the story of Eloff Street
requires a book. But does the thought of that make Johan-
nesburgers pause in awe as they enter Eloff Street? Not in
the least, for they have plenty of other things to think about.
The motorist hoots his way from Plein Street to Fox Street
with a hard face that spells "Profits"; the wedged-in
humanity of the incoming tram sways to the ruthless rhythm
of "Business-business"; and even those fair young Dianas
who seek furs and frills in those wonderfully stocked shops
which line both east and west pavements are too preoccupied
with that other eternal triangle—"Credit-Cash-Discount"
—to marvel at the strangeness of their being there at all.

Fortunately, that is only one side of the picture; the other
is made up of jolly throngs, night-time laughter, bright
lights, brighter eyes, brilliant frocks, merry children, jovial
ancients, twinkling feet, captivating scents, delirious movement, gilded youth. Yes, we can call it a street! But let us

look at Eloff Street through the spectacles of the pioneer. The substantial buildings, the bustling crowds, the racing vehicles oscillate violently in the sun's glare, crumble, disintegrate, shrink and vanish. In the place of it all, there magically appear a few straggling tin shanties, a few wattle-and-daub shacks, a few drooping tents, a few roughly clothed miners. This is how a chronicler[1] has described that early scene:

"As yet there were no buildings more permanent than the mud-and-reed hut called Walker's Hotel; but already the traffic in 'stands' had begun. Corner lots on the pegged enclosures had become gambling counters to be sold and resold half a dozen times in a month. Everywhere there were tents. Reaching forth from the congested nucleus of Ferreira's camp, their far-scattered tilts, bleached by the sun, resembled, when seen from a distance, a litter of paper-scraps strewn haphazard, or a flock of white egrets come to rest on the shoals of a sandy estuary.

"In these tents, without water or sanitation, dwelt men —three thousand of them, drawn not only from the back-wash of Barberton but from Kimberley, from the Cape, from Natal, from the uttermost corners of the earth to which the rumour of easy-won wealth had penetrated. Here were skilled miners from Colorado and Ballarat; Hebrew capitalists from Kimberley; mining engineers from America; builders and blacksmiths, hucksters, panders, saloon-keepers; casual labourers, down-and-outs—every imaginable sort of human riff-raff washed on to that barren ridge like jetsam cast up by the tides.

"To these thousands was added an even greater con-course of natives: Malay drivers from Cape Town, whose carts plied from one end of the reef to the other at exorbitant fares; Griquas, Hottentots, Cape Coloured-folk, and, out-numbering all these, the hordes of raw Kaffirs who, tramping to and from Kimberley, were snatched up like metallic particles by the magnet of Johannesburg and swept, naked,

[1] Francis Brett Young in *The City of Gold* (Heinemann 1939).

underground—to have their lungs eaten away by sharp crystals of powdered quartz—or flung on the tented streets to rot their bewildered brains with Cape Smoke[1] and dagga,[2] or raw potato-spirit laced with tobacco-juice."

Four years go over. It is 1890. Eloff Street has still an unprepossessing appearance. The monotony of galvanised iron roofing has become much greater; an extraordinary number of transport-wagons, loaded with food and mining material, creak and jolt their way towards the Market Square; the trek-oxen, hearing the yells of their Kafir driver and feeling the keen lash of his long whip along their flanks, strain anxiously against the yokes; men in smasher hats, with shirt-sleeves rolled up, and with leather belts holding up trousers without turn-ups, lounge about mud huts; their wives busy themselves over Dutch ovens built in the open; and their children laugh in the sunshine; one-storey structures of corrugated iron are being put together; dumps of bricks await the builders; and on empty lots, even in those uncertain days, temporary places of worship were numerous; but at this time no church or temple had been put up with the exception (Oh, significant beginning!) of a Jewish synagogue.

Suddenly a bugle blares forth and an unusual stir is caused. Men shout to one another and rush towards the sound. The stage coach, drawn by eight spanking horses, flashes across Eloff Street and rattles down Commissioner Street. The guard, with many a flourish, treats the gathering crowd to a musical entertainment, nearly bursting his cheeks in a valiant effort to send the notes to the farthest ends of the mining town. The latest arrivals are welcomed, news is given and asked, nearby bars are invaded—for, by then there were several in Eloff Street, and a total of over a hundred in the whole town.

From then on the metamorphosis is amazing. It is too swift to follow. Eloff Street as we know it to-day begins to take shape. Buildings of two and three storeys rise up;

---

[1] Raw brandy.   [2] A sort of hashish.

Beyond the mine-dumps glitters ever-growing Johannesburg, bustling metropolis of the Golden Land.

In the centre of Kimberley is the Big Hole from which Cecil Rhodes scooped the diamonds that financed the taking and making of Rhodesia, north of the Limpopo River.

imposing shop fronts proudly glitter; smart traps and spiders speed along; trains steam to the north end of Eloff Street; motor-cars roll into town; tram-lines are laid down; skyscrapers tower up at the cost of a million; the thorough-fare roars with traffic, the pavements teem with pedestrians —Johannesburg has been built, rebuilt, and built yet again.

3

Public transport lags far behind the growth of Johannesburg, so that each morning you see long lines of privately-owned motor-cars converging on the city. Usually each large American car is occupied by one man, who sits grimly at the steering-wheel hooting pedestrians out of the way and muttering impatiently at traffic hold-ups. He reminds one of Babbitt in Sinclair Lewis's *Main Street* hurrying fanati-cally to his job of money-getting. In the evening, the reverse journey, after a couple of brandies-and-soda, is done in a happier mood—provided the Stock Exchange has behaved itself. For the Stock Exchange is Johannesburg's heart to whose fast, uncertain beat all the buzzing Babbitts hustle or go bust. It was so in the early days, in the nineties when "everybody talked incessantly and dreamed about gold-scrip and bought it and sold it. Within two years there were more than three hundred gold-mining concerns, some sound, some worthless, some merely existing on paper or in their owners' imaginations, offering shares for sale. Men bought, not with any intention of holding their purchases, but for the thrill of a game of chance that was less scientific than poker. High stakes, quick returns were the rule: tomorrow was 'settlement day', as few brokers took the risk of selling gold-scrip 'to arrive' when, within a week, the buyers might well be gone. There was no reason behind the pro-digious gamut through which shares would go rocketing one day and crashing the next in a market that had the sensitiveness of a seismograph. The first rumour of sub-

I

stantial values would set them soaring; the faintest whisper of doubt bring them down with a run. Representatives of the great Kimberley houses, handling millions, took part in the scramble with men who worked with picks and drills in the mines. . . . Now that the fame of the Rand was noised abroad, foreign buying, by speculators in London and Paris and New York, who barely knew where the Rand was or what shares they bought, continued to keep it spinning at an even more furious pace. They called the Exchange, not unreasonably, the 'Kaffir Circus'."

The Johannesburg Stock Exchange retains its youthful lust and habit of chivvying wild-cats, and its staid London parent sometimes cannot restrain itself from joining in the frolic. When the Orange Free State gold-hunt got exciting, New York sent special correspondents to Johannesburg to find out what it was all about. One of them,[1] discovering a brilliance and blare challenging Barnum's show, wrote as follows: "The architecture of the brownstone, porticoed Jo'Burg Stock Exchange recalls our General Grant period, and so does the prevailing Union ethic, 'Buyer beware'. Indeed, this land no less than the U.S. in the days of the robber barons bears the mark of the frontier. The conditions and mood that powered the U.S. of post-Civil War days past that frontier are today operative in the Union, in all their raw force. Despite the touch of New Deal in the policies of Prime Minister Jan Christiaan Smuts, South Africa is one of this latter-day world's outstanding amphitheatres of ante-Delanian rugged individuals. And the heart of the amphitheatre is the Jo'Burg Exchange, scene of gold rushes that gleam with the color not of virgin metal but of well-worn stock certificates. . . .

"The exchange last April was bedlam. Trading records were broken. Teleprinters lagged, telephone exchanges bollixed, the backlog of orders forced a cut in trading hours. Speculators flocked in from the provinces to trade more conveniently, and hotels were packed as in wartime Washing-

[1] Herbert Solow in the October 1946 number of *Fortune*, New York.

ton. Holders of solid old dividend payers shifted to Kaffirettes (South African slang for cats and dogs). Little men, including many a demobilized soldier heavy with war pay, plunged deep. Big financial houses unloaded cargoes of paper at premium prices. . . . Business offices were crippled as stenographers made little killings and quit their jobs. Wives of lucky men put new buyer pressure on the already tight diamond market. Night clubs were full of spenders. Cape bubbly (*doux*) cascaded. . . . Throgmorton Street, where men have traded in Kaffirs for half a century, howled for them. And, across another sea, a few rich traders put up U.S. chips."

And while the financial music goes round and round, the Whiteman's Johannesburg leaps farther and higher; and the Blackman's Johannesburg, like a great, obedient shadow, does likewise. For there is a Blackman's Johannesburg, and it is made up of back-rooms in the Whiteman's houses, of hideous slums, of depressing locations, and now, since the building of even the humblest sort of houses cannot keep pace with the rate at which the tribal beggars are coming to town, squatter camps: camps of hessian shacks put up hugger-mugger by the Natives as they arrive. The shacks keep out neither the wind nor the rain; but from them the Natives can see the Whiteman's endless rows of lights that sweep up to the hilltops to mingle with the stars —the lights that have blossomed from the footprints of the pioneers of the first rush; and this is a great new rush, with shacks mushrooming hopefully again as they originally mushroomed in the eighties. The Whiteman's shacks of the eighties and nineties are today bungalows, and mansions, and tall office-buildings: so the Blackman's shacks of today may tomorrow turn into—what?

4

The interplay of Johannesburg and its Shadow is always interesting, but sometimes disturbing. White Johannesburg moves in motor-cars along an inner, faster current: Black Johannesburg moves by foot, along the slower stream on either side. But, also on the roads, are buses with black passengers and other buses with white passengers. And, increasingly, Mr. Babbitt sits in the back of his motor-car while Mr. Shadow occupies the driver's seat as chauffeur. White Johannesburg relaxes in the inner gardens, verandas, and living-rooms: Black Johannesburg gossips in the outer streets. Parks, once the close preserve of the Europeans, are now, I noticed, crowded with Natives; and shops, where formerly only Europeans bought (perhaps accompanied by a Native domestic servant to carry the purchases) nowadays are alive with Natives. In the homes of Europeans I noticed another Johannesburg innovation—Native bands hired for the guests dancing in the ballrooms: the musicians come and go in their own bus or convoy of cars, and they dispense swing numbers with all the verve and passion of American Negroes.

The black stream and the white stream eddy into each other at certain metropolitan twists and turns, but their main courses are, for the most part, clearly discernible in the major pattern of the city's teeming life. For the European, the suburbs and the slums; for the Native, the slums and the squatter camps. And the height of European luxury, apart from comfortable homes and lavish feasts, is the cinema. Here is described the impact of a Johannesburg picture palace on the mind of a Johannesburg journalist:[1]

"You enter a marble hallway about ninety feet high and walk up a grand staircase carpeted in rich crimson past life-size nymphs bearing bronze lamps. At the top of the staircase you are confronted with an aquarium. A large

[1] Alexander Campbell in *Smuts and Swastika* (Gollancz, 1943).

glass tank is flanked with giant fish carved out of what looks like crystal, and in the tank real fish swim. Behind the tank is a profusion of real greenery, with real palms and real flowers, really growing. Above you, the roof is glass again, yards of it, scalloped at the edges like gigantic glass water-lilies. You pass along a broad corridor and through a giant door into the inner darkness. You are deposited in a plush air-cushioned seat and breathe deeply of thoroughly conditioned air. The place seats several thousand people. There appears to be no roof, but it has suddenly become night, for though it was only early evening when you entered, stars gleam in the apparently authentic heavens above you, and to complete the illusion light clouds pass gently across them. You look around, and discover that you are apparently in a ruined castle. Towering turrets and stone battlements surround you, all with dimly lighted windows. Beneath the turrets are, somewhat incongruously, huge relief maps of the world, the New World on your left and the Old World on your right. When you have taken in all this fantasy, you may look at the picture you came to see. But not for long. For halfway through the programme, an immense organ suddenly rises from nowhere and commences to play popular airs, and it is followed by a full symphony orchestra on the stage."

The Natives, too, have their cinemas—and their social centres, their newspapers and their sports clubs. Their amateur players even give a version of Richard Brinsley Sheridan's *The School for Scandal*. But the focus, inevitably, is on the slum life that too often is their lot. Those slums are spreading as the Natives and Coloureds push into districts whence the Europeans move on to some new working-class suburb: but at these eddying-points the race-streams mix.

"Around Jo'burg", writes a woman doctor[1] who worked in those slums, "rise mountainous mine dumps, bleached

---

[1] Vera Emanuel under the title *Mis' Lady Doctor*, in *The Saturday Evening Post* 15 June 1946.

by the cyanide process which drained them of gold, until they gleam in the South African sun like stunted Alps. Between the dumps and the spick-and-spanness of the city itself are the outlying slums in which live those of mixed black-and-white blood, poor whites, Asiatics, Indians and Negroes—many of them fresh from the bush or kraal. This fringe lies at Jo'burg's back door like trash swept into an alley. . . .

"I set out to rent rooms for a clinic there. . . . Throngs shoved along the narrow pavements. A fat Basuto woman, her head shaved, her cheeks and nose tatooed with tribal markings, swung her petticoats rhythmically over her swaying hips. On her head was balanced a kerosene tin filled with freshly gathered cow dung. Her arms were loaded with basins of roasted sheep's heads. Tiny, naked, black children with streaming noses sat playing in the gutter or darted after long-tailed Kaffir dogs."

All big cities have their slums, and Johannesburg does not claim to be free of them: on the contrary, I found her citizens busy with improvement schemes. The backlog in building, caused by the second German war, is one of the factors aggravating the problem of the slums and squatter camps. And as European builders cannot keep pace even with the requirements of the Europeans, it becomes clear that the Natives must be taught not only how to live in a house in a congested area (after being used to a hut in the open veld) but also how to build such a house with his own hands.

5

The analysts vouch for the fact that Johannesburg's streets are paved with gold—or rather that they are impregnated with gold-dust that has escaped the devices of the metallurgists. But the Johannesburg station, until a few years ago, was an ugly tin-shanty of a place that smelt of poverty. Now, however, there is a brand-new railway station, with a central concourse of elegant arches, fountains and mural paintings. Under this station a subway has been burrowed for pedestrians. So that now, the subway drag has become a twice-daily habit for many thousands. Along its concrete they pace briskly to and from their city job while the trains rumble overhead.

The young carry sandwiches in their hands and a hopeful heart on the sleeve; the old carry sorrows upon their face and a lost world of yesterday in their disillusioned eyes; the middle-aged—but nobody is middle-aged in Johannesburg.

Every few minutes as the Reef trains roll in after break-fast, herded humanity squeezes down the stairways from the various platforms and strings itself out along the lighted ubway. The concrete cavern is vibrant, murmurous; high-heeled shoes, high-pitched voices; the *thud-thud* of wood and leather. The grand army of office toilers is marching to the attack. But they have time to glance at the posters as they hurry along. Are there any new ones? All the colours of the rainbow, and many that no rainbow could look in the face, are spattered along both walls. In the quieter hours the subway is not a drag for wage-earners: it is a laughter-filled tunnel where children run before their mothers and nurses. The posters become suddenly pretty, thus seen through wondering eyes; small hands, fascinated, wander across the green and gold, the red and blue. The marvel and magic of it all!

A confident tap-tapping heralds the approach of a blind man. No traffic here to hurl itself upon him as it obeys the unseen signal of the street robot. Here and there along the subway's length are boys who sell cigarettes and matches, journals and sweets. They seem conscious of the fact that they are enshrined in the catacomb of the nation's latest temple of transport. Gee, must have cost a mint of money! Too bad they have to sit on soap-boxes. But, as I write, the station is outmoded; and the architects and engineers are already completing the plans of a bigger, better, more glorious station for the city built on gold.

Despite the prophecy of the pessimists that the old post-office clock would become a plaything for wild monkeys, a new and much larger general post office has been built; and the optimists will tell you proudly that Johannesburg has got a new skyline. This is perfectly true; but, then, Johannesburg is constantly acquiring a new skyline. Since it was founded on the harsh outcroppings and koppies of the Witwatersrand, Johannesburg has suffered constantly from growing pains; and those whose lot it has been to live within this lusty, turbulent city have watched its skyline change from tents to tin shanties, from hovels to mansions, from a few two-storeyed offices to a panorama of ten-storeyed buildings varied here and there by a verandaed cottage—relic of the days of J. B. Robinson, Beit, Rhodes, Barnato and the rest of the early birds—or by an outsize in Rand skyscrapers: that is to say, a concrete edifice rising up and up to perhaps fifteen, perhaps twenty storeys.

"Skyscraper" is a word that runs away with the imagination. It conjures up a vision of the cloud-piercing towers of Manhattan, where man has built architectural masterpieces to a graceful, gleaming height of over 1,000 feet by piling upon one another—thrillingly, beautifully—sixty, seventy, a hundred storeys. Like the word "skyscraper" itself, the term "skyline" as applied to a city, comes to us from America. This is very natural, as anybody will agree who has looked upon New York from the deck of a ship entering the Hudson River, or upon Chicago from the shore of Lake Michigan, or upon Seattle from the sea-front, or upon San Francisco from a ferry in the bay. Those cities, from island, plain, forest or hill, have risen up actually to create new spectacular skylines. They cut into the heavens on the same grand scale that mountains do.

Johannesburg's skyline, even today, after two generations of intensive building under the stimulus of increasing gold production, is a modest one, of course, in comparison with the skylines of American cities; but it is a fascinating sky-line nevertheless, for it is a skyline rendered immediately possible by the honeycombed foundations on which it balances—foundations of gold-shot rock which have been burrowed into by miners to a depth of over a mile and a half (that is to say, below sea level) and over an east-to-west length of a hundred and fifty miles.

With the gold standard dropped, the price of gold at record high levels, and new mines being discovered and opened up in far extensions of the Reef that have been traced to the new goldfields of the Orange Free State, Johannesburg is booming. Building activity soon followed the intensified and widening activities of the Witwatersrand goldfields. A cloud of red dust floated up above the city as the razing operations began in order to make way for deeper foundations and higher buildings—razing operations that are going on at a frenzied pace in an effort to keep pace with the demand for more offices, bigger shops, better flats.

Johannesburg—or, rather, the city itself—is hemmed in by koppies and mine-dumps; and so the tendency has been to build upwards rather than outwards. To give full scope to this tendency, the municipal height-limits have been increased by adoption of the stepping-back or zoning system of architecture. So that today its citizens, even though usually they view Johannesburg from the northern heights —that is to say, they look downwards upon it—may well point proudly to its new skyline. And, as a matter of fact, from certain vantage points Johannesburg has a skyline that even Americans would admit as such. From these the city eats into the sky like a vast rip-saw; but they are not easy to find, those vantage points. The best and least known is one I claim to have discovered myself. It is half-way up Stuart Drive, itself comparatively little known as yet, but which, cut into the rocky ridge, now links old Doornfontein with Yeoville. From here, through trees that grow on the slope, you see the central section of the city floating in the blue of the firmament. This is a fine skyline indeed.

Framed between nearby pine-trees, this skyline is strung

between twenty-storeyed Escom House, to the left or south, and nineteen-storeyed Anstey's Store, to the right or north. These two buildings are Johannesburg's highest, being respectively 223 feet and 230 feet. In this special view of mine they balance one another exactly, and between them runs the jagged man-made ridge of ten-, twelve- and fifteen-storeyed concrete blocks, reflecting the sun's light by day and giving out their own electric glitter by night.

Other vantage points from where the city towers up to form a spectacular skyline are on the Main Reef Road as it approaches the city through its south-western industrial segment. It is a stark, naked outline that obtrudes upon the midday blinding sunshine; but in the early morning it is obscured by smoke and fog, which lies heavily upon the city like a blanket, while in the dusk it is revealed mysteriously, romantically in the western light that glistens against the glass windows and gives to the great walls of brick, cement and concrete a rose-coloured warmth.

"The municipal area of Johannesburg is enormous", says a Johannesburg novelist[1] in her autobiography, "and all the time it is spreading and every few years there are new fashionable suburbs and what are today the fashionable suburbs are extremely attractive. The rocky ridges, where people have blasted sites for their houses and gardens, look across many miles of country. Where we live now it took six months of blasting with a rock-drill, and two years of the convict labour one engages, to make a garden; and much of the soil had to be brought. . . . And in Johannesburg, because it is six thousand feet above sea level, and because of this vigorous climate, and because one lives on top of the world's gold, the people, like their city, are new, alive, hurried, growing and perhaps a bit mad. In Johannesburg things happen. Most of the things that happen in South Africa have their origins in Johannesburg.

"The city part of Johannesburg is not beautiful. Johannesburg is laid out like a gridiron. . . . Today the buildings

[1] Sarah Gertrude Millin in *The Night is Long* (Faber & Faber, 1941).

in Johannesburg are eighteen and more storeys high, the streets look narrower and closer than ever and can hardly serve the great traffic; . . . Johannesburg city accompanies its mines from east to west, and, both east and west, it links up with other Reef towns so that now, for a hundred miles, there flows an almost continuous city. In the centre of Johannesburg are the big retail shops; . . . the banks, the offices of mining and professional men, motor-town. . . . After the retail shops come the big wholesale shops, the big warehouses, the industrial concerns. The signboards appear with Oriental names; the shops begin to dwindle from the wholesale to retail; there are native eating-houses, Indian tailor shops, and crazy sheds of discoloured corrugated-iron where the broken-down or the never-risen of all kinds and colours swarm and mingle. . . . Outside the city are native towns, the beneficent work of Johannesburg municipality. So this, then, is how we live in Johannesburg: the people in the suburbs—from upper to lower middle-class; the white-collar men in the heart of the city; the poor whites, the poor backvelders, the down-and-outs, the would-works, the won't-works, the lower Orientals, the half-castes and various kinds of natives, all confused in the slums; the miners in and around the mines that are in and around the town."

The spreading out of the suburbs, over hill and vale where formerly Johannesburg enjoyed its picnics, is as fascinating, in its own way, as the concentrated metropolitan development of the shopping, business and industrial areas. The high-veld bush and the plantations of bluegum trees are being wiped out, to be replaced by Tudor cottages, Dutch Colonial residences and the angular, suntrap houses of the modern architect. From Houghton Ridge one may look down to watch the far northern suburbs growing outwards to the municipal boundary and beyond. It is a strange experience, and a thrilling one, and those who have seen these suburbs spring up in a summer, and watched the city skyline change to the tune of riveting and concrete-mixing, are not surprised when visitors call Johannesburg restless, unsettled.

6

POSTSCRIPT

The Johannesburg Publicity Association, in Plein Street, and the Travel Bureau at the Johannesburg Railway Station will give you brochures and maps and be glad to plan your Johannesburg trips and arrange your Transvaal tours.

Ten hours by train from Johannesburg, the City of Gold, is Kimberley, in the Cape, the City of Diamonds. Its Big Hole, dug by Cecil Rhodes and the Early Birds of the First Rush, gapes up at those who gape down. Against its stark sides, far below, birds show as they fly high above the shield of water that mirrors the sun. Is it the deepest man-made scar on the earth's surface? Into this lucky dip a thousand hands grabbed eagerly for treasure. Now, scientifically, the men of the De Beers company win the diamonds by way of deep shafts and cross tunnels. The blue ground, brought to the surface, is pulverised to gravel and sent pulsating over a graduated series of greased tables to which the diamonds stick.

Around 1870 Schalk van Niekerk, a farmer, met a Native witch-doctor who had a large and shiny charm to which he attributed miraculous properties. The charm was a large diamond. Van Niekerk bought it for cattle worth about £200, and later sold it to a trader for £11,000. This was the famous "Star of South Africa", 83 carats uncut weight. This find caused a rush of diggers all along the banks of the Orange River. Then diamonds were found on the farm Dutoitspan. Dutoitspan and all the neighbouring farms were soon swarming with speculators. The farm Vooruitzicht ("Prospect") — to-day's Kimberley — was found to contain the most valuable "pipe" of diamonds in the world. Prospectors came from all over the world. The historian J. A. Froude described them as "a motley assemblage, among whom money flows like water from the amazing productiveness of the mine". Kimberley became a railway terminus. The mines gave prosperity to South Africa. They produced, besides precious stones, such personalities as Rhodes, Beit, Barnato, Joel, Stafford Parker. The world's largest white diamond, however, the "Cullinan", was found in the Premier Mine, near Pretoria. It weighed $3,024\frac{3}{4}$ carats (about $1\frac{3}{4}$ lb.), and was presented to King Edward VII.

Those visiting Kimberley should go to the Duggan-Cronin gallery. Its thousand photographs, taken over a period of about half a century, reveal the Bantu in their tribal costumes and decorations against the background of their kraals and unspoilt landscapes. They form a unique record of Bantu styles and customs that are now being rapidly modified by European religion, education, clothes, agriculture and industry.

A motor tour of the alluvial diggings, along the Orange River, is well worth while. Here individual diggers still sift and wash for diamonds as their fathers or grandfathers did in the days of the Kimberley rush.

CHAPTER VII

THE TWILIGHT OF THE GODDESSES

I

IN JOHANNESBURG, with its skyscrapers and country clubs, it is easy to accept the solidity and permanence of Western civilisation in South Africa. The diapason of the ore-crushers comes up from the central ring of mine-dumps, south of the town, like a confident, passionate hymn of praise to the Golden Calf; and, in the Kafir Circus, the strong bulls and bears, those sweating stockbrokers, roar religiously as, in ritualistic repetition, they daily disembowel one another for a blood-sacrifice to Mammon. Could economic man be more gloriously powerful and secure, whether in Wall Street or the City, than on the Witwatersrand, on top of the world, hacking off for himself great chunks of the root of all evil—gold?

Yet one day's motorcar-run from Johannesburg, along the Great North Road, there survives in the misty lowveld of the Northern Transvaal the very fount and repository of Africa's immemorial wisdom and strength. Beyond Duivelskloof, which is to say the Devil's Gorge or the Devil's Gate, is the deep Bantu past itself, projected into the present. The Whiteman, two generations after Paul Kruger, is only now venturing to settle in those fertile valleys—not because of Bantu sorcery or savagery, but because of the malarial bite of the mosquitoes. Oil-spraying and bush-clearance have minimised the activities of the mosquitoes, and the farmers are growing more and more vegetables, flowers and sub-tropical fruits for the insatiable Johannesburg market; but on the mist-enshrouded hilltops the rain goddesses still hoard their heritage of secret knowledge and, by using it for joy or sorrow, for weal or woe, retain the allegiance and veneration of the tribes.

Here grow green fever-trees, gold-powdered; and de-formed baobabs, with thick torso and short, disjointed arms bearing cream-of-tartar gourds; and sturdy, shady *marulas* dropping yellow plums so sun-fermented that elephants, having feasted on them, stagger tipsily.

High in the heavens, cupped on a mountain-crest, shines Lake Funduzi, sanctuary of crocodiles sacred to the Bavenda, who adorn themselves with rare blue beads inherited from a place and a past unknown even to themselves. Leading a sure-footed Basuto pony along its easiest approach, I have climbed that mountain to ponder the why and wherefore of that still, heart-chilling body of water that hangs above this far country bordered by mirage and the Limpopo River. My mountain pony shied suddenly from its placid face, and a hunting dog left the heels of my Venda guide to slink away from its edge into the cover of bush and grass. From the bank and water on the far side, flocks of egrets and flamingoes, like white and pink clouds, spiralled straight upwards in the sunshine; and over the rough rim of its pear-shaped saucer, beyond the cliff and quick drop at the broad end, the Coloured lands ran away with long strides of light and shade until they merged with the dancing heat-haze.

As I rode across those lands, through forests of aged, indigenous trees, down valleys and gorges vibrant with the orchestra of a thousand birds, across crystal-clear streams musically cascading over rocks where the rain-doctors place their offerings to the clouds, I came, from time to time, to pools merry with splashing, swimming boys and girls. In this pool would be boys, in that pool girls: and their bodies gleamed and glinted like polished mahogany as they dived under or leapt into the air, framed by a dazzle of liquid diamonds. Sometimes, when the veld was open, two or three pools were simultaneously in view from the saddle; and from them went up such unrestrained shouts and laughter and chatter that the chorus was as fitful and wild as that of the bird-choirs in the echoing gorges.

Out of this Blackman's Arcady, as I rode on, tapered a high sugarloaf peak, guarded by Chief Lwamonda and his clan: it is the Hill of Sacred Baboons. About the base of the hill are fields of maize cultivated by the women for the special benefit of the baboons. The grandfathers of the grandfathers of these baboons earned this privilege of freedom and plenty, and handed down this inheritance of bounty and sanctity, by barking a war-alarm. From the hill-flank they spied the silent-footed regiments of a rival tribe advancing in the moonlight; and the noise of their excited barking, carrying far in the still night, roused the sleeping tribe, whose warriors, seizing their assegais, launched a surprise attack in fields familiar to them. The enemy, panic-stricken, confused by the barking baboons and the sudden war-cries of their assailants, rushed away in broken remnants.

In times of drought, when their own maize stalks shrivel and die, the baboons find, at the foot of their hill, gifts of pumpkins, sugarcane and corn fetched from other districts. The old-man baboon, king of the sacred troop, is grey with age, for the tribal protection gives longevity; and if hunger renders him impatient for his food, he will wander to meet it half-way. Along the winding footpath come three Bantu women from the nearest kraal, straight-backed, each with a grass tray balanced on her head. The maize-cobs, still in their green jackets, are mustered in close formation, and their red beards blow in the breeze.

The old-man baboon takes a short-cut through the long, wet grass to the footpath and there waits for the carriers, breaking off some grass-tops and chewing them to pass the time. The rear file of the fatigue party, an old woman, encourages the front file, a young woman, and the procession continues on its way, though more slowly. The young woman, as she approaches the baboon, lifts the tray from her head, and, stooping with an unconscious grace, as if

Venda women, of the Northern Transvaal, returning home from their kitchen-gardens with hand-woven baskets full of pumpkins.

Women and children crossing a river in Vendaland, Northern
Transvaal, whose hill-country is still untamed by the
Whiteman.

indeed bowing to a king, offers it for his inspection. He grunts and grabs; and then, with two cobs in his right hand and one in his left, he rolls away sailor-style. He rips off the covering of green leaves and bites greedily into the rows of pearly sweet-corn; he ambles up the hill, munching. Then he glances back over his shoulder at the three Bantu women, now walking on again beneath their loaded trays; and, as he barks, his teeth flash in the morning sun—a grey-backed, old-man baboon, dew-bedabbled, who seems to be smiling and saying, "Nice work if you can get it!"

2

Among a cluster of hills in the middle of this land lives Rider Haggard's *She* whom I have called *She-who-never-dies* but whom he called *She-who-must-be-obeyed*. Her real name is Mujaji, and she not only rules over her own clan but exercises power over neighbouring clans; and her magic as a Rain Queen is respected even by the Zulus and Swazis and other far-off tribes. By tradition and common consent she is the champion Transformer of the Clouds; but there are others approximating to her style, which is different from the style of the Swazi Queen Mother, who is the matriarch of the ruling family, the wise parent supporting her son in his chieftainship. Mujaji is the Queen of her people, who have no King, as well as their Rain Queen. She is more than a Queen: she is a goddess. Others seek to rule lesser clans through their guardianship of the rain-making secrets, or are used by the chief to strengthen his own hold over a tribe.

For instance, Chief Chigango created such a rain-goddess; and her story will serve to prepare us for the greater story of Mujaji. Critics, from the distance of Europe, do not often realise that only a short distance separates the White-man's outposts of civilisation from the Africa of superstition. This particular Mount Darwin episode may help to reveal

K

the general truth that Africans live not in our scientific
world, the world of the European, but in a world held
together by magic. Mount Darwin is in Southern Rhodesia;
and there, a few years ago, a modern Abraham solemnly
sacrificed his son to appease the gods of his fathers. It had
become necessary for the Governments of Southern Rhodesia and Portuguese East Africa to effect a straightening
of the borderline between the two territories, and in the
process, a few tribes of Chikunda Natives found themselves
within the country of Southern Rhodesia. This sudden
change was felt acutely by a tribe under Chief Gosa. One
half of his tribe was included in Southern Rhodesia; the
other half was left under the administration of Portuguese
East Africa. His most poignant source of anxiety was "how
to provide rain for those members of the tribe now under
British control".

There had been for many years in Portuguese territory
a family of Natives to whom the much revered ancestral
spirits had granted the right of appointing a virgin whose
presence would, if her chastity were cherished and her
association with other people carefully barred, ensure always
an abundance of rain in its due season. After long delibera-
tion, Chief Gosa allowed Chief Chigango—one of the newly-
made British chiefs, but lately of Portuguese territory—to
assume the position of high-priest and guardian of any rain-
goddess awarded him and his people in Southern Rhodesia.
The terms were that the goddess would be supplied from
the original family that had provided these rain-goddesses
for very many years; that this goddess would be fed at
the hands of Chief Chigango himself; that her chastity
would be kept inviolate; and that her seclusion would be
ensured by Chief Chigango. In return, Chief Chigango
agreed to pay tribute to Chief Gosa for his condescension
in doing so magnanimous a thing.

Chief Chigango soon acquired a considerable reputation
among the Natives in Southern Rhodesia. Although the
secret of the wonderful rainy seasons invariably experienced

by his tribe, the Makore-kore, was carefully kept, the tribes close to Chigango's land suspected that some mysterious power was being used. Many Natives moved from the out-lying districts in order to share in the benefits derived from the never-failing rains.

The rain-goddess allotted to Chief Chigango was a maiden of about fourteen years. She possessed a style of beauty seldom found among the Bantu, her features being more European or Eastern than Bantu. Her complexion, too, was olive, not black, and altogether her appearance was sufficient to instil into the minds of beholders that this, indeed, was a goddess. This child, then, in whose person the rain-goddess dwelt, caused abundance of rain, and consequently splendid harvests; and there was great contentment in the tribe.

Chigango had placed the rain-goddess in a lovely grove of *miti-michena*—white-trees. This grove, situated on a hill which enjoyed a maximum of sunlight, was about fifty yards wide. The lofty and massive trees, with their glittering, sturdy trunks, provided an effective setting for this child-goddess. The outer trees were carefully interlaced with withes to form a fence round the sacred grove, which was quite near Chief Chigango's kraal. About forty-five miles away was the Mount Darwin government post. An old woman, a relative, did all menial work for the rain-goddess except that of sweeping the grove, which was done by Chigango's wives. The old woman cooked the goddess's food, which was daily placed by Chigango himself in the roots of a gigantic white-tree which formed a large, deep basin.

Then one rainy season great disappointment was felt among Chigango's people: the rains failed. Crops and grass withered, the cattle were soon in very poor shape. It seemed clear that the sacred rain-goddess had lost virtue; and one aged member of the tribe recalled how many years ago, this same Chief Chigango—now eighty years of age—had traced a previous lean year to the unseemly behaviour of a rain-goddess. In that case the offence had been purged by the suspected culprit being burnt as a sacrifice to the offended spirits.

Chief Chigango, whose son had been sacrificed on the former occasion, felt that he should accept the blame in this case. But the tribal councillors would not have this, as his great age made it clear that it was not he who had violated the chastity of the goddess; but it appeared likely to them that the culprit was Manduza, Chigango's eldest son. One night Manduza went into his First Wife's hut and was sorrowful; and at about ten o'clock a loud commotion was heard outside. His wife asked, "What is wrong?" Manduza drew out his certificate of identity and handed it to her saying, "They have come for me; take this to the Government and say Manduza is dead." The door burst open, and witch-doctors and headmen swarmed into the hut and charged Manduza with sacrilege. He made no reply. Manduza was bound, and, at midnight, taken to the place of sacrifice known as Nyamakunguwo, meaning "crow's-meat". A high altar of dry logs was built. Manduza was laid on it and more logs were piled on top of him. Soon the flames of the sacrificial fire lit up the country for miles around.

Immediately after the sacrifice of Manduza, rain fell! It fell in torrents and for many days. And so, in the course of the Mount Darwin police examination, it was suggested to Chigango that though his act may have brought rain, apparently he had made no arrangement to stop it. Thereupon Chigango mentioned to an official that a blue cloth had been placed on a bush at the place of sacrifice as a token that everything possible had been done to purge the offence, and that rain would continue to fall until this cloth was removed. In order to prove the stupidity of Native beliefs, the official went to the scene of the sacrifice, found this cloth, and took it away; immediately, the torrent ceased.

Chigango and two other aged chiefs were sentenced to

death. However, as they were very aged men in whose childish minds was no criminal intent, the death sentences were commuted, and they were sent to gaol with two others less directly responsible for the human sacrifice. None denied the act alleged; all expressed amazement that the European authorities were punishing them for it. Meanwhile, the little rain-goddess continued to live in the sacred grove, attended by another member of Chigango's family. But a few months later, she became ill and died.

Chigango did not stay long in prison: during the whole period of his imprisonment—a year—he was in poor health. In his country, too, things were going badly: there was no goddess in the grove, the rains were late, and the Natives were anxious. In view of his failing health, the authorities decided to release Chigango, and, on hearing the news, this old man, frail in body, but with the eagle-light of his eye in no way dimmed, exclaimed, "Now shall you have rain!"

On the day of Chigango's release from Salisbury gaol the sky was pitilessly blue: not a hopeful cloud could be seen, so that Chigango's remark sounded like sarcasm. Chigango, escorted by a few faithful retainers, set off for home; but he had not gone far when rain fell! That whole night there was a torrential downpour—the first of the season. The next day Chigango told his people, "I am here, fear no shortage of rain". Again that night it rained heavily; and till the time of Chigango's death a few months later, there was indeed no shortage of rain.

One must live in that hotbed of superstition to appreciate the difficulties experienced by the authorities in their efforts to enlighten the Blackman—especially when such results as these occur to support his beliefs!

3

The description of Chigango's rain-goddess reminds one of Mujaji and of *She*—her European or Eastern features and her light complexion contrasting with the dusky, Bantu faces of those about her. She came from somewhere across the border of Portuguese East Africa: might she not have been a Portuguese girl, kidnapped as an infant, or part-Portuguese, a half-caste whose father had left her to be brought up by her Bantu mother?

Mujaji's country, the Transvaal lowveld, itself runs into Portuguese East, and it has been suggested that the original Rain Queen might have been a Boer girl captured by the Natives in a raid on one of the Voortrekker parties, or a Portuguese girl from Lourenço Marques, or an Arab girl from Zanzibar. Rider Haggard, in his highly romantic adaptation[1] of the Mujaji reality, turned her into an Arab princess—*al Arab al Ariba*, an Arab of the Arabs—who, with youth eternal gained by bathing in flames thundering from the very womb of Africa, rules despotically through the centuries over a primitive Bantu tribe. His Cambridge heroes, hearing of this beautiful white chieftainess, trek in search of her—and this is *She*:

"The curtain agitated itself a little, then suddenly between its folds there appeared a most beautiful white hand (white as snow), and with long tapering fingers, ending in the pinkest nails. . . . A tall figure stood before us. . . . Not only the body, but also the face was wrapped up in a soft white, gauzy material. . . . The wrappings were so thin that one could distinctly see the gleam of the pink flesh. . . . She lifted her white and rounded arms—never had I seen such arms before—and slowly, very slowly, withdrew some fastening beneath her hair. Then all of a sudden the . . . wrappings fell from her . . . and my eyes travelled up her form . . . instinct with a life that was more than life, and with a

---

[1] *She*, by H. Rider Haggard (Longmans, Green, 1888).

certain serpent-like grace that was more than human. . . .
I might talk of the great changing eyes of deepest, softest
black, of the tinted face, of the broad and noble brow, on
which the hair grew low, and delicate, straight features.
But . . . her loveliness did not lie in them. It lay rather . . .
in a visible majesty, in an imperial grace, in a godlike stamp
of softened power, which shone upon that radiant countenance like a living halo. . . . Yet it had stamped upon it a
look of unutterable experience, and of deep acquaintance
with grief and passion."

Few if any Europeans were allowed to see the real *She*,
Mujaji I and Mujaji II; but Mujaji III, the present Rain
Queen, has found it impossible to retain that studied
secrecy with an increasing race of hunters, prospectors,
farmers, police, officials, railwaymen, explorers and scientists
crowding in upon her solitude as they tame the Northern
Transvaal. But an old prospector, who had lived most of
his life there, told me, as we sat among the derelict buildings
of a played-out goldmine on the borders of the Rain Queen's
domains, that he had once been privileged to see Mujaji
dance in the glow and smoke of her own hearth. It was
nothing like the strip-tease described with such bated breath
by Haggard; but it was, I feel sure, more authentic. His
long residence in that district had made him familiar to its
Natives, who came to accept him as part of their world in a
way that they did not accept more important Europeans
who paid them brief business visits during the healthy,
winter months.

In the course of his life among them, he learnt their
language, their manners, their customs. He hunted with
them and shared with them the lean as well as the fat years:
he belonged to them. And once, after a hunt, the Native
trackers, carrying the divided carcass of a sable antelope
he had shot, led him up the hill-path to Mujaji's kraal.
Fires were lit in Mujaji's open courtyard; and while the buck
was being roasted on spits, maize-beer was passed round in
calabashes and *dagga* was smoked through a leaf-filtered

reed from a small underground oven or covered-in bowl. Hands beat large tambourines of cow-hide, drawn taut over a section of hollowed tree-trunk; and to its varied tattoo the Natives chanted and danced. The hot, fresh meat, the long draughts of beer, and the inhalations of hashish had an intoxicating effect on the company; and when they observed an old hag, one of the royal attendants, taking beer and meat to Mujaji's hut, the drumming, dancing and singing became louder and wilder. Mujaji's hut lay in the shadows on the far side of the glowing embers of the open-air fires.

Some dung and green branches were placed upon the embers and the air became thick with smoke. A team of girls began to stamp their feet and rattle their seed-filled gourds in front of Mujaji's hut: a thrill of expectancy ran through the company—and a great murmur went up as a ghostlike figure suddenly appeared and, after swaying to the beat of the tom-toms, began to glide swiftly, with weaving arms, in the flicker of an occasional brief-lived flame, in the gloom between the huts, and behind the rising smoke that wreathed and floated like many moving veils. Thus for a minute or two Mujaji, her beads and bangles gleaming upon her glimmering, naked body, danced with her dancing people; then the smoke thickened, the girls clustered closer, the drums and voices reached a crescendo—and Mujaji vanished.

4

Like a vision of the prehistoric past, set above Mujaji's kraal and swathing the round flank of a hill with their fronds, are the cycads. They are survivors in reality of a distant geological era, just as *She* was the imagined survivor of a pre-Christian civilisation. With the Hill of Sacred Baboons by way of approach, and the Hill of Cycads as a background, Mujaji, Transformer of the Clouds and Queen of the Locusts, is fittingly framed.

"If you stand among these rugged trunks", writes a South African journalist,[1] "with their glossy green leaves shining in the hot bushveld sun, the huge cones breaking apart and scattering vermilion seeds among the dark fronds, you may imagine—with every scientific justification—that here the clock of geological time has stopped. You have travelled back 100,000,000 years to the Mesozoic Era when giant herbivorous dinosaurs fed on the great profusion of cycads. . . . You pass through three of Africa's most amazing and sudden transformations. First, there are the irrigation canals, the great sub-tropical estates of modern European agriculture. Then you come to the scattered villages of a Bantu society as it has developed since A.D 1500—slowly and witchcraft-ridden through the ages of steam and electricity into the dawn of an atomic world; and then, if you have a spark of imagination, you are jerked back those 100,000,000 years, as if travelling on a Wellsian time machine, to the Mesozoic, the Age of Cycads. . . . It may . . . be asked why so much significance is attached to . . . the cycads of the country of Mujaji? First of all, there is the breath-taking beauty of this luxuriant forest. . . . But there is also the ecological mystery of this profuse growth. Why should these living fossils be crowded so densely on this one rocky spur when the rain mists also drench other south-east slopes of the mountains?"

The thick trunks of these gigantic ferns that look like palms are covered with diamond-shaped scales, marking where the old fronds have fallen away as the tree has grown taller; and crowning them are great cones, which scatter their vermilion nuts among the dagger-edged fronds— unless the baboons have eaten them beforehand. They form, these cycads, a unique decoration for a unique woman, of whom General Smuts says:[2]

"For at least half a century the Rain-Queen and her people and the curious stories about them have interested

[1] Anonymous, in the October 1946 issue of *Libertas*, Johannesburg.
[2] In his preface to *The Realm of a Rain-Queen* (Oxford University Press, 1943).

me. She was said to be very light coloured: was she a descendant of one of a couple of Boer girls who were said to have been spared by those natives, when early in the nineteenth century they massacred the Van Rensburg party without leaving a trace behind? What was the mystery about her which made it almost impossible for Europeans to catch a glimpse of her? Had the Natives adopted a white queen as something divine? . . . I saw that wonderful woman, well over sixty, but strong in body and character —every inch a queen. We exchanged information and gifts in the traditional style. . . . I was . . . pleased to have met a woman who so impressed me with her force of character and intangible air of authority—a woman who really was a queen. No wonder her subjects look upon her as the embodiment of their divine order. And yet that woman is the centre—in the ritual of her tribe—of a great tragedy which awaits her, as it has awaited her predecessors. That ritual carries us back to the most dim and distant past of the human race. . . . Mujaji is one of the high lights of anthropology, and, looking at her calm, strong face, I wondered what she thought of the fate in store for her. Here are the tears in things mortal."

These are dark words of doom for one who has achieved fame through her immortality and who wields supreme powers over the rain and the locusts. We are told[1] that for the Bantu she is the magician *par excellence*, with a far-reaching fame that inspires fear. Against those tribes who provoke her wrath, she can launch dread swarms of crop-devouring locusts, or bring drought that destroys both grass and cattle, or let loose such storms that the very soil and villages are washed away by floods. If she is not provoked but is pleased by the people and their tributes, then she transforms the clouds into gentle, soaking rains to grow maize and millet and to improve the pastures. Also, she is a sort of Lilith, the Mother of All Living, for she is believed to be a wonder with four breasts so prodigiously

[1] Rev. A. T. Bryant, *Olden Times in Zululand and Natal* (Longmans, Green, 1929).

long that she can "slap them over her shoulder and suckle
the infant comfortably seated on her back: the most extraordinary, most powerful and most mysterious female of her
time in all Africa". In addition, does not legend say that
she is eternal?

Partly because it reminds us of Chigango's grove for his
goddess, but chiefly because it sums up popular rumour
about Mujaji as it spread among the Europeans while they
infiltrated into South Africa during last century, the following passage[1] from a letter in 1879 is, I think, worth noting:
"She has her sanctuary in a wooded gorge, where the rites
and sacrifices are performed, which she ordains and presides
over. With the exception of a few privileged ancients, none
dared approach the sacred grove; and if by chance some
head of cattle venture across the boundary stream, whoever
the owner may be, they at once become the property of the
priests in charge, and are sacrificed without appeal. No
stranger is allowed to penetrate into the village of this
chieftainess: it can only be seen from afar, perched upon
the mountainside like an eagle's eyrie, on the edge of a
black forest. She herself is invisible, so that certain individuals take it upon themselves to doubt her existence.
Those best informed assert that Mujaji really exists, and
they even add that she is immortal."

But whence does her immortality derive and how is it
sustained? Deep and dangerous are the practices which are
said to give her its secret. They are concerned with the dark
mystery of final consanguinity, with the blood-relationship
that grows closer and closer until it is one, with an ancestry
so exclusive that it has no divided roots or spreading
branches but only one source and one unmixed, pure
flowering of life.

Compared with Mujaji's strange and complicated control
of the change that brings death, *She's* flame-bath seems a
clean and simple exercise. All *She* did was to turn towards
the moving pillar of a subterranean fire breathed from the

[1] François Coillard, *On the Threshold of Central Africa* (Hodder & Stoughton, 1897).

earth's uttermost core; and it lapped her round with flame
that ran about her body. She lifted it with her cupped hands
as though it were water and poured it over her head; and
she inhaled it into her lungs until she seemed the very
Spirit of the Flame. The mysterious fire "played up and
down her dark and rolling locks, twining and twisting itself
through and around them like threads of golden lace; it
gleamed upon her ivory breast and shoulder, from which
the hair had slipped aside; it slid along her pillared throat
and delicate features, and seemed to find a home in the
glorious eyes that shone and shone, more brightly even than
the spiritual essence."

It is faintly reminiscent, this flame-bath, of Mujaji's
nocturnal dance in the smoke-veiled glow of the hunting
party's fire; but there is no significance in the accidental
similarity. Not external flames but the inner fire of the
royal blood-stream is Mujaji's elixir of life. Does it derive
in some oblique way from the marriage customs of the
Pharaohs of Ancient Egypt?

5

The people Mujaji rules over are the Lovedu, peaceful
tillers of the soil. Against warlike tribes such as the Zulu
and Swazi, Mujaji balances her higher wisdom and supernatural mysteries. The trick has worked and paid dividends.
So much so that they call her the "huckster in her hut"—
the dealer in virgins and rain. For the councillor and ally,
the reward of a virgin from her harem; for the generous
payers of tribute, the gift of rain. Closely guarded within
the royal stockade are the huts of the girls. They are called
Mujaji's wives in the sense that they are her property to be
awarded to the men whose politics and social importance
make them her favourites.

Lesser sub-chiefs and rain-makers, such as Denga, with
whom I talked as she guarded the Pepedi Falls near Sibasa

in a neighbouring area, are also surrounded by virgins whom they give in marriage to men selected to strengthen the established ruling caste or whom they retain as concubines for the chief of the tribe. Denga, like Mujaji, has a strong, good face, full of character and refined by the sorrow and secrets of her life.

The girls of Mujaji's court—gifts from those who seek her rain-making favours and gifts, in turn, to those whose support she values—are not held cheaply by the tribe. They are not mere toys of pleasure, but important factors in inter-tribal economics, diplomacy, and politics. Not their barren-ness but their fruitfulness is prized; and fecundity in the whole tribe is encouraged by rites and customs and by aphrodisiacs brewed from the sap of *malala* palms, from cycad nuts, and from *marula* plums. But this harem system, judged from the outside and by European conventions, may be easily condemned. And if not condemned, it is certainly put in a crude light by one European writer[1] who spent his life in the Northern Transvaal, where the Natives were his preoccupation and his delight. Of Mujaji, he says: "The white chieftainess certainly had an admixture of Arab blood in her. . . . The Arabs travelled far. Did they pick up white women on the slave markets of Timbuctoo, Sokota, or Kano? Were these white women survivors of a conquered race? Both, Arabs and natives, favoured light-coloured women. Had these women been spared on account of their light colour and beauty; because of the knowledge of arts and industries which they possessed? Had her female ancestors, survivors of a conquered race, sold into bondage, not made their wisdom felt by enchanting their masters with sex? Was she not ruling her councillors by remaining un-married, by the intrigues of love? She had never heard of the Borgias, yet she could have taught them much. High diplo-macy, intriguing sex love, orgies, magic, poison, murder were the weapons by which the Rain-Queen conquered.

"The activities as a rainmaker, her stand-by profession,

[1] B. H. Dicke in *The Bush Speaks* (Shuter and Shooter, Pietermaritzburg, 1936).

supplied Mujaji with plenty of girls sent her as presents, who, trained at her court, could safely be trusted to do her bidding. These girls knew that unescapable death was the penalty for failing to do their duty, to fulfil the task set them by their queen. Sent to other chiefs as friendly offerings their duty was to captivate, to spy, to report, to induce their new masters to attend the festivities, dances, beer drinks, orgies, licentious debaucheries continuously held at the rain-priestess's capital.

"When a chief thought it wise to acknowledge the white Queen, Mujaji, as his supreme ruler, he was required to send a daughter to the chieftainess's court, as hostage, and in exchange for a girl presented to him. These daughters sent to the capital were called Mujaji's 'wives'. It was their duty to please visiting chiefs. Although the children of these temporary matings were called 'Mujaji's children', every subject chief knew that he had children at the Queen's court, and grandchildren, and this prevented the chiefs from harbouring the idea of attacking the Rain-Queen, their paramount ruler. . . .

"Of course, it was not the same Mujaji who ruled all the time. But Mujaji never died. Her death was not made known to her subjects. A new Mujaji, a daughter, was substituted. This deception was easily effected as the Queen seldom showed herself. On the occasions that she did so, she covered herself with a kaross and wore a skin cap with fringes which hung over her face. Her features were not well known to her people."

A careful and prolonged study of Lovedu society has been made in recent years by two South African anthropologists—a man and his wife.[1] Of the central figure of that society, the sacred queen, they say: "Against the background of our world, she no doubt appears unreal in some respects, like the baseless fabric of a dream, but in others she is real enough. We can, for instance, readily visualize her, without

[1] Mrs. E. Jensen Krige and J. D. Krige, authors of *The Realm of a Rain-Queen* published for the International Institute of African Languages and Cultures by he Oxford University Press, 1943).

official husband to cramp her authority, bearing her successor by a secret consort; or maintaining her strategic position at the centre of the tribe by re-distributing as favours the wives she receives as tribute. But it is a different and far more difficult matter to depict as real what we regard as mysterious; for, hallowed by a heritage of incest, she is chosen for her role by the ghost of her predecessor, and her destined end is death by her own hands, in order that she may rule by divine right. . . . These mysteries become realities when we see them as means to the supreme end of consecrating her power to make rain, and when we realize that this power implies control of half the cosmic forces and gives men faith to do their daily tasks. . . . Considered as a whole, the culture emerges as a structure supporting and in turn supported by the Rain-Queen. We may think of the royal institutions as the foundations upon which men build for safety against famines and foes; the culture dispenses with reliance upon garden magic for success of the crops and upon a military system for national defence. Marriage cattle and the kin can be regarded as forging a frame which firmly holds the society together, binding its families, foreign groups and territorial units to one another and to the adjusting disputes by conciliation. A cult of masks and man-made mysteries appears to surmount the edifice like spires and pinnacles; we may envisage it as the cultural handling of those enigmas of nature, the exalted themes of growth and fertility."

And then, by turning their historical data into a series of vivid pageants, the authors seek to trace in the tribal pattern its scarlet thread of ritual suicide and royal incest. They begin with the legendary Monomotapa, mighty monarch of the north, whose sons quarrel and hive off, each setting himself up as an independent mambo or chief. Mambo (the mambo[1] particularly important to the future Lovedu tribe) "rules his people, not by force, but through his supernatural prerogatives, for he is a sacred king.

[1]About the year 1500.

Tradition dictates that he should end his reign by ritual
suicide. He is appointed, not in accordance with man-made
rules, but by the spirit of his predecessor, who holds the
door of the hut in which he died against all but the true
heir; and it is only through that doorway that his successor
can ascend the throne. This mambo has a daughter, Dzugudini, and, though she is unmarried, she has an infant son,
Makaphimo. Mambo wishes to punish the seducer of his
daughter, but Dzugudini and her mother refuse to disclose
the identity of the culprit, saying, 'The father of the child
of a king's daughter is not to be known'. Mambo becomes
more and more suspicious. Dzugudini's mother steals the
rain charms and the scared beads, and, feverishly teaches
her daughter their virtues and their use; and before Mambo
can take action, Dzugudini and her infant son flee to the
south. After a long and eventful journey, the fugitives . . .
settle and found the tribe of the Lovedu. We do not know
whether Mambo ever discovered who had seduced his
daughter; but Lovedu tradition records that Makaphimo
was the issue of the incestuous union of uterine brother and
sister. The brother remains as mambo, successor to his
father; the sister, Dzugudini, by virtue of her incest,
justifies the creation of a new people. . . ."

The years, the generations pass: three centuries go over.
In the upper tribal hierarchy the names of Mujaji, a woman,
and of Mugodo, a man, recur in politics, in rain-making
and in statecraft. And then, say the historians, "Mugodo[1]
is the instrument of an inexorable fate. His faith in his
fellow men, in his councillors, even in his sons, has been
shattered. He muses that women also are faithless. But
their faith, however unfaithful, keeps them falsely true;
they intrigue against him as their husband, but they are
loyal to him as their king. Above all, their mystery is allied
to a power, not to blast the tribe to fragments, but to subdue
men and turn their passions to the service of the state. That
is the vision given to Mugodo, and the guarantee of its

[1] About the year 1800.

A young mother of Queen Mujaji's tribe laughs at her kitchen chores.

Mysterious Rain Goddess, model of Rider Haggard's *She*, Queen Mujaji, thoughtful index finger pressed to chin, takes time to answer the Whiteman's question, while her lady-in-waiting gives silent support.

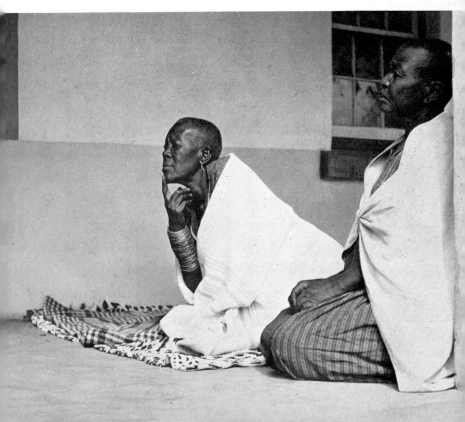

Gigantic ferns, cycads surviving from a distant geological era,
form a fitting background to Queen Mujaji, Transformer of
the Clouds.

divine origin is the far-off past in which Dzugudini origi-
nated the less tribe. That past also suggests how the vision
can be realized. . . .

"Mugodo betakes himself to his favourite daughter. . . .
Simply he tells her of his purpose, but she doubts its divine
source: 'It cannot be, my father,' she says; 'these things
are too difficult.' Mugodo goes again to her, but she remains
mystified that a sin that defiles can be a rite that sanctifies.
Then Mugodo goes to . . . Mujaji, daughter of his wife
Mamujaji. To her also he confides his vision; he tells her
she will be queen if, though celibate, she will bear the heir
to the throne. He is not speaking of a virgin birth, for she
understands that he, her father, will be the father of her
issue. 'You are all-wise, O father,' she replies. 'I am the
servant of your will.' A secret hut is built . . . and in due
course a son, not a daughter, is born. But Fate tricks Mugodo in vain. The son is strangled and a little later there is
a daughter. She is to become Mujaji II. . . .

"Mujaji I has already been on her resplendent throne
for half a century; she has turned the chaos of her predecessor's reign to peace and prosperity; and, surrounded
by restrictions which forced her into seclusion and fostered
the idea of her sagacity and immortality, she has won the
fame and attraction which drew so many foreigners to her
capital. She is 'the white-faced Mankhadeni, radiant as the
setting sun'. . . . Hosts of foreign ambassadors and poten-
tates gather at her court. Some bring cattle, others their
daughters or sisters; these are the gifts with which they show
their homage or supplicate for rain. But the mightiest
tribute of all is the gift from the Zulu king, who, disappointed by the failure of his mission to the great Swazi
rain-maker, supplicates the rain-maker of rain-makers. . . .

"The sceptre, secretly entrusted to Mujaji II on her
accession forty years and more before this pageant passes,
is the symbol of forces that swayed a bygone world. People
are uncertain of their bearings in the new world, their
sense of security has been shaken. The black ants from

L

Swaziland have left a scar. . . . Now the red ants are brought upon the scene. . . . To the workers and warriors of the 'red ants', the sceptre is like a broken reed rather than a magic wand. Some of them with impunity appropriate the country, enlisting in their service the denizens of the soil; others are collecting taxes, exacting tribute and redrawing age-old boundary lines; still others invade the sacred places, even desecrating the drums. . . . The princes still come, but they supplicate surreptitiously.

"The temporary triumphs cannot offset the disastrous defeats, and Mujaji, bewildered by the turn of events, does not know how to adjust her weapons and her diplomacy to the needs of the new situation. . . . When the grave of . . . the Christian kinsman whom she martyred becomes the rallying point of a disloyal creed, when the conspiracy to expel the European intruder ends in the disaster of the deportation of her neighbours, she loses her faith in the gods of her ancestors and adjures her followers to trust the apostle of a creed that was uprooting these gods. Pathetically she presses the poison cup to her lips, conforming to the letter, not to the spirit, of the ritual end ordained by her ancestors. In a world indifferent to the eternal verities, that cup is like an empty sham and that end like a vain sacrifice. . . .

"A cheerless panorama unfolds before us as Mujaji III ascends the throne. To submission is added humiliation. . . . They are faced with the problem of reconciling the claims of two incongruous worlds: is the authority of the queen to be derived from the alien conqueror and his ceremonies or from the spirit of the deceased and the rite of the door? . . . We are left in doubt where the victory lies. . . . The culminating point of Mujaji's power stands out prominently amid the surrounding turmoil. It also challenges it. The drama suddenly ends; it has run its course. In the sequel, the problem of the death-grapple of dualistic worlds has developed too suddenly, too disturbingly, for the powers of the tribal historian."

Paradoxically, does the fact that Mujaji III is now on view, and no longer an unseen goddess like her predecessors, mean that she has entered her twilight? Already the mystery of the lesser rain goddesses has been stripped away by the Whiteman and by the detribalised, educated Blackman. Is Mujaji, the greatest of all the rain goddesses, to be shorn of her magic too? Perhaps even now she is fading away for ever in the Lovedu twilight while, above her, high on the hill-slope, the prehistoric cycads keep their secret still.

In the gathering gloom, Mujaji remains dignified, calm, inscrutable. But the inquisitive Whiteman ponders the puzzle of her end. By self-slaughter, will she contrive to perpetuate the rite of the door for a successor, in whom her blood-spirit and ancestral powers will survive? Thus yet again might life spring from a death that is not death. Now in her seventies, she must either answer that question soon or put it from her altogether; for tradition demands that the queen shall not become decrepit and old before she poisons herself. But she gave no hint of an answer to that question while I was in South Africa, though she granted an audience to an Afrikaner journalist.[1]

"We were sitting on the stoep of the European-style house", he writes, "waiting for Mujaji. Next to this modest place is the royal hut. The old Mujaji slowly mounted the stone steps, and as we stood up in deference to the queen of the Lovedu, she smoothed the blanket at the top of the steps and sat facing us with her hands folded in her lap. Royalty was ready. Her chief counsellor and her interpreter were with us on the stoep. They made obeisance to their queen, crouching before her and pressing their hands together as if in prayer. . . . Mujaji nodded to the interpreter, and the European could speak. We paid our respects to the queen of the Lovedu, and laid our gifts at her side. We spoke to her through her interpreter as she cannot understand English. She said little, her chief counsellor replying to

[1] Stanley Uys under the title *The Twilight of the Rain Queens* in the Sunday Times, Johannesburg, of 13 April 1947.

most of the questions. When the interview was over, we
went down the steps. . . . The meeting with the legendary
Rain Queen seemed almost commonplace, although there is
still a tinge of the fascination of the mysterious about the
royal kraal. It did not seem plausible that the old woman in
the black and grey dress and the black shawl could be the
person who had inherited the rain magic of the Mujajis,
who practised the secret rites in the little rain-hut on the
edge of the precipice looking over the valleys where the
people of the Lovedu lived. Was this the African divinity
whose name struck terror into the hearts of thousands of
tribal natives in the majestic country of the Northern
Transvaal? . . . The daughter of Mujaji III has weakened
the power of the throne by a liaison with a commoner. The
seriousness of her defection will be appreciated when it is
remembered that the Rain Queens may not take husbands,
that a theme of incestuous union runs through the dynasty.
. . . Will her daughter succeed to the position of Transformer of the Clouds?"

Obviously the journalist had not dared to ask Mujaji
the question that was in his mind. But it will answer itself
in the near future. Has Mujaji another daughter of whom
we do not know? Has she with her councillors selected
some other royal virgin by whom to bring into the world
Mujaji IV—or a *She-who-must-be-obeyed*, a *She-who-never-
dies* of some other name, who will begin a new line of rain-
goddesses for the Lovedu people?

6

POSTSCRIPT

The Eastern and Northern Transvaal are very accessible
from Pretoria or Johannesburg by train or motor-car. It
is the country of *Jock of the Bushveld* and *Sarie
Marais*. Through the hills of the De Kaap valley, once

honeycombed by gold-seekers, you go to Barberton, aflame in the summer with tropical flowers. On to Nelspruit, "capital" of the Lowveld, where the cicadas enliven the evening air with their song. Then to Machadodorp, a country hydro where anglers go flicking the pools for trout. Finally to the warm springs at Badplaas in the Carolina district.

Or make for Lydenburg, deep in the lowveld, musical with trout streams. It points the way to White River, one of the most popular of the jumping-off places for the Kruger National Park.

Alternatively, go to the Rider Haggard country, to the Zoutpansberg and beyond. Louis Trichardt shelters under rugged Zoutpansberg, and is the centre for one or two spectacular excursions into the mountain country. Tzaneen offers the angler tiger-fish in the Letaba River. Motor into the magnificent countryside by way of dramatic Magoeba's Kloof. Duivelskloof lies farther north in a similar setting.

CHAPTER VIII

THE GREAT INDIAN INVASION

I

DURING THE winter months of the mid-year, a freezing wind from the Antarctic blows upon Johannesburg and across the plains of the Transvaal and the Orange Free State; but the Drakensberg range keeps it from Durban and its surrounding province of Natal, snuggling low against the warm Indian Ocean. In the late afternoon, wrapped in woollen scarf and greatcoat, you stamp your feet upon the cold platform of Johannesburg's main railway station; you eat enormously in the dining saloon of the Natal train, and warm your chilled blood with the red wine of the Cape; you sleep in your heated compartment; and, in the morning, as you eat breakfast, you watch the flower-bright hills down which the train spins you dizzily to Durban.

The air is warm about you as you motor through the streets, and, above, the great shock-headed palms bow their heads in a lazy welcome. The sky is like blue silk, and the bay deep blue between the town and the Bluff, which reaches its arm protectingly around the ocean liners, the cargo ships, the whalers and the yachts.

In this sub-tropical Eden—they used to call Natal the Garden Colony—of luscious fruits and brilliant gardens and pleasure beaches, three sorts of people mingle in the streets—lightly-clad, pale-faced Europeans, strongly-built, laughing Zulus, and delicately-featured, slender Indians. The Zulus are the original inhabitants, descendants of Shaka's nation of warriors; and the northern section of Natal is still exclusively their own Zululand. The Europeans came next, in the footsteps of that band of English adventurers whom Shaka welcomed to his country as powerful friends. Finally came the Indians, as labourers and traders. Now there are as many Indians as Europeans in Durban —indeed, it is sometimes described as a sort of Indian bazaar framed by Zulus.

Mohammedan mosque and Hindu temple, turban, fez and sari, small flags high on bamboos to drive off evil spirits, teeming markets and religious processions—all, all are India. For Durban is one of the strongpoints of the great Indian invasion of Africa's East Coast. Slowly, but steadily, this migration, southwards across the Indian Ocean, has been going on since before the Europeans sailed their ships round the Cape; but their permanent settlement along the East Coast, like their settlement in the islands of the Indian Ocean (such as Madagascar and Mauritius) has followed the European explorers, pioneers and colonists. As the Europeans have beaten down the opposition of African tribes and cleared a living-space in the African bush, the Indians have streamed in, to help, by their labour and commerce, in the development of the East Coast protectorates of England, Germany, Italy and Portugal. It is an interesting chapter of human history that still has to be clarified and written.

"There has been intercourse between India and Africa throughout history", it is authoritatively stated.[1] "A Roman hand-book to the navigation of the Indian Ocean mentions that trade in various commodities was then being carried on between East Africa and Kathiawar and Cutch on the west coast of India, and Marco Polo, in the thirteenth century, tells of 'the ships of Maabar which visit this island of Madeigascar and that other of Zanghibar'. When the Portuguese reached East Africa in the late fifteenth century, Indian traders were already there, and it was an Indian who piloted Vasco da Gama on his first voyage across the Indian Ocean. This Indian commercial community continued to prosper in Zanzibar throughout the

[1] Lord Hailey, *An African Survey* (Oxford University Press for the Royal Institute of International Affairs, 1938).

seventeenth and eighteenth centuries, under both Portuguese and Arab rule; ... In view of this long historical connexion, it is not surprising that Indians emigrated in large numbers to Africa when the development of sea transport stimulated colonization, and large areas of Africa came under British rule. To-day there are large Indian communities in South Africa, Kenya, Uganda, Tanganyika, Zanzibar, and Portuguese East Africa. In smaller numbers Indians are to be found trading in the Rhodesias, Nyasaland, and in British Somaliland.''

On the heels of the original labourers of 1860, indentured to Natal sugar-planters, have followed fast, and followed faster, Indians of all kinds—snake-charmers, performers of the mango-tree trick, lawyers, hawkers, agriculturists, merchants, priests. And players of traditional plays. Quite by chance it was that I had heard of such a play being staged in the Indian quarter; and so for further information I went to the place where Indian news is to be had—the Indian Market. This place, some maintain, is the most interesting part of Durban. My quest forgotten, I wandered for an hour in and out of the bewildering maze of many stalls. My interest was equally divided between the heaps of strange commodities and the people selling them. For they are of all types and sizes, the Indian men and women who here cry their wares. A heavily-bearded patriarch from the plains smiles blandly from behind his pile of green leaves—those leaves in which the betel nut is wrapped before being chewed—and waves a pair of persuasive, eloquent hands.

A small-featured woman, gaily garbed and decorated, jabbers excitedly while distributing to eager customers weird sweets which form great pillars of brilliant hues on her limited counter-space. From morning to evening the ceaseless activity goes on; for they understand the art of trade, these Indians. They enjoy it. Nothing is so much a part of their lives as is this buying and selling.

In one quiet corner I discovered a dealer in brassware

that is beaten out by skilful hands in the villages of his Indian homeland. Lions and elephants have been shaped by the tapping hammer; and trays worked in delicate, remarkable designs. Then I passed down a row of little restaurants where the hungry buyers and sellers eat dishes of hot curry and pickled limes and tiny, unripe mangoes.

One oily cook, busy over his stove, suddenly—and for no apparent reason—smiles a Mephistophelian smile of glittering wicked teeth, and I suddenly recall the fact that I am in search of information. I tell him so. The cook waves a frying-pan in the direction of a gaudy poster—and there it all is! Several curious pictures illustrate scenes from the play, and below them I learn from a series of misprints just where and when it is being staged.

2

The curtain rose at 10.30 p.m.—an inconvenient hour, perhaps, to the European way of thinking; but in the Orient time is not chopped up into separate chunks by the minute and hour hands of the clock. Two clowns, in freakish costumes and headgears, were grimacing at the audience and dancing like automatons. And, save for brief spells when they disappeared into the wings after a particularly strenuous knockabout turn, these clowns were always on the stage. Sometimes they shadowed the principal actors as if they were their guardian angels (only they were more like imps of mischief!) and sometimes they sat down and watched the play as if they were members of the audience; but, during those awkward spells when scene-shifters must grunt and sweat at their job, these clowns gesticulated and shuffled in the glare of the footlights, worked themselves into a frenzy of delight, indulged in an orgy of humour until the audience came as near to roaring their ribs out as it is possible without the actual aid of a surgical operation. Their object—an object which they certainly achieved—was to prevent the play from dragging by keeping the kettle of fun bubbling.

The manager had arranged for an obliging Indian to sit next to me and explain what was happening. And his skilful interpretation enabled me to follow the general drift of the argument. On this Saturday night of which I am writing the Baratha Natiya Company were acting an ancient play called *Kantha-rupa Kantha-rupi* in that dazzlingly illuminated institution in Victoria Street known as Rawat's Picture Palace. First of all a Rajah, resplendent in a green robe, sat upon his bejewelled throne and recounted, in well-polished periods, the trials and tribulations of the life of the much-maligned autocrat.

For years—so he assured his empty Court in words that pursued the quick throbs of the tom-toms—he had been childless and, in consequence, worried to death about the royal line of succession. But at last his constant prayers were answered, for a son had been born to him beneath an auspicious star. So he was named Kantha-rupa—the Form of Splendour. Now the Rajah was suffering from insomnia because he could not find a suitable and beautiful girl for his son to marry. He thereupon summoned his Lord High Chancellor and petulantly wanted to know what he was paid for if he couldn't arrange for the Heir Apparent a fitting marriage with some fair Princess. Then he thrust a portrait of the Ideal Woman into the hand of the flustered Lord High Chancellor and ordered the reality to be discovered.

The clowns romp up and down the stage, the scene moves to a neighbouring kingdom, and here in the palace is another Rajah, just as resplendent in his robes and just as bothered in his mind. He, too, for many barren years, was childless; and then his prayers were also answered with a daughter, born beneath that same auspicious star, and so she was called Kantha-rupi—this time the genuine Form of Splendour. In all the earth there appeared to be no man just good enough, and handsome enough, and rich enough for her. So this Lord High Chancellor, too, is metaphorically rapped over the knuckles and given a portrait of the Ideal Man, with instructions to wander along the highways and byways, and across the face of the land, until he found the Genuine Article.

Here, then, was the art of repetition exploited to the full to give a balance to the piece which, by now, was like a vivid, though soothing dream; for the rhythm of the pipes, strings and drums—a rhythm dwelling in a sort of half-way house between the realm of bagpipes and the desert of jazz —and the rhythm of the perfect Tamil verses, uttered by the players in sing-song monotonous voices, had long since lulled the senses into a delightful state of rest and brought Nirvana itself to the thoroughly mesmerised mind.

Of course, the two Lord Chancellors, footsore and hope-less, meet by a happy chance, and after comparing notes and portraits, fall upon one another's neck, weep with joy, and hasten on the ceremonies for the marriage of Kantha-rupa and Kantha-rupi. My wrist-watch told me that it was now midnight; but this marriage did not, as might have been hopefully expected, end the play—it merely launched the play into its long middle phase. The mummers—all men and boys, powdered white and touched up with dark pig-ments, and done out in gorgeous, fanciful attire—strutted the boards with greater assurance than ever and rolled upon their tongues (with a keener enthusiasm than before) the playwright's periphrastic prose and poetry.

A castle—all slender minarets and bits of stucco like a pretentious wedding-cake—was built for the honeymooners in a picturesque park, in which there glistened a pool. No duck-pond this, but an artificial pool built of gold; and the surface of its water was brilliant with lotus flowers. About this pool one starry night came tripping and swaying and dancing seven Celestial Virgins whose wings were all yellow like the yolk of a potent egg. Here boys impersonated nautch girls—nautch girls dancing graceful, snakelike dances until the yellow wings quivered passionately. Then the Celestial Virgins entered the palace. In an upper chamber—the faithful clowns and scene-shifters had again done good work—they found the ideal Kantha-rupa and the ideal Kantha-rupi sleeping in their double bed. The sight of the handsome Kantha-rupa proved too much for the chaste Celestial Virgins, and they spirited him away to their Abode of Love in the skies and put a spell upon the unconscious Kantha-rupi. For seven successive nights —there were, you remember, just seven virgins—they keep Kantha-rupa with them; but on the eighth they spirit him back home to his wife. But that eighth night proved more than they could bear, and so, thereafter, Kantha-rupa had to stay for ever in their Abode of Love.

There is a royal scandal when, after the long and mysterious absence of the Prince, the Princess announces that she is about to add another branch to the Rajah's family-tree. Banished by the suspicious Rajah, the distracted Kantha-rupi, in her weary peregrinations, is drawn one night to a funeral pyre of a widow's only daughter. The Princess is about to feed the flames with her own body when the widow adopts her. The widow, however, is annoyed when Kantha-rupi bears a son instead of a daughter, and so, deceiving the widow with the story of a miraculous birth, backed up by a wooden doll as the magic medium, she leaves him at the feet of Kali, that many-armed and malignant goddess who dearly loved a sacrificial dish of tender human flesh. Follows a glimpse of those shuddering days of devil-worship—those days which reach back to before the Vedic philosophers, who reasoned their way through the race's dark superstitions to the comparative light of their mystic creeds. But Kali, when she looked upon this royal baby, grew wistful, whistled up her pet five-headed serpent, and gave him into its efficient care.

So the child played hide-and-seek in Kali's Dravidian temple, with its pyramidal towers and grotesque ornamentations, until the Rajah, coming to worship, seeing him there, adopts him and appoints him his heir. He grows up into a splendid fellow and chancing to meet his beautiful, unknown mother in the forest, he falls in love with her! But the explanations of the old widow clear the way for a happy ending. The Prince, after his long spell in the celestial Abode of Love, has to wander for a while in the Wilderness of Faithless Husbands until an adequate penance has been done. Then he is restored to his beautiful palace, to his picturesque park, to his Pool of Gold, to his lovely Kantharupi, to his splendid son and to his much-harassed father, the ever green-robed Rajah.

It is by now five o'clock of a cloudless morning and the theatre is filled with the smoke of a thousand cigarettes. The sing-song voices of the players, the throbbing tom-toms, the wailing strings, the droning pipes—suddenly are silent; but it is only with a great effort—even out in the chilly street with the sky flushing over with the faint streaks of the false dawn—that the mind can shake itself free of their mesmeric influence.

3

In the outlying residential areas the hovels and the homes of the Indians are patterned over the grass-covered hills. The huddles of hovels are being cleaned up and replaced by pleasant bungalows, well spaced and set in gardens. Lacing the various sections of the Indian community together are their intensely religious and their elaborate social customs; and decorating their society are merchant princes who live in mansions and roll to and from their town offices in large, expensive motor-cars. They have their poor, as all communities have their poor; and they have their schools and clubs and cinemas. Here, in short, is a branch of India flourishing and flowering in Natal, which is thus being simultaneously invaded and colonised by East and West. Can the Zulu people—primitive, barbaric, subjugated —stand the shock of the double impact: or, baffled and bewildered by Western and Eastern gods and sanctions, will they disintegrate like the Polynesians?

In the South Sea Islands, beauty still feeds on beauty; but nothing can stop the rot of the Polynesians. They have only their gift of laughter to sustain them in the dying moment in which they now live. Like those flamboyant flowers that riot to ruin at the coarse touch of a human hand, so the dancing, singing, warring, sinning, smiling Polynesians are fading to swift extinction on contact with an alien civilisation: a lovable, beautiful race killed by the Whiteman's way of life; a race rendered sin-conscious by the imported touchstone of the missionary; a playful race made miserable by being robbed of its toys and given commerce; a singing race made voiceless by having nothing of its old life left to sing about, and by being inflicted with the gramophone and the radio; a race of dancers who no longer dance except at the behest of Europeans—a mere show, empty of emotion, a piece of vaudeville put on for dimes and sixpences and not for the joy of living, a pathetic parade of automatons engaged in what they do not realise, or realise only in a bemused fashion, is their own death-dance. When in the course of another generation or two, Polynesia is definitely of the past, nothing of it will remain but a sad, sweet memory. Will the Zulus go the same unhappy way?

My own view is that the Bantu, like the Negro, has a tough inner core and an outward adaptability that can withstand and, indeed, thrive on Western, and perhaps Eastern, influences. But we cannot help wondering what the ultimate effect on the Bantu will be of the increasing pressure of Indian infiltration. For, crowded out of their own teeming and impoverished sub-continent, the Indians are still spreading across the Indian Ocean to its many islands and to Africa's East Coast whose climate suits them so perfectly. They spread their praying mats on the well-decks of European-owned ships and approach the African shore with hopeful hearts: or they get there singly and in small troupes in the trading dhows that still roam the Indian Ocean, as they have done down the centuries, their sails held in the monsoon by a short, stout mast. Sindbad the Sailor voyaged in dhows such as these. On the southern beat, their bulging belly is loaded with salt or dates from the Red Sea, and with coconuts or cloves on the northward—unless they bring Indians and take away elephant tusks and black slaves.

Strange, frail little fellows, these Arab traders are; and they dress in long robe and turban, such as Sindbad must have worn. Often they sport a thin red beard, and invariably carry the lightest of light canes. Their faces, the colour of desert dust, are delicately Semitic, and their brown eyes, as sharp as a weasel's, dart glances everywhere. They navigate by the stars and by their inherited knowledge of Africa's East Coast, the islands, the currents and the winds of the Indian Ocean, as much as they do by the crude compass many of them now possess. The dhows come and go like curious seafowl, as the weather and the seasons move them, not the calendar and the clock. They anchor by the score in the East African ports, linking Arabia and India with Mombasa, Dar-es-Salaam and Zanzibar; and they lie, rolling in twos and threes, off less frequented shores, to which the Arabs row, pulling on red, round-headed oars, in the quaintly shaped boat that each dhow carries lashed beneath its hood. Indians have made the sugar-island of Mauritius one of the most densely populated places in the world; but in Africa's East Coast they see more elbow-room and scope for their labour and talent.

Indian labourers built the railway from Mombasa to Nairobi; Indian pedlars distributed goods made in Germany to the Natives of Tanganyika, formerly a German colony; Indian workers made possible the establishment of Natal's sugarcane fields; Indian soldiers have campaigned under British generals in Abyssinia, Tanganyika, and Kenya; Indian tailors, money-changers, storekeepers, traders, financiers, farmers, and industrialists are prospering all down the East Coast from the Sudan to Natal. They are slowly flooding into the East Coast like a deep, almost imperceptible tide; but it is a human tide that will have no ebb. For good or ill, the great Indian invasion goes on, reinforced by an average of seven children with whom each Indian married couple is blessed.

4

It is perhaps not without significance that the books and pamphlets about the Natal Indians are all written in terms of politics. About the Cape Malays, the Natives, and the Cape Coloureds there are many books describing their customs and ceremonies, their way of life; but if there are such descriptions of the Natal Indians, they are very few and far between, and certainly hard to come by. Yet the Natal Indians are most picturesque, and should provide a wealth of material for romantic writing. They have not even been used by the fiction writers—not to any great extent, at any rate. Yet short stories and novels about the Natives, the Cape Coloureds and Malays are numerous, and each year sees more added to the long list.

I take this to be evidence that the Indians live much more within themselves and their own religions than the other racial groups of the Union of South Africa. Through Christianity and a more intimate intermingling of interests, the Natives and the Cape Coloureds are brought within the understanding of the Europeans; and even the Malays, Mohammedism notwithstanding, have been woven, through three centuries, into the pattern of European consciousness in the Cape. But the Indians, late-comers to Natal, seem to live secret lives, and the Europeans see them only in their outward and visible form, and know nothing of their inner and spiritual grace. Through their eyes, the Europeans are aware of the Indians in the market-place and in the shops; and passing Europeans idly watch and wonder when the Hindu worshippers hold their great religious processions, carrying elaborately designed and coloured con-

A Zulu pauses to consider the Whiteman's cane fields and sugar factory in the rolling hills of his forebears.

Patterned into suburban Durban are the cottages and gardens
of the Indians.

traptions through the Durban streets in order to fling them into a river as a peace-offering to the gods that preside over their universe.

Even those who write in political terms, however, occasionally offer us a phrase or a paragraph which conjures up some sort of picture of the Indians themselves, their daily life, their work, their clothes. For instance, in 1904, during the early, Ghandi-led demonstrations against the Whiteman's law, Natal Indians, men, women and children, gathered on the Transvaal border with the idea of forcing their way across, despite the ban against their immigration. And the historian,[1] in an aside, tells us that they presented "a striking spectacle in their Eastern garb, the women decked out in jewellery that glittered in the sunlight, the children dressed in garments of gorgeous colours".

Then, after a comprehensive tour of South Africa, a decade after the establishment of the Union, an Englishman[2] has this to say of the Natal Indian: "His very virtues are cause of offence. . . . The Indian possesses an extraordinary capacity for saving. He will live 'on the smell of an oil-rag'. . . . Years ago the promising young man from the large merchant firms in South Africa looked forward to starting a little business in the back country. Each little *dorp* had its store owned and run by a white man. Everything was sold there: 'kaffir truck'—that is to say, the beads, blankets, pots and pans, and the other simple articles required by the raw native—and the jam, biscuits, pickles, ham and tenpenny nails required by civilisation. Now, the white man is no longer there. His place is taken by the Indian. Even the Jew has had to give way to him. . . . If you ask for an explanation, the last of the white traders will tell you: 'Oh, that coolie lives on nothing and saves every farthing. He dosses beneath the counter of his shop in a box of shavings or places his sleeping mat on bags of flour and potatoes. He has no home-life, no recreation, no

---

[1] D. N. Miller in *History of Volksrust*.
[2] Charles Dawbarn in *My South African Year* (Mills & Boon, 1921).

M

standard of comfort—no anything except an unending round of trying to make money. A little rice and rags of clothes content him. You can imagine how the British working man or small trader regards him—he who has struggled hard these many years to emancipate himself, to give his life a little dignity. It is really a conflict in the ideals of East and West.'

"The Indian marries early and hies him to a house which may be built of anything. If he is a town labourer or engaged in the smaller sort of fruit and flower culture, he will inhabit a terrible-looking shanty made of flattened petrol tins. So unsightly a dwelling excites the strong resentment of the white man. It is generally insanitary: the kaffir's hut is a model of order and cleanliness compared with this eye-sore of a dwelling-place. To add to the horror of it, its site is certain to be the prettiest in the countryside— a ridge overlooking wide, pleasant valleys. Thus is Durban, to its very gates, polluted and defiled by these excrescences. . . .

"The Indian admits readily enough that his dwellings are not ideal, that the sanitary arrangements are nil, that the conditions are quite unfavourable to the bringing up of his family. 'But,' he says, 'this is as much as I can do on the money I receive. How can a man live in a *real* house at the present price of commodities, and at present rentals, when he earns but £6 a month! We Indians live as well as the white man—at the same wage.' This is some part of the truth, but not all of it. To express the problem in all its terms, one must say that while the Indian does not earn as much as the white man, generally speaking, for the same class of work, and therefore less must be expected of him in the matter of appearances and house accommodation, yet he is more uncleanly than the native. His womenfolk, however intelligent and industrious, present a soiled and unkempt appearance—even though arrayed in finery—in comparison with the lower classes of the white population and even of the native women. . . .

"Durban shows a remarkable development in the Indian's commercial position. . . . Dark-skinned merchants riding in superb motor-cars driven by white chauffeurs are no uncommon sight to the resentful amazement of the older white residents. Recently, Indians have inhabited the Berea, the most fashionable part of Durban overlooking the town and sparkling bay. . . . Then there is the question of the Indian's capacity. Can he rise to the white standard of efficiency and intellectuality? I think there is no doubt about it. Indian children in Natal and other parts of the country are keenly set upon their work and show sharpness and intelligence. A Durban friend, who advertised for a clerk for architectural work, received the best expressed letter from an Indian. Indians are entering business houses, banks, law offices and, indeed, everywhere where the colour bar is not too rigidly applied. . . . He has made the waste ground on the outskirts of municipal areas to blossom as the rose. He has the art of raising bananas, vegetables and flowers on the most unlikely swamps. *Petite culture* is almost entirely in his hands, thanks to his undefeatable industry and patience. Sammy's baskets balanced on the end of a bamboo pole, like the nests of the weaver bird, go bobbing along the streets and lanes of every township in Natal."

Violent, tragic street-fighting[1] took place between the Indians and the Zulus in January 1949—chiefly in Durban, but to some extent in Pietermaritzburg. There were also minor attacks on Indians in Johannesburg, while, in Kenya, far to the north, the Africans began a boycott of Indian stores. These events suddenly laid bare the deep rivalries and bitter animosities (racial, cultural, commercial) that exist between the Africans and the Indians; and so, representing a London newspaper, an Australian journalist[2] began probing the whole question for the information or the public in England.

"In Kenya in 1935", he pointed out, "there were

[1] Killed, 142; injured, 1,087.
[2] Noel Monks in a message from Durban, *Will the Indians swamp Africa?* published by the London *Daily Mail* of 3 February 1949.

40,000 Indians. To-day there are 85,000 and they are arriving there by hundreds each month. In the same period Uganda's Indians have increased from 15,000 to 27,000, while Tanganyika's Indian population has gone up from 33,000 to 58,000. In the Rhodesias, the only African territory outside the Union that keeps a tight rein on Indian infiltration, figures have risen from 5,000 to 7,000. Even in the British Protectorate of Bechuanaland 66 Indians in 1939 have multiplied themselves into 2,000 to-day. To these figures add 300,000 Indians in the Union and you are getting up to the half-million mark. . . .

"From Capetown to the Red Sea figures reveal the vast colonisation scheme being carried out by Indians that, if unchecked, will do more to drive the white man from South, Central, and East Africa than the hypothetical fear of the Bantu. If you drive the 2,300-odd miles from Johannesburg to Nairobi, as I did, you will come across more Indian officials at the various frontiers than European from Nyasaland on. . . . It is easier for an Indian to get into Kenya these days than it is for a British workman— and the Springboks just cannot understand that any more than they can understand the fact that there are five elected Indians in the Kenya Parliament. The people are just beginning to realise now the impact of Indians on the economic, social, and political life of Africa."

5

Though rapidly growing within the larger framework of the Whiteman's economy prompted by London and Johannesburg, Durban looks to the East Coast and to the East for the widening ambit of its trade. Colombo and Bombay sometimes seem to be sister cities of Durban linked by the Indian Ocean. Commercially, that has been true in the past; and it is likely to be so in the future, despite political differences, for these cities are linked not only by the Indian

Bisected by brilliant sunshine and deep shadow, West Street is Durban's busiest thoroughfare.

In front of his beehive-shaped hut, a Zulu chief smiles
happily among his wives and children.

Ocean but by Indian traders along the East Coast and on the many islands of the Indian Ocean. In climate, too, and in the outward manifestations of life, Durban and Colombo, or Bombay, have much in common.

A witness[1] bore testimony to this half a century ago, and surely the years between have increased their similarity. He says:

"Durban, with its climate, its Oriental servants in the hotels, and its club, reminded me somewhat of Ceylon; and the people have a good deal of the planter element about them. They have none of the Johannesburger's rush, but the solemn sturdiness of the Cape Towner has no part in their composition. They are—so, at least, they struck me—an easy-going, good-natured community, and British in everything. . . . Durban has some wide streets, some good shops and hotels, and—especially as regards its Town Hall —some fine public buildings. Its club is more like one of the institutions one comes across in India than a Colonial club; it has none of the free-and-easiness of the Colonial institution, and much of the Anglo-Indian formality and ceremony."

Precisely the same sort of things are being said and written nowadays about the Natal Indians as ten, twenty or fifty years ago. Their lot is improving steadily; and that they are thriving is proved not only by their rapidly increasing numbers but also by the splendid physique so many of them have. The lean, hungry coolies of yesterday have been replaced, to a very great extent, by tall, well-built farmers in their own sugarcane field or market garden or waiters in the holiday hotels or well-to-do tradesmen of all kinds, whether shopkeepers or carpenters. Their children pack into the schools, which are always expanding and multiplying; and in the new residential areas their womenfolk, with flowing veils and saris, walk with light grace in the sunshine.

Although the Durban authorities have organised social amenities of all kinds for the Indian community—educa-

---

[1] Stuart Cumberland in *What I Think of South Africa* (Chapman & Hall, 1896).

tion, housing, health, sport—angry voices from India continue to say harsh things about the way the Whiteman treats the Natal Indians. It is true that the Whiteman from his *laager* regards the Natal Indians as part of the tide of colour that is rising about him on all sides; but high-caste voices from India ring a trifle falsely from the grim walls of India-Pakistan class prejudices. South Africans do not fail to notice that high-caste visitors from India, instead of kissing the feet of their exiled brothers, whom they say the Europeans should take to their bosom in political and social equality, treat them with utter disdain. An Englishman[1] who became editor of a South African newspaper, puts it in the following words:

"As for the cry that the *amour propre* of Indians in India is unbearably wounded by the thought that their compatriots in South Africa are treated as an alien element in our population, it is no doubt genuine enough . . . so far as it goes. But its sincerity does not go very deep, as anyone who has lunched with one of the high-caste official representatives of India in South Africa, at one of our good local hotels, where there are Indian waiters, knows. There are very few Indians in South Africa whose touch, or even near approach, does not pollute the presence of a high-caste Indian official or visitor here. The manner of these official or visiting Indians to their compatriots who wait on them here is loftily contemptuous. No South African with any claim to decent breeding would dream of treating an Indian waiter as these officials and visitors of their own race, but of superior caste, treat him as a matter of course."

6

POSTSCRIPT

One side of Durban has its grain chutes and its coaling gear and all the impedimenta of a great port; but its other side has its beaches and holiday hotels. The Durban Publicity

[1] B. K. Long in *In Smuts's Camp* (Oxford University Press, 1945).

Association and the Travel Bureau of the South African Railways are centrally situated near the General Post Office. They will tell you how to tour Durban, the seaside resorts on the North and South Coast, the Hluhluwe Game Reserve, the Valley of a Thousand Hills, and the Drakensberg National Park.

The South Coast stretches for 120 miles in a succession of beaches, with small townships attractively sited along numerous small rivers and streams. Townships that have found favour with settlers are Umkomaas, 34 miles south of Durban; Scottburgh 40 miles; Port Shepstone 86 miles, and the numerous resorts on the lower South Coast between Port Shepstone and Port Edward, 122 miles from Durban.

The North Coast, including Zululand, stretches to beyond St. Lucia Lake and Estuary, 176 miles from Durban. Temperature ranges are some degrees higher than in Durban. St. Lucia Lake, False Bay and Richards Bay provide excellent surf, lagoon and estuarine fishing. Eshowe, the old capital of Zululand, and the surrounding districts are favoured as areas for settlement.

Much the same style of clothing prevails in sub-tropical Durban as in large cities in Great Britain and the United States of America, except that there is a general trend towards medium and lightweight materials.

A short distance inland is Pietermaritzburg, the capital of Natal. The Zulus call it Umgungundlovu, the-place-of-the-elephant. Durban they call Tegwene, after a big bird that used to haunt the muddy foreshore of the Bay, while along the South Coast are such place names as Isipingo, Amanzimtoti (Sweet water) and Umbogintwini. And the Zulus call the Drakensberg mountains Quathlamba, which means assegai-heads. Forming a great buttressed wall, rich in thousands of species of flora, these "Dragon Mountains" have major peaks which attain a height of 11,000 feet. Good roads and hostels have turned them into holiday resorts within the Natal National Park.

Monarch of the Drakensberg is Cathkin; but perhaps the most impressive peaks are those known as Mont aux Sources, whence the Tugela River plunges down nearly 3,000 feet in a series of great leaps, to form the highest single fall known in South Africa. The highest point of Mont aux Sources rises 11,783 feet above the sea. On all sides peaks and valleys succeed each other in thrilling succession. Here you can watch the headwaters of the Tugela, Orange and Elands Rivers starting on their long journeys to the Indian and Atlantic Oceans. From here, too, you can see the broad valleys of Basutoland covered with wheat, the great pastoral lands of the Orange Free State and the fertile valleys of Natal.

Rainbow and brown trout leap in the streams, and, beneath the Giant's Castle, roam herds of oribi, rhebuck, klipspringer. Visitors can ride along the mountain trails on Basuto ponies. But for mountaineers there is the ascent of the Sentinel, a 10,700 feet pinnacle, 12 miles from the hostel. A stone hut has been built on the summit by the Natal Mountain Club; and those who want to see a wonderful sunrise spend the night in this hut.

CHAPTER IX

THE FALL OF THE HOUSE OF ZULU

I

NORTH OF the rushing Tugela, Natal's largest river, and circumscribed by the Whiteman's borders, lies Zululand. In the centre of that Blackman's country, high on a hilltop above surrounding hills, is Nongoma, royal capital of the Zulus. Nongoma—the name makes soft, sad music within the mighty anthem marking, just above earshot, the rise of the Bantu. Nongoma, aloof, alone, is the home of the Zulu royal family, whose late ruling scion was Solomon— a modern King Solomon with hundreds of wives—and whose present head, Cyprian Inyangayezizwe Bhekuzulu Solomon Ka Dinuzulu, dreams of the moment when the Whiteman's sanctions will ease and thus allow him to assume more fully the chieftainship made world-famous by the terror of Shaka. Nongoma—is it the melody of failure against the commercial success of Durban, where Zulu herds once grazed?

Before going to Nongoma, I took another look at Durban so that I might compare it with the Zulu capital. For the eyes, in Durban, there are scarlet hibiscus, wax-like magnolia, morning-glory and the flame-tree; and for the inner man there are pawpaw, grenadilla, mango and the melon known as *spaanspek*. Berea, on its long hill-crest, is like a gay garland on the city's brow—a great garland of flowering trees, flamboyants, and brilliant blooms of all colours. From this hillcrest, which is refreshed by the cool airs of the dawn and evening, the residents descend to their business in the solid blocks of offices and in the large and airy shops, to bathe along the beaches at the foot of West Street, to yacht in the Bluff-protected bay, to fish in the open sea or from the rocks of one of the many little holiday resorts that are strung like a necklace along both North Coast and South Coast. In these dreamlike surroundings of sea and shore and sky, where every prospect looks like a delightfully composed and delicately executed watercolour fresh from the artist's brush, you are pleasantly lulled into the *dolce far niente* of Tennyson's *Lotos-Eaters*:

> They sat them down upon the yellow sand,
> Between the sun and moon upon the shore;
> And sweet it was to dream of Fatherland,
> Of child, and wife and slave; but evermore
> Most weary seem'd the sea, weary the oar,
> Weary the wandering fields of barren foam.
> Then some one said, "We will return no more;"
> And all at once they sang, "Our island home
> Is far beyond the wave; we will no longer roam."

Remembering Nongoma, I threw off the gently clinging lethargy and turned north. I was determined to see as much as I could of Zululand, which, in past years, I had roamed with delight. The Zulus, under their autocratic and warlike chiefs, certainly made a stir in the world, so that the world knows of them far more than it does of any other Bantu tribe. *Dolce far niente*, the Natal fever that drugs the European into day-dreaming, had no fascination for the Zulu kings, who were men of action. The hot sun, the subtropical humidity and the malarial mosquito did not tame or kill off their warriors and women: in their heyday, during the nineteenth century, they were numerous, full-blooded and virile. It is possible that the Zulus brought their radiant health and zest for life, their hot blood and lust for fighting from a more bracing climate—from the African highlands, from the Transvaal and Rhodesia, whither one of their military groups, the Matabele, travelled and settled, perhaps by a homing instinct; but, on the other hand, it is possible that the Natal climate suits them as it suits the Indians—in short, that it is their climate.

Now that the Northern Transvaal has been opened up

and widely settled by European farmers, Zululand is the least-known part of the Union—especially its northern and inland areas, away from the European sugarcane-growers whose trimly cultivated plantations pattern—amiably possessive, cosily cuddlesome—the fair flank of coastal Zululand.

Half an hour by motor-car from Durban, on the winding, rising road to the provincial capital, Pietermaritzburg, lies a special Zulu reserve—the Valley of a Thousand Hills. On the veranda of a roadside hotel, I took tea and looked out over that great panorama of valleys and summits, with Zulu kraals clinging to the slopes. Then, leaving the trunk road, with its traffic speeding on the Whiteman's business, my car rolled me along a side track down into that Valley and up over its Thousand Hills. With clouds brushing the hilltops and mists sweeping up from the valleys to greet the sun, it was rather like lolling back in a comfortable cushion of cumulus, and watching the Zulu world revolve and twist and turn in a series of slow stretching exercises and sudden cavortings. The strong-limbed women stooped to their kitchen-gardening in the maize and millet fields, the children ran at play about the villages, and the men, with easy stride, herded their cattle in the pastures or squatted to sharpen knives, cut sandals from oxhide, or fashion a fighting stick. At an open-air smithy, while one old Zulu worked a pair of primitive, oxhide bellows, another heated assegai-heads in the fanned coals and then hammered them out to the requisite point and edge. Only one thing marred this delightful fragment of the Zulu past—an occasional roof or wall of corrugated iron among the round, thatched huts comprising the kraals of that reeling landscape.

Zululand itself does not lie here any longer—it did in the days of Shaka and Dingaan—but beyond the Tugela. The Valley of a Thousand Hills and the rickshaw-boys of Durban are all the Zululand that most Europeans ever see. In the summer there is the danger of malaria in Zululand; the healthy winter is short; and there are many other pleasant places to visit where hotels and other European amenities are not to be despised. So Zululand remains off the beaten track of the holiday-makers and apart from the main stream of progressive South Africa. Out of Zululand come the muscular giants who, to make money for their hut tax or their next wife, pull rickshaws in the streets of Durban. They fix on their heads ox-horns for strength and massed feathers for speed; and they have dangling about their lightly-clad bodies all manner of decorations and charms. Anklets of dry seed-filled beans and small gourds rattle as their naked feet hit the street; and as they race along, with one or two passengers, they ring a small handbell which they hold against one of the shafts. Their legs are white-washed with fanciful designs, which give the effect of gaiters never yet made by man. Downhill, the skilful rickshaw-boy balances his weight against his passengers, and thus he can rest on his shafts for many yards, while his happy feet dance in the air. At the end of a run, he carefully puts the money he has earned into a leather wallet, and then, with the ends of the shafts planted on the ground, he sits on the footrest of the rickshaw to cool off. With an oxtail-switch he drives off the flies, and with a wooden spoon he scrapes the sweat from his face and neck. He is a barbaric warrior in drag-harness; but he seems to enjoy himself, judging by his high-spirited prancing and his shrill whistles and shouts as he boasts his prowess in the Whiteman's streets. When he gets bored, he puts away his rickshaw and his regalia and goes back to Zululand.

2

But we must run away from Durban if we want to get closer to the Zulus and their way of life. Down into one of their own valleys—that is where I have gone, whenever the chance has occurred, to feel the earth vibrate with the songs and dances of the Zulus. And always those joyous songs and

Ringed by stockades, the villages of the Zulus perch on the ridges of the mountainous landscape.

Pier at St. Lucia estuary, Zululand, where the boats await
their complement of anglers.

vigorous dances do something more than remind me of a
bloody past: they prompt me to ponder the doubtful future.
But the dancers, significantly enough, are not worried by
any doubts as they come streaming down the hill in long
lines, their oxtail mantles dazzlingly white in the sunshine.
It is a thrilling moment when these descendants of Shaka's
warriors, in all their elaborate and savage finery, leap forward from the long grass and swarm upon the dancing
ground. With their shields flung up into the air, and
brandishing their fighting-sticks and battle-axes, they rend
the air with an ear-piercing yell. This is the beginning of
a wonderful series of dances: not only war dances, but dances
of joy and dances celebrating various Zulu customs and
perpetuating different Zulu beliefs; but they are all barbaric
in their vigour and form and fury. Delightfully beaded and
decked out in a hundred monkey-tails, their chiefs are
resplendent in headgears of scarlet and black feathers which
shake violently to the rhythms of the prancing feet. Leopard
skins are draped round many of the headmen, who, with
their shouting and gymnastics, present a most effective and
inspiring spectacle of an Africa that is still tribal and
primitive.

The shrill whistling of the warriors works up to a climax
of stamping feet, swaying bodies, assegai-beaten shields,
and surging songs. The leader of each *impi* does overtime
as conductor and ballet-master, signalling his commands
violently and making his voice heard hoarsely above the
general din. Most dramatic of all is the mock revolt of an
impi against its leader, who is charged down until he at last
reasserts his authority and forces back his warriors foot by
foot. Then it becomes a cabaret of Darkest Africa as the Zulu
women dance forward. A few beads and loin strings suffice
for the *intombis*, the maidens, while the wives wear the
marriage belt, which they keep on throughout their lives,
like a European wife her wedding ring. Led by a matron
waving a wooden ladle emblematic of the home and kitchen,
they step out the measure that is the basis of all such music-

hall dances as the can-can and the cakewalk, and their splendidly proportioned bodies sway and sweat in the scorching sun.

Then, while the women sing, the men perform a ballet of the kraal and hunting field. Squatting on their haunches, leaping high into the air, they mimic the denizens of the bush, while comic relief is supplied by a comedienne and a clown, who burlesque the show with fantastically funny antics. And as a reward for all, Kafir-beer flows, oxen are killed and roasted whole. It is a spectacle mirroring a savage world, which, surrounded on all hands by European influences, still survives by nourishing itself on a conquered but not annihilated yesterday.

Here and there in such a great crowd of dancers are usually a few Zulu men dressed in long, girdled robes; and in one hand they carry a long, cross-tipped staff. They are the strange Christians of Ekupakameni, and Shembe is their prophet. Shembe, as we reckon Shembe, is now dead; but Shembe lives in the new Shembe, his namesake and successor, just as Mujaji, the Rain Queen, lives in the new Mujaji. The huts and houses of Ekupakameni—literally "the High Place" and symbolically "the Place of Spiritual Uplift"—pack cosily on a hilltop at Inanda, not far from Durban, and struggle down its slopes towards broad sugarcane fields, undulating to far-off horizons. Here live the new Zulus: Shaka and bloodshed have gone from their land, but mighty Jehovah may give it power and wonder again. The village of worshippers receives the sun's first swords of light and is touched by the dusk's after-glow when all its surrounding valleys are in such deep shadow that the windows of their scattered houses shine with artificial light; and when the moon rides the night-sky its streets and roofs and walls are all washed with silver. Yet neither the sun nor the moon ever finds Ekupakameni lifeless; white-robed Zulus seem always to be moving this way and that in fewer or greater numbers, according to the hour.

Life in Ekupakameni has little relation to the twentieth

century; it is the life of Bible times. Uninfluenced by a formal education or by the theology of missionaries, Shembe, after having psychological experiences very similar to those of Paul, Joan of Arc, or Mormon Smith, came to see in himself another of the long line of prophets—a prophet whose special mission it was to wean the Zulus from the breast of Darkest Africa and feed them on the strong meat of Christianity. He is just one of the hundreds of Bantu religious teachers who are interpreting the Bible, according to their own light, for the multiplying sects.

A regiment of girls sways rhythmically along an Ekupakameni roadway. Their hands move in special gestures and their legs carry their swinging bodies forward in a series of graceful movements. They are practising a form of eurhythmics that Shembe, the first Shembe, distilled from the wild dances of savage Zululand. One of them beats a gigantic tambourine to give the time as, led by a clear soprano, they harmonise a song whose words and music were composed by the prophet of "the High Place":

> See the Zulus dancing for God.
> Be smart and dance for God!
> We know by the Word coming from the clouds,
> By the Command coming from the heavens,
> We know by the Word coming from the clouds,
> That the trumpet of the Lord is sounding.
> The earth that we tramp will shake
> At the Vision and Voice of the heavens.

Each day brings new followers to Ekupakameni. They come to learn, and return to their kraals all over Zululand to teach. On its dancing pitch grey-headed warriors, complete with shields and assegais, together with almost naked girls straight from their kraals, leap and sing beside the initiated followers, who dress in elaborate and symbolic regalia. Some of the men wear kilts to convince the barbarians that trousers do not constitute a *sine qua non* of Christianity. Some of the women wear bridal veils as a sign

of purity newly gained by baptism. Responsible Europeans
—among them ministers of orthodox Christianity—are
inclined to the view that Shembe's form of Christianity is
proving of great value to the Zulu nation. Hard-bitten
warriors of the old savage school who were left untouched
by the ordinary Christian teachings have been completely
won over by the Shembe method, which encourages them
to retain their tribal mode of existence, to sing their folk
songs, and perform their ancient dances. Then their barbaric promptings are cunningly sublimated into spiritual
fervour through his songs and dances to the "Great Great
One".

The Shembe movement is gathering such strength that
it cannot be ignored by those who take an intelligent
interest in the game being played out in South Africa's
checkerboard of black and white races. Shembe's apostles
teach, as he did himself, by parables borrowed from the
workaday world of the Zulus; and they think and live as
the prophets thought and lived in those Bible times when
mankind was first achieving the idea of God. Thus it is
that Jehovah still broods and thunders and smiles in the
heavens above Ekupakameni.

3

Northwards into the hills I went to visit the royal family
at Nongoma—past Stanger, where the hugger-mugger
grave of Shaka is contemptuously neglected by the nation
he savagely shaped into a war-machine. By torture and
murder he nazified it beyond the limits of human endurance:
his short, stabbing assegai, which never missed like the
thrown assegai, had returned home from its massacres of
the neighbouring tribes to drink Zulu blood itself in a Night
of the Long Knives too oft repeated—then it bit into his
own heart, for the Zulu hierarchy could stand no more self-
slaughter. But the grave of Dingaan, the brother who

guided the assegai to Shaka's heart, is still looked after in its honoured grove of euphorbias. It is right and proper that the protective wire fence about Shaka's grave should have been put up in recent years by a European settler—for whatever else one may say about him, Shaka was always very good to visiting Europeans and seemed to have not only a diplomatic respect but a lively affection for those first British settlers—Farewell, King, Gardiner, Fynn and Isaacs—whom he entertained generously at the royal kraal and encouraged to settle at Durban.

Shaka was certainly no stick-in-the-mud—he was always ready for a new idea. He had no sooner heard how the British soldier employed the bayonet than he armed his warriors with its equivalent—the short stabbing assegai. When Shaka invited Nathaniel Isaacs[1] to watch an army of six thousand warriors being drilled, he was not happy until he had persuaded the visitor to transfer his straw hat to the head of a warrior, who was elated (or pretended to be elated) with this odd new style of battle headgear! And, without any fear of their possibly harmful magic, he took to soap and razor instanter. As Isaacs tells us, Shaka "used to bathe every morning at the head of the kraal; first he anointed his body with bruised beef made up into a paste with ground corn, then rubbed it off again, and threw the water over himself. After indulging in bathing a short time, when dry he a second time anointed himself with sheep's-tail fat or native butter. When we introduced soap he thought it a wonderful discovery, and afterwards used it in preference to his own method of cleaning himself. We presented him with a razor, and showed him how to apply it; and no sooner had he become acquainted with the mode of using it than he threw away his own instruments for shaving, used those we presented to him, and seemed greatly delighted with them."

In the end Shaka was a pathological victim of the mur-

---

[1] Author of *Travels and Adventures in Eastern Africa* (Churton, London, 1836). Reprinted by the Van Riebeeck Society, Cape Town, 1936.

N

derous Zulu system, which he did not invent though he
practised it, and perhaps was forced to practise it, in excess.
It would require the author of *Macbeth* to reveal the majesty
and madness of Shaka. From his magnificent prime, he
declined into a terror-filled, mind-haunted murderer of his
own people, whom he feared like avenging angels. But in
his happier moods, he had a great sense of fun and could
be joyful in the midst of his army. For instance, after an
impi of men and boys had formed in a crescent at his kraal,
"the King", Isaacs says, "placed himself in the middle of
the space within the circle, and about 1,500 girls stood
opposite to the men three deep, in a straight line, and with
great regularity. His majesty then commenced dancing,
the warriors followed, and the girls kept time by singing,
clapping their hands, and raising their bodies on their
toes. The strange attitudes of the men exceeded anything I
had seen before. The king was remarkable for his un-
equalled activity, and the surprising muscular powers he
exhibited. He was decorated with a profusion of green and
yellow glass beads. The girls had their share of ornaments;
in addition too, they had each of them four brass bangles
round their necks, which kept them in an erect posture,
and rendered them as immovable as the neck of a statue.
This ceremony was performed with considerable regularity,
from the king giving, as it were, the time for every motion.
Wherever he cast his eye, there was the greatest effort
made; and nothing could exceed the exertion of the whole
until sunset, when Shaka, accompanied by his girls, retired
within the palace, and the warriors to their respective
huts."

Shaka's seraglio of hundreds of girls was in the Zulu
royal tradition of polygamy *in excelsis*. Dingaan, too, delighted to dance with his damsels, displaying "extraordinary
power in throwing himself in particular attitudes, which
must have required great muscular strength to have accomplished, and this in fact his frame evinced". In our own time,
the late Solomon carried on the custom of royal polygamy

while revealing a Shaka-like eagerness for new notions, such as motor-cars, gramophones, pianolas and resplendent European uniforms.

4

It is not known how many wives and concubines Solomon, King of the Zulus, numbered in the many kraals of his domains. But it is said that no matter where he might travel in his kingdom, there would always be young wives to greet him in the kraals where he elected to sleep. He publicly married his forty-first wife as unconcernedly as an old-time French courtier might have taken snuff. Yet he was then only thirty-four years of age! Indeed, it is unlikely that his Old Testament namesake had a better-filled harem when of the same youthfulness; and so his later record of wives, concubines and girl-friends may well have been challenged by his Zulu namesake before he died. The relatives of his forty-first bride, however, shouted from their hilltops the statement that this was Solomon's first Christian marriage and therefore would be his last matrimonial venture of any kind. The forty previous spouses, they pointed out gleefully, had been taken to the Royal bosom merely in accordance with barbaric custom, and paid for on the nail with fat cattle from the tribal herds. But Solomon himself did not appear to lose any sleep about this Christian sanction cutting across barbaric practice. He made no official pronouncement on the subject, contenting himself with pleasing his young bride by lavishing on her the most expensive frocks, lingerie, shoes and hats to be found in the fashionable West Street stores of Durban.

Provided polygamy did not bring him trouble, King Solomon must surely have been one of the world's happiest men. The Europeans, in their wisdom, administered Zululand for him in an unostentatious but efficient manner, keeping the subsidised Solomon at the head of his people.

And so, while freed of most of the annoying details of
government, King Solomon enjoyed the plums of office.
He lorded it over his robust and picturesque people, occupying four million acres of pastoral and agricultural land.
Solomon's royal kraal, in the midst of this land of milk
and maize and innumerable dusky belles, was situated at
Nongoma, a district beloved by his forebears; but his home
there was not a grass hut, like that of his forebears, but a
house of plastered brick furnished in European style by a
Durban shop. Far below Nongoma the countryside is gay
with the yellow and green of those beautiful but evil fever
trees. From their fleshy trunk drips a red sap that looks like
blood—a reminder of those days of massacre, murder, and
rapine when Solomon's great ancestor was terrorising all
the tribes of Natal.

It is no doubt largely due to the fierce wars which
characterised the life of the Zulu nation for over a century
that its men and women are today so physically perfect.
The weak, the sick, the crippled, were simply killed off,
and even the strong could survive only by beating the strong.
The days of wholesale killing are now over; but the Christian
missionaries have not yet weaned the Zulus from the
superstitions and barbarities of their forefathers. Witchcraft, torture, black magic, trial by ordeal, and human
sacrifice to the rain goddess, are still practised in the heart
of Zululand in the same way, though happily not to the
same extent, as they were in Shaka's day. And occasionally
faction will fight against faction with spears and shields in
time-honoured style.

It was over this lusty nation, then, that King Solomon
ruled in all his glory. He lacked nothing. At his royal kraal
he was surrounded by dozens of wives and hundreds of
servants administering to his every want. When sick for a
change, he journeyed to one of his many villages which nestle
in his undulating lands, there to be enthusiastically welcomed—in general by the residents and in particular by a
company of his wives whom he had, with careful strategy,

distributed throughout the country. His Christian marriage took place at Ekupakameni, that Place of Spiritual Uplift —a significant fact, linking the Shembe cult with the royal household. Solomon's bride was Zondi, Shembe's daughter. The prophet, therefore, considerably strengthened his sect by this marriage which he consecrated himself in flowing robes of blue, in the presence of a thousand men and women then in residence at Ekupakameni. His active followers throughout Zululand were then reckoned to be thirty thousand. But Zondi lost favour in King Solomon's eyes, and they separated. The royal relatives quickly closed their ranks against other rivals from the various religious and political groups of the commoners: the blood royal must not be weakened. That blood royal already flowed in the veins of Solomon's infant son, Cyprian, whose mother was now more clearly discernible as the First Wife.

Twenty years before, Shembe, after soaking his mind in the Bible as translated into Zulu, prayed to God to show his nation that the words he spoke constituted a divine message. He claims that he was then endowed with the gift of healing by the laying on of hands in order that his people might recognise him as a prophet. A girl was stung by a puff-adder and he maintained that he saved her from death by curing her of the effects of the poisoning by his mere touch. There is little doubt that Shembe was a man of great piety, an idealist and a visionary who gave up his wives, wagons and flocks to live the ascetic life of a wanderer in the wilderness. Even in the days of his success, as the head of a powerful sect and a thriving settlement organised on a communal basis, he made pilgrimages to far-off mountains for prayer and meditation.

Just before the marriage, the Zulu king and his delicately featured bride visited Durban to do their shopping. Zondi bought an elaborate and expensive trousseau at the best stores. Solomon, wearing a decorative uniform, caused quite a stir among the Europeans in West Street when he drove up to a bank in the latest model of a shining American motor-car and collected sufficient cash to do a round of the shops, in order to add to his already extensive and fanciful wardrobe.

Beer, song and women still constitute the Zulu idea of happiness, despite the undoubted strides made among sections of them in the matter of education. The *indunas* or headmen surrounding Solomon, however, were all of the conservative or even reactionary school. They hungered for the good old days when the law of the Whiteman did not cramp their style—those days of bloodlust and violence, of feasting and drinking. Then, if the Zulu warriors desired more women and cattle, the kraal of a subject tribe was wiped out, quite simply, and all the maidens and cattle rounded up and driven home. Solomon was careful, however, not to allow himself to be egged on too far by these diehard barbarians; for it was only in 1915 that the late General Botha, as Prime Minister of the Union of South Africa, and Lord Buxton, then Governor-General, allowed him to return to the flesh-pots of Zululand. For Solomon inherited the state of exile which his father, Dinizulu, earned by his political intrigues which caused internecine strife and little wars. Dinizulu, a mountain of flesh, had not the patience to keep steadily along the peaceful path of Imperial policy. He kicked over the traces and so was imprisoned on the island of St. Helena from 1887 to 1897. He was then allowed to return to his people; but owing to a rebellion by a section of the Zulus in 1906 he was confined to a remote region of the Transvaal where he died not many years later.

Fascinating indeed is the story of the Zulu race. In the middle of the eighteenth century the heir to the chieftain-ship—known as the Wanderer—had to escape from a band of assassins by leaping the fence of his kraal and fleeing into the bush. A barbed assegai found a billet in his side. In the bush he chanced upon a maiden collecting firewood and she removed the assegai and bound up his wound. He wandered on from tribe to tribe as a fugitive, becoming such a mighty

hunter that he once killed a lioness single-handed as he
wanted to capture her two cubs. Finally he returned to the
royal kraal, murdered his brother who had been installed as
chief, and then revealed the scar in his side. "The wound
is his witness!" shouted the tribesmen and acclaimed him
their king.

The Wanderer's line of succession was broken at the
beginning of the nineteenth century by Shaka, a brilliant
and brave young warrior, whom the Zulus enthusiastically
chose to be king. He reorganised the military system with
remarkable results. *Impis* or regiments were placed under
the severest possible discipline, each being recognisable by
the distinctive colour of their long, oxhide shields or by a
special animal skin about their loins, or by a bunch of
feathers on the head. The light assegai, which had been
thrown at the enemy when at a distance, was forbidden,
being classed as a cowardly weapon, and the short stabbing
assegai with a heavy blade was introduced instead for use
at close quarters. Shaka became the scourge of the country
encircling the royal kraal for some hundreds of miles. His
bloodthirsty young warriors, who were forbidden the sweets
of matrimony until they had proved their valour in several
fights, swooped down on the subject tribes inhabiting the
adjacent territories and drenched the country in blood. In
the formation of a crescent moon, they advanced shouting
their savage war-songs and making thunder by beating a
tattoo on their shields with their assegais. The two horns of
the regiment closed in about the doomed kraal; its old
women and men were quickly and ruthlessly stabbed to
death, its screaming girls were caught, ravished, and, together perhaps with a few likely-looking children, driven
back as slaves of the all-conquering Zulu nation; and
finally its huts, by then blood-bespattered and with the dead
and dying lying against them, were fired.

These perfectly trained soldiers in all killed—how many?
Some say a million human beings, others three million. I
believe myself that these figures are greatly exaggerated;

but from this welter of slaughter emerged the great Zulu nation, with its well-built men and its women, beautiful after their fashion. Shaka for years made a practice of having his sons murdered soon after birth in order that they might not grow up to rival him; and when it was discovered that his own mother had one of his sons concealed in her hut, she was killed instantly. Shaka then ordered the nation to go into mourning. That the weeping might be genuine he had a number of other mothers slaughtered; and so there went up a ghastly tumult of mourning, for cows and calves were also killed that the living animals might call sorrowfully for the dead.

With poetic justice, Shaka was assassinated by his brother Dingaan who then assumed the chieftainship. The same Dingaan, this, who in 1838 entertained Piet Retief and his band of sixty-nine Boer trekkers from the Cape; and, then, in the moment of his promising to abide by a treaty ceding them a strip of land, had them massacred to a man as they sat without arms in his circular courtyard. The other Boers in Natal soon after avenged themselves at the planned battle of Blood River where three thousand Zulus were slain. Dingaan fled to the northern reaches of Zululand and was there done to death by the Swazis.

Cetywayo was the next chief to make a name for himself in Zulu history. He was installed as chief by Sir Theophilus Shepstone in 1873 in pursuance of the British Government's policy of encouraging the Zulus to rule themselves. But he failed to keep a check upon his bloodthirsty tribesmen who first fought one another and then raided Natal in 1878. A British punitive expedition set out from Natal. About ten thousand Zulus surrounded the main column at Isandhlwana and eight hundred and fifty-eight Europeans and four hundred and seventy-one Native auxiliaries were killed. The invasion, however, was successfully carried out, great slaughter being inflicted on the Zulus, and Cetywayo was captured and deported. So the ill-starred reign of Dinizulu, already described, was reached, to be followed, after a period of exile, by his son Solomon, who was too happy to risk his kingship in a vain attempt to regain the vanities of the old-time barbaric despotism.

When the Prince of Wales visited Zululand in 1925 he gave Solomon a walking-stick which the black potentate proudly carried at the Place of Spiritual Uplift on the occasion of his wedding. A great chorus of girls sang with downcast eyes and danced with a wonderful rhythm as they escorted the bride to the canopy of palms beneath which the ceremony was performed. They wore red kilts, blue tunics, and crowns of purple. Zondi, the bride, a typically handsome Zulu girl, had on a light blue pleated, brocaded skirt surmounted by a shimmering white silk jumper. On her head was a crown of madonna blue silk topped with white feathers. A handsomely embroidered tulle veil floated from the crown, the end of two long streamers of brocaded lilac being carried by two Zulu girls in almond green silk. The bride walked with the majestic bearing which all Zulu women acquire in youth through their habitual task of carrying water in clay pitchers on their heads. In her right hand was an assegai head, symbolical of her new station.

Solomon was dressed in orthodox top-hat, grey-striped trousers, morning coat, patent leather boots, and lemon suede gloves. "*Bayete! Bayete! Bayete!*" yelled the crowd in the traditional royal salute. During the reading of the marriage service Solomon's manly "*Yebo!*"—the Zulu affirmative—reverberated in the hills. After the blessing Solomon took his wife's arm and led her away amid a great shout of "Solomon!" and motored with her to his European-style house at Nongoma.

Zululand is full of such incongruities and startling contrasts for it contains, as it were, a nation of savages at the half-way house to civilisation and Christianity. Only in the untouched heart of Zululand do the tribesmen and their womenfolk still cling to their original savagery in all its naked reality. In the virile maidens who sway in the sun-

shine clad only in a square of beads the size of a fig-leaf
and a few brass bangles, in the lusty warriors who stamp out
their inspiring war-dance while brandishing assegais, in the
Zulu songs of love and hate which thunder from a thousand
throats, in the beehive-shaped huts of grass which are the
homes of this primitive people—in all this is glimpsed a
vivid picture of that Darkest Africa in which the Blackman
was cradled.

5

To left and right, as the motor-car swings and switch-
backs round and over the hills beyond the Tugela, are small
Zulu kraals; but they are so much part of the broken landscape that the eye may easily fail to notice them. It is a
foreign sheet of corrugated iron that spoils their camouflage
of thatch among the outcropping boulders and bleached,
winter grass.

Nongoma, with its little hotel and street of far-spaced
houses, is a Whiteman's village of officials and shopkeepers: a setting for the magistrate's court, solid and smug
beneath the South African flag. The Zulu royal family
lives a few miles farther on, and higher still, as if to be in
the very heavens from which the tribe derives its name.
Its various branches occupy separate groups of houses and
huts, like chessmen on a checkerboard; and, as a matter of
fact, they are engaged in a sort of never-ending game of
chess. There is about this habitation of the royal family a
stifling air of stalemate, a weary frustration of life and effort.
This heavy atmosphere of futility befogs the mind, while
the harsh, bright sunshine lays bare the apparent emptiness
of the bleak faraway.

Where is the king? Nobody is quite sure, for the king is
in check; and he, in turn, blocks the path of the regent, his
uncle; while, cross-legged on the ground, the *indunas*, heads
of a dozen Zulu factions, sit in a circle of fruitless *indaba*.

The debate goes on and on, and all that seems to come of it are the shadows of the *indunas* which lengthen themselves throughout the afternoon and then merge with the nothingness of night. Some *indunas* sulk in their huts or segregate themselves in their own villages; others console themselves with beer or Cape brandy. The old men of the tribe stagger uncertainly in the sun, seeking a purpose in the world about them as it divides and divides again. Cry *bayete* for the king—but where is he and who?

The home of the ex-regent is made up of a collection of round rooms and square rooms—a compromise between Durban and Nongoma. In one of the large *rondavels*, furnished with upholstered settees and deep armchairs from some West Street store, I take tea with the ex-regent's wife. Big and jolly, she is dressed in European clothes—a smiling matron who talks entertainingly about her family. Her daughter, a modest, good-looking girl in her late teens, dressed in a high-school uniform of blue, is bare-legged and bare-footed; and when she has poured out the tea, she serves a cup to me on bended knee, like a graceful medieval pageboy, staying in that easy attitude, with head bowed, while I help myself to sugar. Her mother discourses on the photographs hanging on the wall—Queen Victoria and the obese Dinizulu, among other portraits linking Buckingham Palace with the House of Zulu. The front-door of this home in which a black princess kneels as she hands me a cup of tea bears the legend, "Zulu Royal Family".

Elsewhere, in a hut near Solomon's suburban house, I find Cyprian Inyangazizwe Bhekuzulu, the new chief,[1] with his young wife nursing her baby. They seem very happy; but when Cyprian takes me about the village, and shows me his horses, and Solomon's house, which is his house now, it becomes clear that he is worried about the Zulu hierarchy with its jealousies and rivalries. It makes his own position,

[1] Installed as Chief of the Usutu section of the Zulu people in August 1948, when he was twenty-five and owned two wives. The Minister of Native Affairs, in a message, told him that the question of declaring him Paramount Chief would be considered later if his conduct merited it.

difficult in this preparatory period, doubly difficult; but he is the son and heir of Solomon and draws strength, presumably, from faithful royalists. There are the ex-regent and a former acting chief and the *indunas*; there are the pastors of various religious sects in the kraals, and the Zulu politicians with authority from the urbanised tribesmen whose mandate they hold in their dealings with trade and government officials. While he is learning from his elders and while his chieftainship is in a state of limited animation at Nongoma, the tribal and family intrigues and feuds go on; and in the background there is the higher authority of the Whiteman's government. In all this tangled wilderness of interests and sanctions, where stands the House of Zulu?

As we enter Solomon's house—a bungalow of four or five rooms—a gramophone with a hoarse sound-box is grinding out a once-popular European tune. At the dining-room table a visiting Native politician sweats in a thick suit of blue serge; and he and a henchman are eating a large lunch served by a black Martha of the establishment. Whenever a record ends, she puts on another and quickly winds up the gramophone, so that the room is always noisy, either with the strains of a dance-band or of a church choir. Between mouthfuls, the politician laughs and tells us the answer to the Native problem—the Natives must be given equality of rights and opportunity in the Whiteman's towns and rural areas, but the Whiteman must have no rights or opportunity in the Blackman's territories. The flies buzz over his neglected plate of meat and vegetables.

Cyprian shows me through the house. In the living-room Solomon's pianola is dusty and neglected: the European prints and family photographic portraits hang askew on the walls. The wallpaper is peeling off, here and there, and the paintwork is blistered and tarnished. Indeed, about the whole house there is a look and a feeling of decay and dry rot. Are the white ants, I wonder, having fun with the books and the timber? A dog is lying in the passage, some clucking chickens are scratching and pecking on the

veranda, and on a windowsill a cat sits watching from beside
a vase of artificial flowers. Nobody ever plays Solomon's
pianola now; but his gramophone scrapes and concatenates,
and the politician sits and eats at his table. Light-footed,
gentle-voiced Cyprian, the man born to be chief, is like a
ghost in his father's house. Now in his middle twenties,
will he manage to bring back unity to the House of Zulu,
and give it meaning once more, or will it finally fall before
his puzzled eyes? Solomon's house—it occurs to me as I
wander round it—needs more than a spring-cleaning to rid
it of its dejection as well as its dust and disrepair: and so
does the House of Zulu.

We go outside and there, as the high sun beats down on
the baked earth, Cyprian throws off the depression pervading
the house that Solomon built, but from which Solomon in
all his glory has departed. The transition from the Zulu way
of life to the Whiteman's way of life is not merely by way of
a bungalow's front door; and, knowing that, the sensitive
Cyprian, with his mind in two worlds, wonders and worries
about the future of the House of Zulu and of the Zulu
people. When he leaves idle Nongoma to visit bustling
Durban, the crowds bewilder him by day and the lights
dazzle him by night.

"When I approach the city by car," he says, "I see its
lights afar off looking like stars. This reminds me of the
words of my ancestor, Shaka, who said to his assassins as
he lay dying: 'You will not rule this land. I see the Whiteman coming like swallows over the waves of the ocean.
This land will shine like stars in the starry heavens.' And
I find the city very crowded. I see too many people in the
buildings and in the streets. It is wonderful to me to see how
this city is drawing all classes of people to live together within
its walls. Yet I do not think that most of these people are
happy. I have seen a few of my own people who have become
city dwellers. They, too, are not very happy, although they
do not want to go back to their homes again."

Yes, Shaka's dying eyes saw far—but not far enough.

For the Zulus still have their land, and his own descendants still have authority and rule by family and tribal sanctions. Their destiny is still in their own hands as they rise with the rising Bantu. Polynesians and Red Indians may moan and turn their faces to the wall—but the Negro and the Bantu seem to have that tough inner core and outer adaptability which sees them through suffering and removes the hurt from an alien civilisation. In this belief I find myself supported by one[1] of much African experience who, after listing the lost peoples of the Pacific, North America and Australia, goes on to say: "How comes it that a single aboriginal stock, the African negro, continues to survive and flourish, side by side with us, while all others decay? This solitary exception to an otherwise universal rule is one of the strangest facts in ethnology. If ill-treatment could exterminate any people, or altered habits impair their powers of breeding, the indigenous tribes of Africa must have been an extinct, or at least a dying race by now, for no natives in past times have ever been so mercilessly exploited or subjected to greater changes in their environment and mode of living. The ravages of the slave trade in East, West, and Central Africa, during the latter part of the seventeenth century, the whole of the eighteenth and much of the nineteenth, are beyond computation; yet notwithstanding the gigantic drain on the population of the continent which this traffic involved, and the fact that such of its victims as survived to reach the coast were shipped thousands of miles overseas, there to labour among surroundings, and under conditions, entirely strange to them—notwithstanding all these tremendous experiences, which more than cover every ground that has been put forward to account for the extinction of other native races, the Bantu stock continues to flourish and multiply, not only in the country of its origin, but equally in the West Indies, the states of the North American Union, and wherever else its imperishable blood has been introduced."

[1] Sir Hector Duff in *African Small Chop* (Hodder & Stoughton, 1932).

Even Cyprian, forgetting for a moment the dissensions of the House of Zulu, appears to know prophetically that Zulu life will go on, not despite but because of the shining Whiteman; and so, in his grey slacks and polo shirt of golden silk, he runs to his horse and jumps into the saddle. His wife, her baby straddling her right hip, watches happily as Cyprian puts his mount through its paces.

Cross-legged on the ground, the *indunas* are still at their *indaba*; and one with royal blood in his veins, who once led his *impi* in battle, staggers to his feet. Befuddled with drink, he totters forward, and stretching out his claw-like hands, this grey-headed scion of the House of Zulu begs for half a crown.

The horse's cavortings over, I shake hands with Cyprian and say good-bye to him and to Nongoma, through which the afternoon wind is sighing sadly. In the countryside the Zulus and their cattle are astir; and between the kraals, sometimes singly and sometimes in pairs, young men run like herculean athletes. They are clad in loin-skins and adorned with feathers and wire-bangles. In their hands are oxhide shields and fighting-sticks; and they have anointed their bodies with oil, so that they glisten. Each runs hopefully to a neighbouring kraal to lay claim to the heart of an *intombi*, a Zulu maiden, and to offer her father ten or perhaps fifteen cattle as a bride-price. And from those herding their goats and cattle on the hill-slopes or crushing maize in the kraal, the word goes forth, "Behold, a bridegroom cometh!"

6

POSTSCRIPT

The wind sighs among the giant yellow-wood and stink-wood trees of the forest—"e-Shooowe", "e-Shooowe". That is how Eshowe, the European capital of Zululand, got its name. Like the Nkandla forest to the north, where

King Cetywayo lies buried, this forest of 200 acres in the middle of the township is on preserved ground. Sixteen miles away is Gingindlovu, once Cetywayo's royal kraal. The name means "Swallow-an-Elephant" to tell the might of Cetywayo's person. Zululanders sometimes refer to it as "Gin-and-soda". Only the circular kraal sites remain to show the extent of Cetywayo's establishment. These floors were a compound of anthill, cow-dung and ox-blood which, when polished smooth with round stones by the womenfolk, shone like dark satin. The hut walls of reeds woven over bent sticks have long ago disappeared; but the floor circles remain, as they do also, after a hundred years, at the earlier King Dingaan's royal kraal to the north which was called Umgungundlovu (a name later applied by the Zulus to Maritzburg because, for the conquering Whites, that was their capital).

Spreading away to the coast from Gingindlovu are the sugarcane fields which resemble a deep-piled green carpet undulating over two hundred miles of countryside. Around Eshowe lie the hills and valleys of "kwa Zulu" (home of the Zulu). Time moves slowly in Eshowe. The tempo is made by the Zulus for whom a visit to a store is a day's outing, and the purchase of one article the excuse for endless gossip at the counters. The dignified men haste not, neither do they toil. Work is for the women, and the more wives a man has the richer he is in leisure. True, to obtain a new wife cattle must be paid—ten is the normal number. That may mean that a man has to work on the sugar estates for a few years, or find employment in Etegwene (Durban) or even in faraway Goldieburg (Johannesburg) in order to earn money for more cattle. Most of the tribesmen have, at some time or other, gone to the towns to work. They seek not only wages but the excitement of town-living. They acquire a taste for city ways and city clothes.

But the green hills call them home again. Then, very often, away go the trousers and shirts of civilisation, to be replaced again by the *betshu* and *umutsha* round their waists. Their womenfolk celebrate the homecoming by dispensing foaming beer brewed from sprouted Kafir-corn. Guests and relatives appear from the bush. There is singing and dancing.

The kraaled cattle low, and amid familiar scents and sights and sounds the Zulu knows (as surely as the Cockney back in London from foreign parts or the New Yorker back in Manhattan from overseas) that there is no place like home —kwa Zulu.

CHAPTER X

THE ANIMALS FROM NOAH'S ARK

I

ALL THE animals from Noah's Ark still roam the African wilds; and throughout the continent there are reserves where they live in great herds as they were living before the advent of the Whiteman and the rise of the Blackman.

After the European nations had scrambled for their African slices, there was a distinct chance that all the wild animals would be shot and crowded out of existence. Where the Whiteman went farms and mines and factories sprang up; forests and bush were cleared for timber and to give space for the cultivation of crops and the building of towns; the Bantu labourers crowded in on the heels of progress; and the wild animals were shot in increasing numbers for their meat and skins, driven off their pastures and prevented by fences and human occupation from trekking freely across the land to escape severe winters and drought and to find grass and water across free horizons.

But, just in time, the idea of marking off extensive tracks of forest and desert, of mountain and river, of bush and valley was suggested to the various governments; and, despite strong opposition from those who wished to colonise and develop those areas, the authorities, during the past generation, have created an increasing number of wild life sanctuaries, from the tropics to the Cape.

These animals may indeed be regarded as the animals from Noah's Ark, for anthropologists, geologists and other scientists are steadily adding evidence to evidence to show that much of Africa was once flooded over by the sea, that its character has changed, here and there, from swamp to forest and from forest to desert, that animals and sub-men and primitive men followed the vegetation as it spread from the fertile, flowering highlands to the middle plain and low-lying deserts, and wheeled again as droughts and famines struck them. The records of the rocks are slowly revealing their story, and in caves and petrified forests and in deep-buried strata, links in the chain of Man's evolution are being pieced together; but still, deep in the Congo forests north of Lake Tanganyika, the gorillas walk upright as they pursue their vegetarian way of life, while, high on the slopes of the Drakensberg and in the low-lying bushveld running down through Zululand to the sea, the baboons gracefully swing themselves into the tree-tops for a feast of wild berries and nuts.

"Walking in the gorilla forest", an Italian traveller[1] tells us, "is not so much walking as fighting every inch through an almost solid wall of trees, bush, and heavily matted vegetation. It seems that the gorilla has chosen for his home just that corner of the world where nature herself aids him in his evident desire to put up an insurpassable barrier between his life and the life of every human being, and in so far as possible every other living being. Entering that forest seemed to me like passing through a door into another world, a world that had existed intact and isolated since the dawn of life. I seemed to have stepped into some prehistoric epoch. . . . There I beheld the scene I had so long dreamed of. . . . A huge female gorilla was luxuriously basking in the sun, while a young one of perhaps three years was jumping on her, worrying her, and making every kind of mischief until the mother grew annoyed and gave him a powerful smack which sent him spinning, rolling over and over in a clumsy ball of flying arms and legs. A little distance from them were two other females and one enormous male covered with long, black hair tinged with grey across the centre of his back. They were quietly, with almost human deftness, devouring bamboo shoots and strip-

[1] Attilio Gatti in *Tom-toms in the Night* (Hutchinson, 1932).

ping away the peeling from high stalks of a sort of wild
celery. Another female near a tree was busily digging in the
ground. . . . A female and a male were sitting side by side
resting their backs comfortably against a tree. Their long
arms dangling, their enormous heads sunk on their chests,
their monstrous bellies entirely obscuring their short legs,
they looked like a fat old couple completely absorbed in an
afternoon nap. The last of the group, a half-grown gorilla,
grasping two lianas, was swinging back and forth."

On the very summit of the Drakensberg, in the Mont-
aux-Sources area, I have watched a troop of baboons frolick-
ing and eating berries in that perfect freedom and happiness
from which machine-enslaved *homo sapiens*, despite his
dreams, is getting farther and farther away. On all that sun-
kissed, sun-soaked mountain-back, there was nobody to
dispute the right of liberty and the pursuit of happiness to
these creatures picnicking between the floating clouds and
the villages of the humans, deep in the bush-screened valleys.
The mother baboons foraged for fruit with their babes
riding pickaback, small hands gripping firmly; while the
leader of the troop, an old-man baboon walking upright a
little apart from the rest, kept glancing about him like a
keen and dutiful picket, and barking in my direction from
time to time to make it clear that I was not particularly
welcome in the baboon-land of which he was lord.

In the lowveld of the Northern Transvaal and in the
coastal area of Zululand, I have also watched baboons at
play and at their business of food-gathering—and food-
stealing from farms and houses if the bush is niggardly in
providing for their needs. Though ungainly on the ground,
they are extremely graceful as they climb up or descend from
trees. They are then like circus acrobats, swinging from
one branch to another, lightly, expertly, and with all the
rhythms that make up the poetry of motion. They are
cunning and skilful raiders, too, for they reconnoitre carefully before making their lightning attacks on farmlands
and homesteads and even on town gardens and kitchens.

A Zulu sculptor modelling Africans and wild animals in clay.

A lonely, lordly elephant in the long-grass of Kruger Park, about to enjoy a wallow in his favourite stream.

By doing the splits, a giraffe, with tick-birds feeding along his spine, necks a long drink at a Kruger Park waterhole, while a baboon turns away impatiently.

Their periodical raids on the British Navy's base at Simon's Town in the Cape are described in the newspapers and sometimes made the subject of editorials.

"The august atmosphere of the Simon's Town naval base", one such editorial[1] states, "has once more been disturbed by the attack of a commando of baboons, who advanced in open formation, preceded by their scouts. It appears that the baboons penetrated the defences of the naval base and actually reached the town before counter-measures broke the cohesion of their attack. The baboons, however, were not yet beaten and retreated across the house-tops, pillaging and looting as they went. The position in the naval base appears to have been restored, but it is definite that the baboons merely made a strategic withdrawal, that their forces are still intact, and that they took their booty with them. For generations past Simon's Town has had to cope with hit-and-run raids from these intransigent baboons, and it is indeed likely that Nelson, during his sojourn there, was a spectator, if not a participant, in one of these engagements."

Within memory of the passing generation of South Africans, the whole sub-continent was a wonderland of game of all kinds. Their great migrations made a most marvellous sight. In the case of springboks, those fleet antelopes that leap high in the air arching their back, that is to say *pronking*, so that their short white mane and spine-protector gleam in the sun, their migrations meant millions and tens of millions on the march across the face of Africa.

That mighty hunter and fearless explorer, Gordon Cumming,[2] who trekked across the Karoo and into Bechuanaland in the early forties of the nineteenth century, "beheld the plains and even the hillsides, which stretched away on every side, thickly covered, not with herds, but with one vast mass of springboks; as far as the eye could strain,

[1] *The Cape Times* of 29 September 1942.
[2] Author of *The Lion Hunter in South Africa* (John Murray, 1904).

the landscape was alive with them, until they softened down to a dim mass of living creatures."

"This morning," remarked a Boer to Gordon Cumming, "you beheld only one flat covered with springboks, but I give you my word that I have ridden a long day's journey over a succession of flats covered with them as far as I could see and as thick as sheep in a fold."

Even at the turn of the century, according to one[1] who made a study of these almost unbelievable migrations, the springboks "trekked in such dense masses that they used sometimes to pass right through the streets of the small up-country towns. I have known old people who have walked among them and actually now and then touched them with their hands. Men have gone in armed with only a heavy stick and killed as many as they wished. Native herdsmen have been trampled to death by the bucks and droves of Africander sheep carried away, never to be recovered in the surging crowd. So dense is the mass at times and so overpowering the pressure from the millions behind, that if a *sloot* [gully] is come to, so wide and deep that the bucks cannot leap over or go through it, the front ranks are forced in until it is levelled up with their bodies, when the mass marches over and continues its irresistible way."

Out of the wilderness these antelopes emerged, herds being added to herds until, as a magistrate[2] puts it, "one might as well endeavour to describe the mass of a mile-long sand dune by expressing the sum of its grains in cyphers, as to attempt to give the numbers of antelopes forming the living wave that surged across the desert in 1892 and broke like foam against the western granite range. I have stood on an eminence some twenty feet high, far out on the plains, and seen the absolutely level surface, as wide as the eye could reach, covered with resting springbucks, whilst from over the eastern horizon the rising columns of dust told of fresh hosts advancing."

[1] S. C. Cronwright-Schreiner in *The Migratory Springbucks of South Africa* (Unwin, 1925).
[2] W. C. Scully in *Further Reminiscences of a South African Pioneer* (Unwin, 1913).

And the same magistrate tells us elsewhere[1] that "it is not many years ago since millions of them crossed the mountain range and made for the sea. They dashed into the waves, drank the salt water, and died. Their bodies lay in one continuous pile along the shore for over thirty miles, and the stench drove the Trek-Boers who were camped near the coast far inland."

As mysterious in their periodical migrations and in their vast numbers are the locusts which still swarm out of the wastes of the Kalahari and the Western Transvaal. In the *voetganger* or hopper stage, they creep across the veld like an undulating red carpet stretching for miles and miles. I have travelled by motor-car for days on end watching the *voetgangers* invading the farmlands of the Transvaal like an army of a size that no king or general ever mustered or dreamed of mustering in all the long history of the human race. The farmers, reinforced by Bantu tribes, the police, the general public, soldiers and airmen seek to stem such invasions—but in vain, for always they are overwhelmed by the bewildering myriads of the enemy. The men dig trenches across the landscape, hoping that this will stop the hoppers; but the red plague oozes into the trenches, fills them to the top, and then the seething mass from the rear lurches over them—and the march goes on. Poisoned edibles are strewn in their path; but the living stream over the dead.

The locusts, full-grown a few days later, wing into the sky like a storm-cloud and fly on over the whole country. Far-off, they are like a dark smoke; nearby, their brown bodies and transparent wings glint like gold in the sun. Aeroplanes fly against them, spraying gas and fog; and round their maize-fields and gardens and orchards, men, women and children beat tins, light fires of grass and sticks, beat the ground with branches—but no matter what noise and smoke they make nor how they flagellate the ground, the hungry locusts settle everywhere. As they settle, their

[1] *Between Sun and Sand* (Unwin, 1898).

voracious jaws grind grass, corn and leaves with a ceaseless, machine-like speed; and nothing green is left in the country-side. They eat all vegetation, trailing, as it were, a desert behind them. The springboks trekked in their millions; but the locusts still swarm in their million millions. Only the Bantu make the best of a bad business by eating the eaters. They collect the locusts in sacks and baskets, roast them, and devour them with much satisfaction. ,

We can believe in the myriads of insects, such as white ants and locusts, fairly easily; but the mind usually registers a doubt when antelopes are measured by the million. However, a South African writer[1] with great knowledge of the African wilds makes a clever comparison and removes that doubt when he explains: "There are in South Africa about fifty million goats and sheep, and when the lion and the Bushman were the chief meat eaters perhaps twenty-five million springbok grazed where now the sheep and the goats range for a scanty living. At any rate, the springbok grazed from the grass flats within a mile of the Indian Sea at the Kowie to 'Ngami, and from the west coast to the limit of the grass veld on the east. The veld maintained its strength because the game trekked with the growth and decline of grass and the Karoo bush. They did not remain in one locality to cut furrows like the sheep; they did not eat out the best grasses and the ghanna and the most nutritious of the Karoo bush, but when the grazing failed at one place they trekked to another, and swung back to the old spot when the veld had recovered there. And with the springbok were battalions of wildebeest, and brigades of blesbok, and squadrons of elands, and regiments of hartebeest, sable, roan, and koodoo—a vast multitude of grass-eaters, who followed the rains and moved away from the droughts."

[1] Ernest Glanville in *The Yellow-Maned Lion* (Cape, 1925).

2

Red elephants and white rhinos are among the surprising
creatures to be seen in the African bush—if you know where
and how to seek them. I have known men who, after seeing
a red elephant in the bush, have returned to camp with a
scared look on their faces and unbelief in their hearts. Rather
than credit the evidence of their own eyes, they were ready to
explain it away by blaming the Cape brandy or the African
sun, or an alliance of the two causing *delirium tremens* and
sunstroke. But their eyes did not deceive them at all: the elephants they saw were red, and for a very good reason. They
had been taking a beauty bath in red mud to smooth and ease
their dried, cracked hides. The red clay or red earth is like a
mud-pack or face cream to European women or like the fat
with which the Bantu rub their sun-scorched skins.

In the indigenous forest of the Addo near Port Elizabeth
the protected elephants are not red, for the soil there does
not have the colour, but they enjoy their mud-bath, all the
same. One hot morning an Addo farmer saw a troop of
these elephants enjoying a bathe in his dam. "They were",
he told Deneys Reitz,[1] "drawing up water with their trunks,
sluicing their bodies with obvious enjoyment. He swears
that an old bull started to squirt the sloping wall of the dam
until he had a mud slide. Then he clambered out and went
along the crest until he reached the top of the chute he had
made, and sitting on his hams he slid down. He hit the
water below with a tremendous splash and he was so pleased
with his performance that he began afresh and before long
the other elephants followed his example, each making a
slide and tobogganing into the dam. They continued at
their game for more than an hour; then they marched off
into the bush, flapping their ears, waving their trunks and
pushing and jostling each other in high good humour."

When I saw white rhinos in the Hluhluwe reserve, a

[1] *No Outspan* (Faber, 1943) whose author, when Minister of Lands in the Union
Government, held authority over South Africa's game reserves.

few hours' motor-car run from Durban, their colour seemed no different from that of black rhinos—nor was it. For white rhinos, although now a recognised species, obtained their adjective in the same way as the red elephants. Dutchmen, while on a journey of exploration in Cape Town's hinterland during the rule of the Dutch East India Company, were surprised to see white rhinos in the bush; and not only were they white, they were larger than the black rhino that had upset Governor Tulbagh's coach in what was to become Adderley Street. It was perfectly true that they were larger—and later it was discovered, more particularly, that they had higher withers and broader shoulders; but they were only white because of the clay or dust with which their hides were smothered. The rays of the sun, playing upon a powdered rhino in the green bush, will complete the illusion that he is white. But although, under the powder, his hide is the same colour as the smaller rhino, the so-called white rhino is different in that he grazes on grass, whereas his black cousin feeds on acacia leaves and reeds, for which purpose his lips are prehensile.

Out of the Hluhluwe plains, dry and austere in the winter, this Zululand reserve bubbles up like a green oasis of hills, held in the sky by a boiling, shimmering mirage. As I stood on one of its crests and looked over its beauty of form and colour, I saw that the valley slopes were patched with herds of buffalo, zebra and wildebeest, and that the lively pattern was completed by warthog, white rhino and baboon. Some of the animals seemed to be grazing on the edge of pearl-grey lakes deep in each valley; but these lakes, in reality, were made of morning mist. The sun, rising higher, drew up this mist in slowly turning wreaths, until those lovely lakes faded and vanished, leaving behind them on the grass a numerous treasure of diamond-glittering dew.

Field-glasses brought the animals close to me, so that I could see two white rhinos settle down to rest in the grass, tucking their forelegs under them as they arranged themselves flat on their bellies. As I wandered down into the valleys, dark brown baboons, balancing on branches as they ate their breakfast, made faces at me and then, swinging from bough to bough with their long, strong arms, they leapt to the ground, scampered across a clearing, and disappeared into a denser part of the forest. Farther on, a rarely-seen antelope looked at me from between the grass tufts, and then pranced away—a lovely nyala ram, its dark body a-flicker with white stripes, a wild fringe flying from throat and back, his horn-tips glinting like gold.

Rounding a hill by way of a baboon-path, I nearly ran into the enormous, greyish bulk of Waltzing Matilda, a rhino male, seventy years old, who inquisitively lifted its snout, armed and decorated with two horns, the anterior one being three feet long. Satisfied that I was a human being, Matilda waltzed round to face me and then, assuming from long experience that I carried a camera, he trotted forward to have his photograph taken. This is the famous charge concerning which visitors regale their families and friends with hair-raising stories. But, in my case, not hearing the expected click, Matilda, his short forelegs kneeing high like a trotting pony, stopped suddenly, disconcerted and disappointed, and froze into a granite statue, as if now inviting a time-exposure.

Fingering the air with the divided flanges of their wings, vultures circled low above the bush where some beast lay dead; while, higher up, geese and cranes flew eastwards to Lake St. Lucia. I followed after by car, wheeling down out of the high-bubbling hills and across the flats to the even, blue sheet of a long lagoon. Here hippos floated—fat, lazy behemoths, which blinked at me like sleepy, stupid, overfed puppies. From time to time they sank like rocks below the surface and then bobbed up again to blow spray through their nostrils or show their ivory teeth in an unchecked yawn. In a small boat, piloted by a Zulu piccanin, I by-passed the peaceful school of hippos and drifted between fountains caused by fish leaping like quicksilver in a sparkling shower; and on the sandbars and near the banks, a great variety of birds waded and swam, dredged and dived for their dinner, and took off on sudden, urgent flights. There were herons and storks, spoonbills and cranes, Egyptian and spurwinged geese, flamingoes, pelicans and sacred ibises; and, as we passed a mangrove-shaded shallow a goliath heron stalked about his business—grey, man-high, solitary.

As we neared a bank, I saw with pleasure a tall tree whose boughs were laden with large white flowers—magnolias, I guessed; and then I was startled to see that tree silently explode and all those magnolias hurl themselves into the air, collect in one great bunch, and fly off to the opposite bank—a flock of egrets! The weather was humid and warm, and my senses were lulled into dreamy repose, into drowsy inertia. Africa had me in the hollow of her hand, and for the moment, after too much turmoil in the madhouse of Europe, I was very content to be her prisoner.

Towards a singing pontoon we slowly drifted, in the piccanin's own good time, delayed here and there, on this shallow sheet of water—part river, part lake, part sea—by shoaling mud. But, once on the pontoon, I was caught up into the vigorous beat of its song as its Zulu crew, in follow-the-leader style, ran forward and dragged on the cable until they were aft, and then danced forward again, rhythmically hauling to the quick rhythm of their chant.

3

When the moon is full the lion families sometimes gather on the banks of the Sabi River for a dance. To the murmuring and whispering music of the river and the bush, with improvisations by calling jackals and hyenas, the lions shake their yellow manes and the lionesses flash their teeth and switch their tails. Up and down the clearing they lope, swinging and swaying; shoulder to shoulder, they mill this way and that, playfully advancing and retreating, cuffing

Riders guide their horses across the source of the Tugela River, high in the Drakensberg summits of Natal National Park.

Old and young Afrikaners, dressed for the occasion in Voortrekker clothes, watch their relatives and friends performing folk dances in the veld.

one another affectionately, rolling over on the grass, leaping up to beat the air with their forepaws, and generally
behaving like exponents of the jitterbug. On the fringe of
the dancing ground, the cubs roll one another about and
skip like the kittens they are; and if they venture into the
centre of the clearing, the big cats dance over them, fanati-
cally preoccupied with their own crazy measure. So the
high-jinks go on, call it cat-romp or lion-dance.

All this is due north of Hluhluwe, north of Zululand,
straight north through Swaziland along the line of the
Lebombo hills; and there, between the Lebombo and the
Drakensberg, lies the Kruger National Park. It is in the
lowveld of Louis Trigardt's trek through the Valley of the
Shadow of Death, in the hunting paradise of Percy Fitzpatrick's *Jock of the Bushveld*, in the wild fauna sanctuary
of Colonel Stevenson-Hamilton and his game rangers.
Stevenson-Hamilton, after a lifetime spent in establishing
and developing Kruger Park, has retired to put his knowledge
into books. He has been lionised, and justly so, in England
and South Africa; and, when he writes, it sometimes seems
to me that he does so by scratching a lion's impatient claw
across the page—indeed, that the author has actually got
under the skin of a lion, whose mane he shakes, resentful
that his domains should now be invaded by human sightseers
and always ready with an apologia for lions who must kill
to eat—just like men, as he is quick to point out.

That, like the lion, Stevenson-Hamilton is more at home
in the wilds of the Sabi than in a town house, may be deduced
from the following description:[1] "Wild life is just awaken-
ing from its afternoon siesta. Francolins are calling all
around, and from a nearby donga comes the sudden clatter
of guinea-fowl; bush babblers are chattering among the
trees, their cheerful din serving to render yet less definable
the vague sounds which here and there are beginning to
rise from the distant forest. It is the voice of Africa, and with
it comes to me a sense of boundless peace and contentment."

[1] *South African Eden* (Cassell, 1927).

The lion, it appears, no more attacks a sleeping man than a sportsman shoots a sitting bird. In fact, the lion, as such, is not a man-eater at all. Normally, again like a gentleman, it is a venison-eater; and the "man-eater is an anomaly, originally driven to an unnatural diet by circumstances, and persisting in it from depraved instinct, like a habitual criminal among human beings". Stevenson-Hamilton here seems to imply that what a man-eater needs is not a bullet but a psychiatrist. And he chides himself for an earlier heresy in believing that the lion did not have sufficient intelligence to connect motor-cars with mankind. Of course the lion knows that men drive through the Sabi country in motor-cars; but he knows more. For "our lions having argued out the position in their own queer way, decided that so long as the people stayed in their cars they might be permitted to drive up to within a few yards, talk, gesticulate, shout if they liked, without necessitating any interruption of the midday siesta".[1] But when they get out of their cars, then they resume for the lion "their natural hostile role".

Lions, and indeed crocodiles and all the other animals, are not the enemy of man: man is the enemy of the animals. *Without* man there is peace, thus:[1] "Hippos splash and grunt; crocodiles float lazily about among unheeding fishes; otters protrude their heads, turn over in the water like seals, or lie lazily on stones by its edge; a pair of Egyptian geese are preening themselves on a sandbank; kingfishers poise and dive, bush pheasants strut about, and call raucously to one another; a bateleur sails overhead; two fish-eagles perch side by side on a dead bough; a long line of impala makes its slow way towards the water, stealthily watched by a leopard extended along the horizontal limb of a great fig tree."

With man there is terror, thus:[1] "The hippos and crocodiles dive; the otters disappear in water or burrow; the birds fly away; the impala snort and rush off; the leopard has simply vanished. In a few seconds not a sign of animal

[1] *South African Eden.*

life is left visible to the human eye. Unvarying reaction to
the recognition of wild nature's arch enemy. If and when
Man should ever disappear from Earth, there is no form of
nature but would benefit by his departure."

Though further proof of animal and reptilian innocence
is scarcely necessary, the famous game warden enlarges
upon the delightful playfulness of lions, their frisky frolics
in the bush, their intelligent examination and use of man's
utensils and tools, so that they soon come to quench their
thirst at his water buckets and troughs or strike music with
their paws from the labourers' gong.

Mane-growing, too, apparently presents much the same
sort of problems as beard-growing. "Male lions up to
about three years old in a wild state", Stevenson-Hamilton
explains,[1] "have not had time to grow full manes" but
"these tend to become more ample and darker with age,
while they [the young lions] often display the character-
istics of aggressiveness, untempered by discretion, common
to most adolescent animals, including Man. Certain lions
never succeed in growing manes of any consequence. . . .
I think so far from there being any typical difference between black-maned and yellow-maned lions, or lions with
large manes and those without any, that they bear about the
same relation to one another as fair-haired to dark-haired
men, and as those who are able to grow heavy beards to
those who cannot do so."

And again I begin to have doubts: is this a man writing
about lions or a lion writing about men?

4

I spent many weeks in Kruger Park before it was opened
to the public, and I have spent many weeks there since; and
I must support Stevenson-Hamilton by saying that the first
major impression it made on me was its unexpected peace.

[1] *Wild Life in South Africa* (Cassell, 1947).

There were no camps of rondavels when I first journeyed through it, and I slept in a bell-tent pitched on a river-bank or in the middle of the bush. In the night green eyes, like iridescent emeralds, shone out of the long grass and the thickets as some wild creature gazed at my smouldering log fire in uneasy surmise—or was the uneasy surmise mine?

Before dawn I would be comfortably settled in a hide-out usually high in the fork of a tree overlooking a pool. And down to this pool, throughout the morning, would troop antelopes, warthogs, monkeys, zebras and wildebeeste. Birds settled there, too; and, when one was very lucky, a giraffe would come to drink, its long neck reaching far down to the water as its front legs stretched themselves widely apart to bring its mouth to the water.

I remember asking myself, as I watched these friendly proceedings at the pool, "Where is Nature red in fang and claw?" The smaller antelopes, such as the impala, trod with dainty wariness, it is true, and all looked about them with professional alertness before drinking; but the bigger antelopes, such as the nobly proportioned sable, walked to the edge boldly. One lone sable, with far-curving scimitar-like horns, knelt in the shallow water along the edge and arched his neck as he drank from the deeper part—knelt as if in thankfulness as he quenched a great thirst; and on his shoulders and rump two tick-birds rummaged his chocolate-dark hair with their beaks.

Once a furrow led from the pool along the sandy bed of the dry river; and, foolishly following it, I came upon a dead waterbuck, dumped in a ravine as if in a larder. The kill had been dragged by a lion through the sand and up the ravine to the top of the bank. Blood was on its neck, which was twisted. From the opposite bank, which I climbed hurriedly, I could see a lion lying on the edge of the long grass while, deeper in, a lioness sat gazing across at me, her tail twitching and switching—with impatience, probably at my clumsy intrusion. Had I interrupted the lions' breakfast or were they reserving the waterbuck for dinner?

Buffaloes, deep in grass and meditation, slow-moving but terrible in their power and threat of action; and giraffes, their heads in the tree-tops, their necks like great serpents, weaving as they walked—these, too, I vividly remember. And I never ceased to wonder at the curious lope of the giraffes. As their forelegs lever together on the ground, their hind legs come forward, kicking out on either side: the sloping back buckles up and the long neck waves back and forth like an enormous snake striking.

Across the footpaths or over a small bush, the impalas leaped like a golden chain, close-linked, with perfect grace and timing; and in the middle of a river, on a sand-bar, a crocodile basked in the sun, his mouth gaping wide to enable his dentist-birds to hop about his numerous teeth, picking them clean.

There were insects, too, whose skill and cleverness fascinated me. The ant-lion, for instance, whose death-trap pocks the hot sand everywhere. He excavates a precisely symmetrical funnel in the ground, its inward-sloping walls of fine, loose sand. The ant, hurrying about in search of bits of dry grass for the communal nest, steps over the crater's edge; and at once there is a miniature landslide as the loose sand rushes the ant to the bottom. There, beneath the crater, buried out of sight, the ant-lion is waiting; and as he feels or hears the landslide, he reaches a tentacle up into the crater, seizes the ant (whose efforts to climb the sloping walls only result in further landslides) and drags him into his subterranean parlour for a quick lunch.

Then there are the tree spiders who spin out their yellow silk in the wind until it floats into the branches of another tree and anchors there to complete a bridge for its owner and builder to cross. These silken bridges sometimes span roads; and from its web for catching flying food, the spider has a getaway to either of the trees. Another sort of spider lives in the ground where its dug-out is protected by a round door which it carefully keeps closed when it is at home.

P

Quietly, efficiently, the trapping of insects by insects
and the killing of animals by animals goes on in this wonderland of wild life; but the butchering is not wanton nor for
sport, but for food so that insect and animal life may go on.
The majority of the animals, however, are vegetarians and
fruitarians—the antelopes, from the great eland that is
weightier than an ox, to the tiny klipspringer which leaps
nimbly from rock to rock on the slopes of the koppies, and
the giraffes, the elephants, and the grass-cropping hippos,
the buffaloes and wildebeeste and zebras, the monkeys and
baboons, the warthogs and bush-pigs.

5

In the Cape there are game parks for the elephant in the
Addo and Knysna forests, for the bontebok near Bredasdorp,
for the zebra in the Cradock hills; in the Orange Free
State there is the Sommerville reserve for the blesbok and
springbok; in Zululand there are sanctuaries for a wide
range of animals at Umfolozi, Hluhluwe, St. Lucia,
Mkuzi and Ndumu; in the Transvaal there is Kruger
Park, the largest of all, reaching from the Komati River
near Swaziland to the Limpopo River in the tropics—the
border between the Transvaal and Southern Rhodesia;
there is the Drakensberg park, mountainous home of
elands, baboons, leopards and eagles; and there is the
reserve in the Kalahari desert for the gemsbok and—the
Bushman.

In all these reserves there are many species of animals
besides those for which each is specially noted; and, indeed,
from Hluhluwe straight north, whether in reserved areas
or not, it is game country all the way through eastern
Swaziland, through the eastern Transvaal and western
Mozambique on both sides of the Lebombo hills, eastern
Rhodesia, Nyasaland, Tanganyika with the Congo, and
Kenya with Uganda.

Frederick Courtney Selous has described[1] all that hunter's paradise, first as a killer and then as a naturalist. There may have been greater hunters in Africa, but none with such a sustained record of far-ranging interest in its animal kingdom, of zealous spying-out of its known and until then unknown denizens, of keen pursuit not merely of the quarry but of the living creature and its family and way of life, of painstaking measurements and descriptions for the greater knowledge of Europe's zoologists.

To all this Percy Fitzpatrick has added an intimate picture[2] of the intermingling of man's life, of the pioneer's life, with the wild life that abounded along the ox-wagon roads from Lourenço Marques to Barberton in the eighties of last century—the rough roads over veld and mountain that led through what is now Kruger Park. The urgency of supplies for the newly discovered goldfields took the transport-riders to the last great refuge of those man-shy creatures of the wild where, hitherto, they had been protected from the rifle by the tsetse flies and malarial mosquitoes.

Finally, in this generation, we have the writings[3] of an Afrikaner, A. A. Pienaar, who goes into the wilds not as a passer-by with a job to do for a different world, like Fitzpatrick, nor as a professional hunter and expert collector, like Selous, but, quite simply, as a watcher. He identifies himself with the forest and becomes part of it, a nomadic tree with eyes: and then he takes notes for his biographies of lions and rhinos and elephants, and his stories of animal loyalties and friendships, such as the friendship of a rhino and a hippo, orphaned by bullets. (The rhino, left alone on the river-bank, could never understand why the hippo spent so much time swimming.)

And we are reminded again, when reading Ernest

[1] *A Hunter's Wanderings in Africa* (1881) (Macmillan, 1911), *Travel and Adventure in South-East Africa* (Ward, 1893), and *African Nature Notes and Reminiscences* (Macmillan, 1908).
[2] *Jock of the Bushveld* (Longmans, Green, 1907).
[3] *The Adventures of a Lion Family and other Studies of Wild Life in East Africa* (Longmans, Green, 1926).

Glanville's books, that, despite pythons and crocodiles and other killers, whose law is eat or be eaten, there is much joy within the man-free marches of the animal kingdom. In one of his graphic pen-pictures[1] he tells us: "The birds dance, the shaggy wildebeeste manœuvre like cavalry, the blesbok thread the maze, the springbok bounds high in pure exuberance, the grim leopard will pat at a dry leaf, and a party of lions will roar for the pride and glory of the tremendous uproar they make without thought of hunting. The young furry creatures play like kittens, and if they do not laugh they seem to grin. Nursing mothers often extend their nourishing care to the forlorn young of creatures they regard ordinarily as foes, or prey. Buck stand at dawn to catch the first rays of the sun before seeking their forms, and there is a general feeling of satisfaction when the hours are passing in quiet and beauty. The songs of the birds are in rejoicing. They are flung on the air in an ecstasy, but in the intimate social talk as they go about their daily occupations there is clear enjoyment. The black and white sociable birds go flitting through the woods in a continual conversation, blithesome and gentle, and other birds, like the starlings, and the mousebirds, and the long-billed creepers, and the shrill-voiced parrots, all interchange a continual joyous conversation."

The birds have their sanctuaries in South Africa, too, but need them far less, of course, than the earth-bound animals. While the birds have enjoyed the freedom of the air, from Europe to the Cape in some cases, all the animals of Noah's Ark have been shot out of the Whiteman's path and given notice to quit his towns, lands and farm fields; and that notice to quit would have run them out of Africa altogether but for these extensive reserves where they have been granted their reprieve. Here Africa remains as it was when the Bushman, before the Bantu, came hunting the herds of antelopes that spread over the plains after the seas had subsided from the shell-strewn rocks of the Drakensberg.

[1] *The Hunter: a Story of Bushman Life* (Cape, 1926).

6

POSTSCRIPT

Kruger Park, larger than Wales, is the world's greatest natural zoo. It is a monument to the forethought of the old Transvaal Republican Government of President Paul Kruger which, in 1897, proclaimed an area of some 1,800 square miles lying between the Sabi and Crocodile Rivers of the Eastern Transvaal to be a sanctuary for wild animals. In 1903 the area was extended northwards to the Rhodesian border, and to the east and south. With certain later adjustments it now covers 9,000 square miles. Skukuza, in the southern part of the Reserve, is a favourite haunt of lions. A rough guess puts the lion population at between 400 and 800. This is out of an estimated total of 500,000 head of game. Half of these would be the graceful, high-leaping impala buck, upon which lions prey to the extent of 20,000 a year.

Skukuza is the largest of the eleven picturesque thatched rest-camps dotted along the 200-mile length of the Park. Here there are rondavels for bedrooms, baths, kitchens and cook-boys—all for hire at a small charge; but tourists should carry food supplies in their motor-car. Statistics show the leap to popularity of the Park since the twenties. In 1928 only 183 cars passed through. By 1938 the figure had risen to 10,000. When the Park was reopened in June, 1946, after the war years, over 100 cars were queued up waiting to enter. Included in this group were American magazine representatives. Only closed cars are permitted along the Park's 12,000 miles of earthen roads, and a maximum speed of 25 miles an hour is imposed so as to disturb the animals as little as possible as they promenade or browse close to or even on the veld roads.

For the greater part of the Park the tourist season is restricted to the months from June to October (the winter months) owing to the great heat of summer and the danger then of malaria. But a section of 200 square miles in the south-western part is healthy in summer and so remains always open. This region includes Pretorius Kop. It is said that the real menace in the Park is not the lion but the tourist who, on sighting a lioness with cubs at the side of the road, wants to leap out of the car to pat the "little darlings". In over twenty years since records were kept, however, there have been no casualties, but there have been narrow escapes among venturesome people who ignored the advice placarded in the rest-camps.

CHAPTER XI

THE NEW FOLKS AT HOME

I

THE SAVAGES and the wild animals, seen in their sun-scorched, storm-shaken scenery, so fascinated me and stirred my wonder that I found myself being caught up into the heart of primitive, untamed Africa—the Africa outside the Whiteman's *laager*; and, in order to find my way back to urban civilisation, I had to free myself, with reluctant determination, from the uncanny spirit that took possession of me in such places as Swaziland, Zululand and the Transvaal low-veld.

What I mean is explained by General Smuts when he says,[1] "Wild Africa makes a very subtle appeal to our emotions, and fortunately for us much of Africa still remains wild. Civilization has barely touched it at a few selected points, and in the course of the ages the contacts of Africa with civilization have never been permanent or long-lived. After a casual acquaintance with her sister continents she has always shaken herself free and returned to her wild ways. Her spirit has been alien and aloof from that of the rest of the world, and her charm continues uncontaminated by the conventions of civilization. The European invasion which began in more recent years has to some small extent affected her peoples; her wonderful fauna has suffered severely at the hands of civilized man; but in her heart of hearts she is and remains wild and free and unaffected by the invading influences. Nowhere is that mysterious presence of Wild Africa felt more deeply than in the Transvaal low-veld . . . greater even than its wonderful

[1] In a foreword to *The Low-Veld: Its Wild Life and its People* (Cassell, 1929).

fauna, its sub-tropical flora, its unrivalled scenery, is the mysterious eerie Spirit which broods over this vast solitude, where no human pressure is felt, where the human element indeed shrinks into utter insignificance, and where a subtle Spirit, much older than the human spirit, grips you and subdues you and makes you one with itself. To those who wish to experience a thrill—a thrill which is unlike any they have ever experienced before—I venture to recommend a visit to this secluded home of the Earth Spirit."

I had come to South Africa not to commune with the earth-spirit or guess Mujaji's secret but to visit the new folks at home. Of this fact I reminded myself as I sat under the green canopy of a *jakalsbessie*, whose mighty trunk of Transvaal ebony had its roots in a farspread anthill. It was pleasant making a lunch there off great, golden pawpaws, sun-ripened to a honey-sweetness, and resting my eyes upon the majestic brow of the Drakensberg at precisely that point where Voortrekker Trigardt had tobogganed his wagons down cleft and cliff. They were the first of the new folks in these parts: Louis Trigardt, his wife Martha, their children, and the rest of that ill-starred trek—"seven families of forty-six individuals, but only nine men who can handle guns".[1]

A century ago they had tumbled down from the *krantzes*, the rocky crowns of those towering mountains, into the lowveld, the bushveld, and put themselves together again; and when the wheels were back on the axle-ends and the oxen inspanned again, they trekked on, past this spot where the *jakalsbessie* had since taken root and grown to a height of fifty feet, across the Olifants River and on through the Valley of the Shadow of Death to the Lebombo Hills and Lourenco Marques. The tsetse flies killed off their cattle; and the *anopheles*, the malarial mosquitoes, spread fever and death among the trekkers; and many of those new folks found their homes in graves by the sea at the end of the long, long trail.

[1] Claude Fuller, *Louis Trigardt's Trek across the Drakensberg, 1837–1838* (The Van Riebeeck Society, Cape Town, 1932).

As they journeyed hopefully, one of them, Gabriel Buys, attended by a Knob-nose Kafir called Waai-Waai, went on ahead with a letter "to the Honourable Gentlemen and Friends at Delagoa Bay" in which Trigardt, after saying he had slaughter cattle, sheep and cows, wool and oxhides and skins of wild beasts to trade, added, a little pathetically, "If you can trust us up to a matter of 50 or 60 dollars [each 48 halfpennies] worth of clothing, linen, thread, needles, some thimbles and sewing rings, please give the goods to the bearers. . . . My wife asks for three lbs. of tea, five lbs. of coffee, and five lbs. of sugar".

Alas, these little comforts were not sent as the Portuguese could not read Dutch; and Martha was among those who died of malaria at the journey's end. In all Afrikaans literature perhaps nothing is so poignant as the last entries in Trigardt's *dagboek*, his diary, wherein, before he himself died in exile, he records his wife's death.

"My wife", he writes, "became so bad that we almost gave up every hope. But the Governor's wife, who had much knowledge of malaria, came to her, and got her so much better that she regained consciousness."

From under the wagon-hood, her home during all that courageous journey, she was carried to the Portuguese Governor's house to be nursed.

"I found her conscious but very weak," Trigardt continues, "and I hoped with God's help that she would recover. Even though I could not feel sure that she would, I offered my praise unto God for all His mercy." And then, "When I saw my wife, I could not hide my grief. I told her that she was keeping herself back by being so despondent, and begged her to take cheer from the others who, she could see, by the grace of God had recovered."

Leaving her bedside at sunset one day, he is recalled because Martha had collapsed.

"I rushed to her room", he records, "and found her speechless. I gathered her in my arms and she revived a little. After the Governor's wife had given her some medicine, she recovered slightly. Then they told me to go and sleep in peace. The Governor's wife felt sure she would be stronger in the morning, and said that she did not wish us to sit up with my wife, but would prefer to do it herself. I was so overcome with grief that I felt as if I could not live through the night."

And the next day: "I got up at cock-crow to see if there was any news of my dear wife; but as all was quiet at the Governor's house, I went back to bed. I could not sleep, and at second cock-crow I got up again. It was still dark as I waited impatiently for the doors to open. When they did, I sent Carolus to ask about his mother. He came back and told me she was a little better but very weak. I went at once to her, to wish her good-morning. She answered me so softly, that I could not understand her words. 'Does my dear wife know me?' I asked, and she answered: 'As if I would not know you.' She spoke with such difficulty, that suddenly it came over me, that all I dreaded was coming true, and that I would never see her well and strong again. Then I lost all hold upon myself and, in the depth of my sorrow I knew not what I said or did. The children wept with me, and their grief made mine the harder to bear.

"I bade my wife farewell in this life and told her of my hope to meet her in the home of the Heavenly Father. I no longer bemoaned my fate, but prayed for strength. All our sorrow and care was in vain. The will of the Lord be done.

"About 11 o'clock, Almighty God called her away—in Him I place my trust. My worthy and adored love had entered into blessedness. Of that, indeed, I felt sure, but the thought brought me no consolation. Grief overpowered me so that I hardly knew what I did.

"The Governor and his wife both did their best to comfort me—but for me there is no solace left in this world.

"My dearly beloved is taken from me for ever."

But along that trail into the Northern Transvaal, others followed, Boers and Britons; while the Bantu stayed; and today, after combating the tsetse flies and the mosquitoes, the Whiteman is at last taming great areas of this low-veld, which is yielding up its fruits in an ever increasing measure. The oil-drums of the mosquito-killers mark the pattern of their campaign as they spray stagnant pools in the river-beds and even the rain-water cupped in the rocks of the koppies. Elsewhere, the tsetse-destroyers skirmish slowly through the bush, burning a disinfectant whose heavy smoke settles upon the leaves where the flies are resting. And the Whiteman is also showing the Bantu how to grow wheat in the valley of the Olifants River above the Drakensberg—along the Trigardt-trail—and all manner of fruits and vegetables below the Drakensberg in the fertile soil watered by the Letaba and Makoetsi Rivers. Here the new folks are teaching the Natives to plant and to eat carrots and potatoes and tomatoes; and to drink the sugared tea and coffee which Martha Trigardt had to do without.

2

The Boer profile, framed with beard and pipe, is still to be seen against the background of the veld; but it has been replaced, for the most part, by the new look of the clean-shaven, cigarette-smoking Afrikaner. There is often nothing to distinguish this Afrikaner from the colonial Briton who has evolved into the independent South African. They share the common heritage of the Union and wonder how they are going to trek forward into an industrial future wherein the Blackman and the Indian are already pegging out claims. *Skof*[1] by *skof* they have moved forward in time and space, from three hundred years ago until today, from the Castle at the Cape to the Karoo, and from there to the plains across the Orange and the Vaal and down into the sub-tropical valleys of Natal and the Transvaal lowveld as far as the Limpopo. Others have gone on even farther, into

Stage of a trek, from outspan to outspan.

Rhodesia and East Africa as far as the Great Lakes—seeking their fortunes, like Trigardt, away from the main body of their small, semi-nomadic community. Can the *laager* do without them—or is the *laager* now only a memory of the past, a figment of the imagination prompted by yesterday's reality? As they trek northwards to new farms and pastures, and also westwards for diamonds and karakul pelts, the Bantu press in upon their old outspans and the trails between. But each trekker, as he moves over the next horizon, turns his heart into a *laager* and hopes that it will see him through.

Motor-cars have, for the most part, replaced the ox-wagons and the horses of the pioneers—but not everywhere, and, again, certainly not in their hearts. Because of the Great Trek and the frontier way of life, they linger on in the South African's psychology and, sometimes, in the farming practice of the back-blocks; and the rifle, not the pistol, is still his great comforter and companion. In times of political difference, the Boers' procedure, up to General de Wet's civil war against General Botha in 1914, was[1] "to talk it over with his own kind, saddle a horse, sling a rifle, clap on a wide-brimmed hat, and go out to protest his grievance. As Delarey said, 'It is the way of the Boer'. Very often he had no intention at all of using his rifle. He had become so used to the weight and feel of it that it was as necessary to speech as liquor is to the tongue-tied. He was at home in his saddle, more comfortable there than anywhere else, and even to-day he will ride out of his dorp to meet a prominent leader miles out of town, bring him in and, still in the saddle, listen to what he has to say. It reminds him of the old times."

Although these present-day commando-rides are a show, put on to please and divert, they are not a mere pageant of a bygone mode. In the outlying farms, the mode goes on to some extent; and the house the farmer lives in is often self-made, the tricks of elementary building being done by

[1] G. H. Calpin, *There are No South Africans* (Nelson, 1941).

unskilled hands. There may be no ceilings below the roof, and no flooring boards underfoot, but the good earth smeared over with a mixture of dung and ashes. The Bantu woman who smears the floors has a trick of doing so in a pattern made by the semi-circular sweep of her hand; and, when it is dry, she polishes it with the oily leaves of the wild castor-oil bush, and sometimes with ox-blood. A house with fresh-smeared floors has a distinctive aroma, not un-pleasant, but clean, sharp and cool after the dust and enervating heat out-of-doors. In the case of a poor family, the wife herself will smear the floors of the house.

Such a house is described by Pauline Smith, who, although using English, has written some of the best Afrikaans stories there are. In *The Pain*,[1] which is a Trigardt-like tale of a grieving husband's care of his dying wife, she says: "The three-roomed mud-walled house in which the old couple lived stood close to a small stream behind a row of peach-trees. Every year from these trees they took a thankoffering of dried fruit to the Thanksgiving at Harmonie, and year by year they had beaten the stones of the peaches into the earthen floor of the living-room. Every morning Deltje sprinkled this floor with clear water from the stream and swept it with a stiff besom. The floors of the kitchen and bedroom she smeared regularly with a mixture of cow-dung and ashes called *mist*. The little house smelt always of *mist*, of strong black coffee, the beans of which were ground with peas to make it go farther, and of griddle cakes baked in the ashes of the open fire in the kitchen.

"The living-room, with its three chairs strung with thongs of leather, its table scrubbed a bright yellow with the yellow-bush that grew on the mountain-side, and its gaily painted waggon-box, was a small square room with a half-door opening on to the yard behind the peach-trees. This was the only door the house possessed, for the doorways between the living-room and the kitchen and the living-room

[1] *The Little Karoo* (Cape, 1925)

and the bedroom were empty. The partition wall, built like the outer walls of mud, did not go up to the reed-and-thatch roof, but ended, within reach, in a flat ledge on which pumpkins, twisted rolls of tobacco, little bags of seed, bars of home-made soap and water-candles, and various odds and ends were stored. From the rafters hung cobs of dried mealies, and just outside the door was the worn mealie-stamper, cut out of a tree-trunk and shaped like an hour-glass, in which the mealies were pounded into meal. There was one window, in the wall opposite the half-door. It had no glass, and was closed by an unpainted wooden shutter."

3

Dorps, too, when off the beaten track, have changed little, despite the garage and the petrol-pump. The store and the hotel with its stoep are still its two main structures —always excepting the church which is its very core and centre. In the large dorps there is a cinema nowadays, called bioscope still from its earlier name; and often a Greek shop —where they sell fruit and sweets and serve tea and perhaps meals. This is the backveld, and many like it that way: the real activity is on the farms, and the dorp is a meeting place for *nagmaal*, the quarterly celebration of the sacrament and confirmation in the Dutch Reformed Church, for an occasional cinema or dance, and for mailing and marketing. When G. W. Steevens, the celebrated correspondent, was looking for the Boer War, he spent a few days in Burghers-dorp—half a century later the census credits it with two thousand Europeans—in the Eastern Cape; and to his quick eyes, it appeared to him like this:[1]

"The village lies compact and clean-cut, a dot in the wilderness. No fields or orchards break the transition from man to nature; step out of the street and you are at once on rock-ribbed kopje or raw veldt. As you stand on one of the

[1] *From Capetown to Ladysmith* (Blackwood, 1899).

bare lines of hill that squeeze it into a narrow valley, Burghersdorp is a chequer-board of white house, green tree, and grey iron roof; beyond its edges everything is the changeless yellow brown of South African landscape. Go down into the streets, and Burghersdorp is an ideal of Arcady. The broad, dusty, unmetalled roads are steeped in sunshine. The houses are all one-storeyed, some brick, some mud, some the eternal corrugated iron, most faced with whitewash, many fronted with shady verandahs. As blinds against the sun they have lattices of trees down every street—white-blossoming laburnum, poplars, sycamores."

The lonely farmhouse and the small dorp have given a frail European framework to the long-distanced South African landscape. Some have regretted that the South Africans did not copy the cosier method of the French peasants who build their houses in the villages and go out each day to work on their farms, which radiate from such centres of their community. It is more progressive, too, for it enables public services to be organised economically, whereas the lonely farmhouse must manage as best it can —that is to say, with comparatively primitive services and comforts. The French method would have given a totally different social pattern to South Africa; but the Boer did not want it that way—he wanted to be solitary, away from the smoke of his neighbour's kitchen, afar in the desert with his own family and his ranging cattle.

4

It is in the Orange Free State that this spacious style of living chiefly survives as a social order. More than any of the other three Provinces of the Union, it retains its early character and maintains its early way of life and thought. Cut off by the Karoo and the Drakensberg from the main streams of Cape and Natal commercial progress, and from Johannesburg hustle by distance and inclination, it remains a series of scattered ranches, with some light agriculture, in the shape of maize planting, on the side. Right in the middle, a sort of out-size in dorps, is Bloemfontein, citizened by 38,000 Europeans: its administrative capital and commercial hub.

A recent portrait of a vanishing type of Orange Free State burgher is that given in the course of a mining engineer's memoir[1] in an English magazine. He calls him August Kritzinger who "was tall, bewhiskered, somewhat unclean, deeply religious and God-fearing (as distinct from man-fearing), indolent, quite unambitious and perfectly happy. For most of the day he sat on the stoep of his house smoking, expectorating and drinking strong sweet coffee. In common with his kind, and not unlike the Irish peasant, he was courteous, and, considering his poverty, showed remarkable hospitality to every European irrespective of nationality. He had inherited a farm of some 8,000 acres, and considered it far too small for his requirements. He never appreciated the fact that the light rainfall, sandy soil and low quality of the herbage would always make it 'small', until such times as bovines developed Marathon qualities and were able to travel at least twenty-six miles daily to get a bellyful of grass. . . .

"The farm had been in the Kritzinger family since the time of the Voortrekkers. The floors of the house had become appreciably nearer the ceiling by liberal applications of cow-dung extending over many years. To stoke the fire one had only to dig up squares of it. . . . There was a badly sited dam of enormous dimensions, but very little catchment area, invariably dry or little more than a muddy puddle; a cart and waggon shed in the last stage of disrepair; and one gaunt and solitary *eucalyptus viminalis*. Mr. Kritzinger always pointed it out with pride as the sole survivor of fifty planted by his father many years ago.

"Every twelve months or so Mr. Kritzinger gathered together the survivors of his flock of sheep. . . . They were

[1] "The Gold Standard" by P. F. Wall, in *Blackwood's Magazine* (February, 1933).

European and Bantu cutting lucerne at Golden Gate in the Bethlehem district of the Orange Free State.

A Pretoria suburban home, thatched and embowered, with features borrowed from Cape Dutch architecture, mushrooms from the lawns of a sloping site.

driven near the house by members of the numerous Kritzinger family, and, irrespective of size, sex or condition, caught by the hind-leg, thrown to the ground and shorn of their dusty or scabby wool by Morolong natives, who masqueraded under the self-bestowed title of 'shearers'. Mr. Kritzinger did not take an active part in this strenuous work, but supervised from the stoep or the shade of the lone gum-tree. All but the more agile of the sheep were shorn, their fleeces dumped on the stoep, and thrown into bales with such items as the local fuel, sand, dust, grass and small bushes, ancient sacking and other matter. . . .

"For years, Mr. Kritzinger's wool clip had averaged £75 per annum. He had managed to live on this and raise a family of ten sons and daughters. Several of his and his wife's relations also lived on the place. . . . He delivered his clip at the local store kept by a Jew who had migrated from Riga. A mutual valuation was agreed upon. . . . Mr. Kritzinger might insist on £15 in cash, the balance of £60 to be taken in goods. Most of the goods consisted of groceries, such as 'Boer-meal', sugar, coffee-beans, a few tins of condensed milk and other luxuries. There would be a sack of cut tobacco and a few dozen rolls of strong molasses-treated tobacco, various medicines, of which Beecham's Pills and Mother Siegel's Soothing Syrup formed the bulk, with a case of Epsom Salts as being equally good for sick sheep or ailing infants; clothing for himself, his wife and children, and the relatives. . . . Receiving £75 for his year's output probably put it into his head to ask £75,000 as appropriate compensation from those who desired to dig holes on his farm and eventually help themselves to some 900 acres of it. . . .

"Buck were there to be shot. Fresh it was delicious, salted it was not quite so delicious, but when turned into biltong[1] it was more delicious than when fresh! Every winter Mr. Kritzinger would shoot about a dozen of these antelopes. . . . He had saved from the Anglo-Boer War . . .

[1] Cut into strips, salted and sun-dried.

Q

a few hundred cartridges of British manufacture and a
rifle of the same origin. . . . When a man and his numerous
dependants live on 30s. per week, one might suppose that
a proposal to pay him £75,000 for a bit of his farm would
cause some little excitement. Not so. I informed him that
we proposed exercising our option; he continued to smoke
and expectorate, and called to Mrs. Kritzinger to bring a
cup of coffee."

The transaction was long-drawn-out as August Kritzinger, distrusting cheques and notes and banking accounts,
insisted on being paid out in golden sovereigns; and even
when these were brought to him in seventy-five bags each
containing £1,000, he refused to weigh them in scales
but counted them one by one—while the mining engineer
and his principals from Johannesburg were kept cooling
their heels for five days!

Alas, this grand sense of time being no object cannot
endure much longer in the Orange Free State, for now it
fairly abounds in mining engineers, geophysicists, borehole
drillers and shaft sinkers. I saw them already in possession
of the corrugated-iron hotel in the tree-planted village of
Odendaalsrus, careering across the dusty but auriferous
veld in American automobiles, and dropping out of the
skies in aeroplanes that take off from Johannesburg to a
regular schedule. I arrived there by aeroplane myself,
skimming over the busy and congested Witwatersrand and
flying downhill, as it were, into the empty, smokeless skies
over the empty, desert-like plains of these new goldfields.
Johannesburg and its *uitlanders* completely changed the
Boer character of the Transvaal; and the goldmines being
opened up across the Odendaalsrus veld will do the same
for the Orange Free State. The Kritzingers there will no
longer have springboks on their ranches to turn into biltong,
and they will have to take payment for their land in bank-
notes, no matter how much gold the miners win from the
mile-deep reefs of ore. Already the many myrmidons of
Johannesburg's Seven Golden Houses are rushing in. They

have their plans and their techniques. On their heels come the Bantu, with pick and shovel and jackhammer. From the flat earth the chimney-stacks of the engine-rooms are piercing the sky like neat pencils. The wheels are turning over; the deceptively sagging belts circulate powerfully; and the clay and rubble are coming up as the shafts go down to the pay-rock.

The maize stalks, scorched in the sun, the sheep and cattle grazing on the dried-out grasslands, the pathetically precious little puddles of rainwater, cupped by the clay-bed six inches below the sand, the windmill bringing up nothing but air to the air that turns it—all these things will not matter very much tomorrow. But what about August Kritzinger's children? Well, his children, at the moment, are collecting tidy sums in options and in the sales of their corn-patches and sheep-runs to the Seven Golden Houses; and there will be more money for them in township lands and all the commerce that must develop from new railway tracks, water schemes, and producing mines. Also, the children of Kritzinger's children, one way or another, will be in the developing gold business up to the neck—and like it! But old Kritzinger will find it difficult to recognise them, and when he does, he will shake his head sadly and yearn for the twelve springboks he used to shoot each year, and the dust-laden saltpan at the far end of the farm that provided him with all the salt he wanted—free, and the golden sovereigns with which the Johannesburg Jews used to pay and which a man could keep safely buried beneath his bed.

The sons and the grandsons of the Johannesburg *uitlanders* are moving across the Orange Free State veld like *voetgangers* and flying locusts: that is what the survivors of the old-time Boers are thinking as they sit on their stoep and spit over its railing. For deep down within them they know, even as they cash in on the gold boom, that the last of the Boers are checking out.

5

The Briton, the *rooinek* as the old Boers used to call him,
is checking out too. Physically, he is no longer recognisable as a *redneck*. Born and bred in the country which,
with the Boer, he has pioneered for a century and a half,
the pink pigmentation of his skin has been altered by the
sun which has given it a permanent tan. In the pastoral
and agricultural areas, the South African of today presents
a similar picture to the eye as does the Afrikaner—both
have leathery skins, both dress casually in similar clothes,
both talk and think in the same sort of way. In the towns,
too, the professional and business men are of similar appearance, whether they are of Dutch or British descent: they
have been to the same schools and universities, played
cricket and football in the same teams, and often there is
intermarriage among their families. The South Africans
have not branched from one stem: they have grown into
one stem from two main roots.

The British settlers of 1820, who were flung ashore at
Algoa Bay in surfboats, form the main cadre of British stock
in South Africa. They were the frontiersmen who held back
the Bantu migration as it pressed into the Eastern Cape;
they held that front while the Voortrekkers flanked away
northwards into the Orange Free State and the Transvaal;
and they pressed on into Natal and later to Kimberley,
Barberton and Johannesburg—and, under the leadership
of Cecil Rhodes, to Salisbury and Bulawayo north of the
Limpopo.

In the seventies the descendants of these British colonists
were visited by R. M. Ballantyne, the famous author of
books for boys, such as *Martin Rattler* and *The Coral
Island*. By then the pacification of the Eastern Cape was
complete; and the colonists, healthy and prosperous, with
no more Kafir wars on their hands, could take time off to
enjoy themselves. With the residents of the village of Salem,

one of the frontier settlements, the adventure-loving Ballantyne went for a picnic, concerning which he writes:[1] "One
of the peculiarities of this pic-nic was that the invitation to
it was publicly given, and embraced the entire population.
Another peculiarity was that the population, almost in its
entirety, accepted the invitation. . . . The place of rendezvous for those who dwelt in the village was an open space
in front of the church. Here, at an early hour, there assembled
numerous equestrians, as well as vehicles of varied shape and
character. . . . Among the cavaliers there were stalwart
men and fair damsels—also little boys and girls, prancing
in anxiety to get away. There were carts, and gigs, and
buggies, or things that bore some resemblance to such
vehicles, in which were the more sedate ones of the gathering; and there were great 'Cape wagons', with fifteen or
twenty oxen to each, containing whole families. . . . It was
a truly grand procession, as, after toiling up the slope that
leads from the valley of Salem, we debouched upon the
wide plain. . . .

"As we advanced, groups and couples of cavaliers and
carts and wagons joined the line of march from outlying
farms, so that when we reached the rendezvous we must
have formed a body of two hundred strong, or more. The
spot chosen was the summit of a woody knoll, from which
we could survey all the country round, and look down upon
the river with its miles and miles of dense bush. . . .

"Was there plenty of food at that pic-nic? I should think
there was. South Africans do not live upon air, by any
means—though air has a good deal to do with their living.
These comely maidens and strapping boys had not been
brought up on water-gruel. . . . There were pies and joints,
buns and beef, cakes and coffee, tea and tongues, sugar and
sandwiches, hams and hampers, mounds of mealies, oceans
of milk, and baskets of bread and butter."

One of the descendants of the 1820 settlers was Kingsley
Fairbridge, poet and founder of the child emigration scheme

[1] *Six Months at the Cape* (Nisbet, 1878).

from the United Kingdom to the Dominions and Colonies. He was born in 1885 in Grahamstown; and his parents and grandparents had been born in South Africa. A land surveyor, his father sometimes sent him for a change of air to a farm—"wild and rocky and surrounded by great hills"; and it is interesting to note how many Afrikaans and Bantu words he uses in his poetry and prose. The farmer, he says,[1] "showed me where the wild-dogs had driven a flock of ostriches over a krantz, and where, in the early days, he had shot a Hottentot who had stolen and was skinning one of his sheep. When I saw the place it looked quite ordinary —just a bare rock and a clump of asgaaiboom behind a stone wall, where a yellow kokkeviet called to his mate. He taught me how to follow the little grey and white honey-birds that take you to wild bees' nests, and showed me the spoor of jackal, porcupine, and rhebok, and where the paddavanger had built her home by the stream. . . . The farmhouse was built of stone, and on the walls hung knob-kieries, assegais, battle-axes, and the bows and poisoned arrows of Bushmen."

Responding to Rhodes's call for pioneers, his father went off to spy out the land north of the Limpopo; and thither his family followed after to build a shack and make a home in the region of the Umtali river. There the boy Kingsley grew up amid the scene that he later described in the following stanzas:[2]

> The dust lay thick on the burning road,
> And thick on thorn and umsasa too;
> All thick it lay where the bare rock showed,
> And the rough roadside where the long grass grew.

> Less than a mile away my eyes
> In the wilder early days had seen
> The charred sticks on the sloping rise
> Where the Shangaan impi's camp had been.

[1] *The Story of Kingsley Fairbridge by Himself* (Oxford University Press, 1927).
[2] *Veld Verse* (Humphrey Milford, 1928).

He lived a life familiar to many South African and Rhodesian boys—even nowadays, though in a diminishing degree. He explored the veld, was much in the company of the Bantu, hunted and came to know the wild animals, suffered from sunstroke and fever, and did a little farming, surveying and office work. But he was depressed by the great emptiness of the veld and wished it could be filled with farmhouses occupied by British settlers. This became his vision; and to realise it, he made the great resolve—to go to England and somehow launch an emigration scheme: the scheme from which stem today's Fairbridge Farm Schools, where British boys and girls are trained in the Dominion or Colony of their choice. So the boy Kingsley says good-bye to his father, out there in the wilds, and courageously follows the gleam. And just as the last entries in Trigardt's *dagboek* are poignant, so Kingsley Fairbridge's account of his last meeting with his father, in the Rhodesian hills, is very moving. In his biography he writes: "The next day I set out in the direction of Old Umtali to find my father and bid him good-bye. I found him on the road beyond Christmas Pass.

"I said, 'Good-bye, Dad; I am going to England.'

"He said, 'Why are you going? What is behind the Rhodes Scholarship?'

"I loved my father, but I hated laying bare the dream of my boyhood. But I had known that he would ask me, and I meant to tell him. My heart beat heavily, so I waited a little, just as one waits before shooting, after a long and tiring stalk.

"Then I said, 'I am going to England to try and get farmers here. I want to get poor children from the orphanages and the towns, and I want to train them here.'

"My father looked steadily at me. 'How will you do it?' he said.

" 'I don't know yet,' I answered. . . .

"My father understood at once, and I was very glad to see him look pleased. 'But it will be a hard job,' he said. . . .

" 'I've got some money,' I said 'and I'm trying for the Scholarship. If I get that it means three years in England.'

" 'Yes, yes,' he said, 'I think they'll give it to you—if you can pass the exams. But you will come back to us soon?'

"He looked round at the great sun-baked hills with a little gesture.

" 'I don't know how long I'll be,' I answered, 'perhaps only two years. Perhaps it will take me all my life.'

"My father's face turned suddenly very serious.

"After a while he spoke again, very quietly, and with a little laugh. 'These people,' he said, 'all these people you are working for, they may never know what you have done, they may never thank you.'

"I remembered my dark hours. 'I know,' I said.

"We were both silent awhile. . . .

"We did not say much more, but my father told me again to come back soon. We looked at each other for a little while; and then my father took my hand and kissed me, and turned away.

"When I had gone some distance I stopped and looked back. It was blazing hot, the dry road quivered under the sun, and the dry red dust lay deep. My father was standing in the middle of the road, looking after me. His grey flannel trousers to the knee were red with dust, for he had come some miles to meet me. He wore a soft felt hat, very battered, and carried a cheap white sunshade. He usually carried the sunshade in hot weather, and had often asked me to use one too, but I preferred my rifle. We waved our hands, and I went on; and that was the last time I saw him."

The job did take Kingsley Fairbridge all his life; and when he died it was, as with his hero Rhodes, a case of "so much to do, so little done". Some of his new folks are now at home on the lands of the Commonwealth; but his South African and Rhodesian lands, if not still empty, have been occupied not by the British but by the Bantu.

6

POSTSCRIPT

When you visit a South African farmhouse it will not be long before your hostess asks you, "n koppie koffie?"—"A cup of coffee?" This is a traditional invitation, especially among the Afrikaners who make up the bulk of the White population in the rural districts. And it remains a custom in the administrative capital, Pretoria. Much of the old Transvaal Republic's business of State was done over a cup of coffee with President Paul Kruger on the stoep of his single-storeyed house in Church Street West. That building, guarded by two white plaster lions, is kept just as it was in the days when Oom Paul was alive.

The spire of the "Dopper" Church across the street where President Kruger worshipped is one of the landmarks of the city. The two greatest monuments, however, stand on the opposing lines of koppies between which the city is built. One is the Union Buildings, superb £1,180,000 block of State offices designed by the late Sir Herbert Baker, which crown Meintjies Kop. The other is the £300,000 Voortrekker Monument which was begun in 1938 at the time of the centenary celebrations linked with the departure from the Cape of the early Dutch pioneers who opened up so much of what are now the Transvaal and Natal Provinces.

Government House lies well back from the road on the upper side of the arrow-straight sixteen miles of Church Street, and borders the fashionable suburb of Bryntirion in which are situated the houses of Cabinet Ministers, the High Commissioner for the United Kingdom, "Libertas"—the official residence of the Prime Minister—and high officials from the diplomatic corps. Below Bryntirion and Government House stretch intersecting miles of jacaranda-lined avenues. It is said that there are 25,000 of these trees with the exquisite clusters of bell-like flowers that make the sky, roads and pavements a sunlit purple in October. Jacaranda Week is a carnival in Pretoria.

In January special trains ("Zoo trains" as they are

called) convey Ministers and their Secretaries, clerks and files from Pretoria to Cape Town for the parliamentary session, which lasts to May or June.

Nine miles south of Pretoria is General Smuts's "blik-huis" (tin-house) at Irene, where he farms. General Smuts calls his house a "blikhuis" because, originally, it was a British Army cantonment of corrugated iron which he bought for a few hundred pounds after the Anglo-Boer War, carting it to his farm in sections. Here the veld, where he loves to botanise, comes right up to the door, and the bees make their hives each year in the house-walls.

Pretoria is linked with Cape Town by the Blue Train, the fastest train in South Africa. It covers the 999 miles between the two capitals in 29 hours 18 minutes, which is 7 hours 17 minutes faster than the ordinary main-line service. The average speed, omitting stops, is 40 miles per hour, but at times the train travels at 55 miles an hour, the maximum speed allowed on the South African Railways. The train is 906 feet long, its load 760 tons and the passenger complement 92. The all-steel, air-conditioned coaches are 65 feet 5 inches long and 9 feet 3 inches wide. Each unit of two coaches has 8 compartments and the same number of coupés, providing a total of 28 sleeping berths.

Whether in the Karoo or in the Hex River Mountains the temperature inside the Blue Train remains the same. Every car has its own air-conditioning equipment and a complete change of air takes place every three minutes. The double windows, which are fixed in position for air-conditioning purposes, also serve to eliminate soot and dust. In the compartments are coat-hangers, cushions, notepaper, wastepaper baskets, a folding table for books, running hot and cold water, and in each coach a hot or cold shower. In the observation car periodicals are available. Excellent meals are served in the dining car which seats 44 passengers: and in the lounge car, tea and cocktails.

CHAPTER XII

THE RACIAL REARGUARD

I

SWALLOWS NESTING under the portico and curving colon-nade of Union Buildings reminded me that I had travelled far since I saw them limbering up in Regent's Park and winging it down the Atlantic. To Herbert Baker's dignified architecture their mud homes, stuck between pillar-top and porch-roof, added a touch of nature that, while doing it no harm, made the whole world kin, linking the northern with the southern hemisphere to point a political moral. But the swallows, flashing from sun to shadow and from shadow to sun, did not know it, despite the inherited wisdom of their world-unifying wings: nor did the public servants, those lovers of files, who, beneath the high ceilings within, bent their heads to the desk as if in prayer or slumber.

It was certainly hot: the gardens, reflecting the high sun, were blinding rather than bright; and each European gardener, seen against the spray as he directed a hose over the flower-beds, was enshrined in a rainbow. Terrace by terrace, the gardens ran downhill to throw joyous garlands about the lawn where the bronze Botha now and always rides his bronze charger out of past bickerings into future hopes.

In his spacious room in the Union Buildings, the late Hertzog's former lieutenant, Dr. Malan, now Prime Minister, busies himself with his statecraft, after a broken partnership that death, in a sense, has mended. The Boer tradition and practice go on, modified by the ruthless, tick-tocking pendulum of time that, year by year, interjects its armies of events.

Botanist and philosopher, Smuts, the late Botha's lieutenant, gazes out of his farmhouse window at Doornkloof to ponder the puzzle of the uno-tree with its holistic fruit. Is it bitter, that fruit, or merely unripe? Perhaps it will mellow as the pendulum swings into a milder world epoch—as he himself, through many sour defeats and many sweet victories, has mellowed.

Through another Pretoria window, from a slightly different angle, young Hofmeyr formerly looked out over the same prospect—but he was no longer young, except comparatively, for he was in his middle fifties. For years Smuts's deputy, one never knew whether he would turn anchorite in the political wilderness or become Prime Minister one day, when, in parliament, the Bantu *yebos* might have it. His distinguished forebear and namesake, Jan Hofmeyr, planned a new South Africa with Cecil Rhodes, until Jameson "upset the apple-cart": would he, could he, with the patchwork mantle of Onze[1] Jan, Rhodes, Botha and Smuts flung untidily over his shoulders, knowing, by then, more of the past, seeing farther into the shaping future, design and build better than his masters? Whiteman, Blackman, Brownman and Coloured-man looked up at him, surmising. They surmise no longer, for "young Hoffie" is dead, and they have buried him in the good South African earth.

It is only the swallows who don't care: they and their unchanging kind built before Herbert Baker, they are building after and upon him, and they will be building and zesting when all Hofmeyr's political contemporaries are good grass for grazing cattle. To be about their business in the world, they do not need the vote or a trade-union's ticket. From their mud homes within the portico, they dive over the amphitheatre and down into Pretoria's jacaranda-bowers where, if they had ears for such things, they might hear the complaining murmurs of the Bantu politicians, speech-training among themselves for parliamentary and

[1] Our.

administrative responsibilities—one of these days. Africa has been patient: be patient still.

Classically proportioned of sandstone, rose-red in the sunshine, Baker's building glows like a beacon above the valley that cups Pretoria. In that huddle of offices and homes is Paul Kruger's old house, his whitewashed lions, the gift of Barney Barnato, that *uitlander* from Whitechapel, guarding the presidential museum. On its stoep at dawn he drank coffee and uttered judgment for those burghers who sought it. When two brothers asked him how they were to share the farm left them by their father, he said, "Let the elder divide the farm and the younger have first choice".

Alas, Kruger did not know how to divide the South African inheritance between the Dutch brother and the English brother. Today, behind the push-buttons of authority in Union Buildings and in supreme command of the reunited Nationalists, Dr. Malan still seeks the solution by means of a Hertzog-plus policy.

On the slope opposite are the State-controlled steel works, their furnaces and rolling mills served by white artisans and semi-skilled black labourers; and thirty miles away are the Witwatersrand goldfields, alive with black workers directed by white miners—goldfields that go on and on, deep underground, south-eastwards, until they reveal themselves again in the up-tilted strata around Odendaalsrus. Kruger thought the miners would be done with their gold-getting quickly—and be over the hills and gone with their glint. But they became and still are the very core of the Transvaal community; and as they flourish at Odendaalsrus they may become the very core of the Orange Free State community.

Malan, lifting his eyes from the crowding industries that breed industries, sees, high in the heavens, with a conical hill for its pedestal, the massive monument to the Voortrekkers. They found the way: have their descendants lost the way? Hertzog perhaps came near to finding it again, as he shared the soul-secret of de Wet and the other

Boers of the Orange Free State. But the earth gave another twist, and there was chaos. Now, somehow, one must fight one's way back to the centre of Afrikanerdom, and divide South Africa anew.

And the Kafirs? The Kafirs are packing in on the old Voortrekker trails and outspans. Must they be fought off, their encroachment delayed, as the trek drags itself forward?

From the Voortrekker monument Malan lowers his gaze to Kruger, dour and stolid in bronze, who stands on guard over his capital; but the old President's wisdom, which failed his own purpose, fails to give answers to the problems of a world shaped and re-shaped long after his day. He could divide a farm for Boer brothers to share; but the division of the country is not only between Boer and Boer, or even between Boer and Briton: it is between Boer and Briton and Bantu; and Coloured and Indian—and Jew.

2

Jew? Yes, as if there were not enough racial groups already, the Jew, ninety thousand of him, counts as another. As lone pedlars of English manufactured articles, Jews penetrated into Bantu countries even before the British flag had fluttered out to protect them as they exchanged blankets for ivory, beads for gold-dust, and knives for animal skins. When the Boers trekked from the Cape into the unknown interior, the Jews followed after as sutlers with a stock-in-trade of little luxuries and necessities for the delight and comfort of those nomads in covered wagons. As South Africa developed to the tumult of Bantu wars, it provided a wonderful opportunity for the Jews who bartered and prospered and multiplied. They helped to uncover the fabulous wealth in Kimberley's diamond-studded blue ground; they followed their star of fortune to the Rand where the world's greatest gold reefs were laid bare beneath the veld.

It is easy to understand, therefore, why Jews are today so firmly entrenched in the Union of South Africa. They were early in the field with the English and Dutch pioneers; the talents that Providence put into their hands they did not bury but used, so that they have increased to riches. Now South Africa has become a Land of Fulfilment, with Johannesburg, whose earliest place of worship was a synagogue, as yet another New Jerusalem.

The offspring of the pedlars and sutlers have become shopkeepers and merchants, mine-owners and farmers, politicians and lawyers, doctors and dealers in real estate. Indeed, they have inherited so much of the South African earth that there has developed a "Jewish question". As symptoms of this, such organisations as the League of Gentiles and the Greyshirts periodically break out like angry boils on the body politic. The League of Gentiles, now defunct, was organised in Johannesburg between the two great German wars on Ku Klux Klan lines. The old familiar accusations were put forward: the Jews were getting away with too much in Johannesburg, they were succeeding by unfair trading methods, they were defrauding the public by insolvencies that left them with fat purses, they were taking possession of city buildings by a ruthless exercise of bonds and a cunning exploitation of company law, they were seducing Christian girls. Masked, and wearing Ku Klux Klan gowns and cowls, the Gentiles swore vengeance on the Jews, worked for a commercial boycott, intimidated a few individuals by kidnapping and bullying them. Then the enthusiasm of the Gentiles flagged and their League collapsed.

Today, guided more ably than were the Gentiles, the Greyshirts are waging war on the Jews in South Africa. They have carried the fiery cross of their hatred into the countryside, in the hope of rallying behind them the farmers who, often carried by Jewish money through bad seasons, sometimes have had to forfeit the ownership of their land by not being able to meet their bonds. The feud between

borrower and lender is older than the Shakespearean injunc-
tion to be neither—that is to say, it is infinitely older than
the Union of South Africa; but in the present feud there
are subtle political factors which seem to link it with the
recent persecution of the Jewish race in Europe that sprang
from the Nazi creed.

The influence of Nazism also bore on South Africa from
the neighbouring territory over which it had been given a
mandate by the League of Nations—the territory of the
South-West, a German colony before General Botha invaded
it during the first Great War. As Germany went from
strength to strength under the Hitler regime, the Nazi
spirit flamed brighter and fiercer in South-West Africa.
New German colonists immigrated to farm and trade and
mine there, thus reinforcing the old German colonists; and
they brought with them, from the very fountain-head, the
false water of life with which Hitler crazed all Germans,
heavy-laden with the burdens the Kaiser's war had put upon
them.

By a strange chance of history, there exists a sentimental
link between the Boers of the diehard school and the
Germans. The Kaiser showed his sympathy with the Boers
by sending President Paul Kruger his famous cable of
congratulation when Starr Jameson and his Raiders were
beaten in battle by the Transvaal burghers; and when the
Kaiser's war broke out, de Wet's Boers rebelled against their
pro-British Government and linked up with the German
forces in South-West Africa who took the field against
Botha. These liberty-loving Boers (who still pathetically
yearn for a mythical freedom in a world that is closing in
upon itself) could not stomach German overlordship for a
single day; but that does not alter the fact that there still
exists this sympathetic bond between the Boers and Germans
that was established during the complicated little game of
colonial politics played by them with the English in those
adventurous years of the scramble for Africa.

It was easy, therefore, for the Nazis to establish through-

Designed by Sir Herbert Baker, Union Buildings, on
Meintjes Kop, overlook Pretoria, administrative capital of
South Africa.

The Blue Train going through Tulbagh Kloof in the Hex
River Mountains, which separate the Great Karoo plains of
the interior from the Cape Peninsula.

out South Africa points of contact from which to prosecute their campaign of peaceful penetration. And so, to the disheartened backveld of the bonded Boer, the Nazi agents brought their hatred of the Jews as a common interest for the dissatisfied, as an emotional cause for the frustrated, as a rallying-point for those crusaders of the fractured cross who rode from the white light of reason to the darkness of medieval prejudices.

The results of general elections in South Africa tend to show that anti-Semitism is a poor kind of bread to offer the backveld. What these elections prove is that anti-Semitism, so often the subject of angry argument in South Africa, is in the final analysis only a small factor in the general politics of a country that each day and every day fights the battles of the Boer War over and over again. Wars in France, the Near East, Poland, South America, Morocco, Abyssinia, Spain, and China may come and go; but the Boer War goes on for ever by means of a fourth-dimensional mystery, to understand which one must know the whole South African story. While such a war eternal engages them, they are unlikely to have much breath to spare for minor wrestling bouts with the Jews.

Despite this, the Jews in South Africa are very perturbed from time to time by social movements against them. These make them unhappy often, and sometimes afraid. Their great possessions do not help them to rest any easier at nights. The cautious send some of their capital to other lands against the possible coming of the deluge. The cunning entrench themselves with the mighty who give laws to the land. The wise play the man and let the wild dogs of anti-Semitism return to their own vomit. For these last, South Africa remains the Land of Fulfilment, for in it, out of the ranks of their race, lawyers have become judges, soap-box orators have become Members of Parliament, itinerant pedlars have become merchant princes, and penniless prospectors have become farmers, financiers, and mine-owners.

R

3

There would have been still another racial group in South Africa if it had not been for a political agitation in Great Britain and the Transvaal. In the post-Boer War period of reconstruction, it became the practice of Johannesburg's mining-houses to import coolies to provide cheap Chinese labour. Westminster's political friends of the mine-owners were thus lampooned:[1]

> To protect him from harm and his money to save,
> We'll send out and catch him, and make him a slave.
> Oh! then in a "compound" how happy he'll be!
> Who—who is so blest as the Heathen Chinee?

There are about two thousand Chinese in the Transvaal today and most of them are in Johannesburg itself. They are not the remnants of that yellow battalion which, by labouring in the Witwatersrand mines, provoked such an angry song from the throats of Transvaal and British politicians in the first decade of the century. Those coolies, recruited from the northern reaches of China, rioted furiously for a while across Johannesburg's crime-sheets; and then they were shipped back home to a man.

Before they left they dug up their dead and burned them on funeral pyres whose black smoke wreathed up between the mine dumps. They put the ashes of their loved ones in bright urns and carried them back to China. Johannesburg's present Chinese colony has been formed slowly, gradually through the years as the enterprising spirit of those bold men of Canton has moved them to make the immigrants' hazard. At least a hundred of them sifted through to Johannesburg with their Chinese wives; and a few, by devious means, have won their way over the intervening fences to become possessed of European wives. And from

[1] Sir Wilfrid Lawson and F. Carruthers Gould, *Cartoons in Rhyme and Line* (Unwin, 1905).

a depressing urban district there rise up those drab buildings which are the three Chinese clubs. If you ring the door-bell of any one of these clubs the result is much the same. There is a long wait; and while you cool your impatient heels upon the pavement you can hear the murmur of voices inside. Then at long last a pair of slippered feet will come shuffling tardily along the corridor or across the room, there will be a great to-do of a key turned in the lock, of a bolt shot back, of an ancient handle scraping round the catch. Then the door will be gingerly pulled ajar and from the gloom of the interior an utterly incurious voice will demand your business. No, they do not welcome you effusively at the door of these dreary clubs. And so you peer through the half-opened door into the gloom of the interior; and out of the gloom there gradually shows up the ghost-like face of a Chinaman, an unsmiling face, wrinkled, wasted, in which black eyes gaze blankly through you like the eyes of the blind. The door opens a little wider; you step briskly inside. But there is a lack-lustre about the loafing members, about the ill-furnished rooms, about the poorly hung pictures—even about the few pathetic chrysanthemums that droop help-lessly in the open courtyard. For even flowers, they say, are susceptible to their surroundings. Ancient and decrepit men squat here and there where the sunshine washes the flags, or weakly drag their way from wall to wall like those dead-and-alive prisoners in the dungeons of a former epoch. However, all men's clubs are dreary places to everybody except their members.

As with the clubs so it is with the Chinese homes. You find them run in the humdrum European style; and some-how you had hoped to encounter something out of the ordinary, something exotic, perhaps, or weird and wonder-ful. You do not even stumble across a humble slave of the poppy pellet—or, if you do, you do not recognise him, for at the coming of the European the opium pipe is quickly thrust out of sight.

The Chinese in Johannesburg are certainly not happy

folk, for they feel that they are indirectly hampered by laws which were made for the primitive Bantu; but still, despite this cramping of their style, there is, contrary to general belief, too great a fund of fun in the heart of your Chinaman for it never to rejoice. They gather in one another's homes and clubs from time to time to feast and frolic and forget and laugh the hours away.

It is at night-time that Chinatown is seen in its most romantic aspect. For then the dust and dirt, the squalor and ugliness of the place are mercifully cloaked by the darkness. At the street corners the gaslamps describe their little yellow circles of mellow light and reveal nothing but themselves. In the side-streets, during wintry nights, braziers burn fiercely soon after dark, and when the coal is reduced to a red-hot mass of embers they are gingerly lifted by fat, lumbering negresses and taken indoors to turn some ice-chest of an overcrowded room into a fetid den of unhealthy comfort. Gas-lamps, stoves and braziers, with an occasional square of illumination filtering with difficulty through foggy window-panes—these are the lights which guide the footsteps of Johannesburg's yellow men at night. Here in their homes devout patriarchs and virtuous maidens may solemnly burn prayer-paper, but the tragedy of this Chinatown is that, having no temple, it is vague about its gods. However, it does have its own newspaper, printed in Chinese characters.

"In a modern building in Becker Street, which runs through the Chinese quarter, will be found something which is unique in Africa—a Chinese press." Thus two topographers[1] of Johannesburg, who go on to say, "There is nothing to distinguish the ground floor office from those of any other small newspaper, but downstairs, in the basement, is a handpress, specially imported from China, and two Chinese compositors are at work setting the paper by hand. As there are 40,000 different characters for them to

[1] Patricia Knox and Thelma Gutsche in *Do You Know Johannesburg?* (Unie-Volkspers, 1947).

deal with, the task presents to European eyes incredible difficulty. The paper, *Chiao Sheng Po*, which is published three times a week, has a circulation of approximately 1,100 and serves, not only the whole continent of Africa, but the Belgian Congo, Reunion, Madagascar, Mauritius and the Seychelles. There are over two thousand Chinese on the Rand alone, but, as the majority of them earn very little, one paper does for several families.

"Another instance of the progressive spirit of the Chinese here is their interest in their little school. It is at present housed in two small houses in Alexander Street, but plans are in hand to move it to less cramped quarters. The ordinary South African holidays and festivals are observed by the Chinese and the only event with an essentially national character is the occasional performance of Chinese opera. This may be held in the school or any other suitable hall and, as the Chinese are passionately fond of the theatre, the audience is always large and enthusiastic. The streets are deserted and even the restaurants are closed when Chinatown goes to the opera."

In those little shops in the area surrounding the intersection of Commissioner and Wolhuter Streets you may buy quaint ornaments and strange goods and elaborately printed books from China; and you may also, if you understand their way of thinking, get into endless conversation with keen-minded Chinamen. And when you glance at your watch you find that you should have been home several hours before; and you look round to find that you and your Chinese companions are seated in a rough-and-ready restaurant, hung all about with ducks dressed ready for the pot. Through an open door you see the cook busy at his fire making all manner of unfamiliar dishes. On the tables there are bowls of rice—rice which is rapidly being transferred to hungry mouths by bickering, clicking chopsticks of ebony—and pots of steaming tea.

Scarcely any of Johannesburg's Chinamen are homesick. They tell you that they have no desire to return to their own country. Gloomy and dreary as is this Chinatown, they philosophically accept it as their lot, while gently suggesting that perhaps conditions for them will improve in the general racial and social uplift that the politicians promise for tomorrow. I hope so, for the Chinese, given the right conditions, make law-abiding and excellent citizens: San Francisco is proud of and pleased with its Chinese colony.

Dingaan, at the height of his power as King of the Zulus, seemed delighted with a Chinaman who visited his royal kraal in 1830. He was a survivor of a Portuguese sloop wrecked on the Natal coast—a slaver bound for Mozambique. The Chinaman, a servant of one of the passengers, then journeyed with the other survivors overland to Mozambique, with the permission and help of Dingaan. Nathanial Isaacs happened to visit the royal kraal when the survivors were being entertained by the Zulu king, and he tells us, "In the afternoon there was a good deal of dancing and singing, when the king sent for us to look on. A Chinese exhibited his long black tail, which was greatly admired, and attracted the admiration of the sovereign and his people."

4

Durban with its Indians, Johannesburg with its obscure Chinese and conspicuous Jews, Cape Town with its Malays and Coloureds, and all with their Europeans and Bantu, Bantu, Bantu: it is a crazy quilt of human complexions and creeds such as none ever dreamed of while South Africa was being seized and shaped.

King Dingaan and his Zulu maidens praise the long, black pigtail of a shipwrecked Chinaman; the Boers drive their cattle into the high grasslands; the Britons delve joyously for diamonds and gold; and, when we look across the land again, it reels with a confused scrimmage of the races.

Nobody planned this; and everybody is displeased with

the result; but, somehow, it has all happened. In the beginning was the Word; and in the end is this Babel. Only the animals of Noah's Ark say little as they herd themselves closer and closer to escape another Flood—the rising flood of the People.

Back in Cape Town I looked over the grim old Castle, where Jan van Riebeeck began it all when, like God, he first planted a garden. From its vegetables the Coloured-folk flowered and spread their seed in the desert places of the hinterland. Around Kimberley—before Kimberley had a name or knew of its hidden treasure, before the Boers had inspanned their oxen for the Great Trek—they farmed the lands of the Orange River; and, far downstream, other Coloureds made the still more arid Namaqualand of its westward course their habitation and their home. The Griquas, bought out by the Boers and Britons, trekked to colonise the wilderness in the undefined borderland of the Eastern Cape and Kafirland, naming their republican capital Kokstad, after their leader Adam Kok.

Summarising that remarkable adventure, a South African journalist[1] says, "The trek of two thousand Griquas over the Drakensberg, with their twenty thousand head of cattle, their three hundred wagons, and harassed by the constant attentions of the warlike Basutos, must still be counted as one of the great treks of South African history. It could never have been accomplished at all but for the tenacity and courage of their leader Adam Kok III, who, when he reached the slopes of Mount Currie, built a sort of mud-and-thatch citadel that was school, church, common meeting-place, and fortress combined; on which he mounted three cannon, which he had dragged with him over the Drakensberg, with such good effect that the fierce native tribes never dared to attack him. He formed a Volksraad or Parliament, and strange tales have been told about that Parliament: of how beef was roasted just outside the Parliament and sessions lasted just as long as and not a sitting longer than

[1] A. W. Wells in *South Africa: A Planned Tour* (Dent, 1939).

the beef lasted: of how old Piet Draai, who was the Father of the House and had an odd knack of getting up during the most serious moments of debate and lighting his pipe at the fire, would suddenly feel the sweet fumes of the smouldering beef overpower him and cause an abrupt adjournment of the House by suddenly crying: '*Kerels, die kos is gaar!*' "[1]

Alas and alas, the Griquas were bought out again; but nobody has bought out the Coloureds in Namaqualand and Gordonia, where the Orange River, dry or flooded, courses through the western wastes. There they are still the undisputed lords of the drought-land.

Time has gone backwards for the rural Coloureds; but for the few Boer families who climbed to a hidden valley through the grim gorges of the Swartbergen, the Black Mountains, it has stood pleasantly still. Here, bordered by the gushing Gamka River, in the Little Karoo but not of it, is a community of twenty families bearing such names as Marais, Le Cordeur, Mostert, Botes. Their ancestors, trek-Boers heading eastwards, found this little paradise quite empty and claimed it for their own. Carrying their children, helping their women, prodding on their pack-donkeys, they followed the Gamka through a deep, narrow rift in the mountains—wading from bank to bank, climbing over great boulders, plodding through sand; and, in that haven from the turmoil of Anglo-Boer politics, they built themselves rough, solid houses from the trees growing there and green bricks or daub. About their homes they planted fruit-trees—fig and pear and banana; and in their fields they raised vegetables, maize, lucerne and a few cattle. Also, breaking it up into its component parts, they carried a wagon into the valley.

All still use this wagon for harvesting their crops; and, in order to get sugar and coffee, about the only commodities they need from the outer world, they load their donkeys with fruit and maize and drive them along the Gamka River, between the high cliffs that shut out the sun, to

---

[1] "Chaps, the food's cooked!"

country stores on the roads running to Ladysmith and
Calitzdorp and Prince Albert. Happy in their fertile valley,
their sons and daughters, as they grow up, go to find wives
and husbands for themselves in the Little Karoo or beyond
—and some stay there, caught up into the larger, faster
life of today. But, otherwise, the Gamka folk, Boers of the
Boers, pre-dating the Orange Free Staters, are content to
continue the simple, pleasant way begun by their trek-Boer
ancestors. They live in precisely the sort of way that the
trek-Boers and the Voortrekkers wanted to live—independent, self-supporting farmers, far from the madding crowd.
Now, however, Progress is poking its nose into their
business, and, by putting a dam across the mountain-
gateway, the waters of the Gamka are being furrowed into
their valley. With the water-furrow goes a road; and the
road will link the last of the trek-Boers to all the world's
roads from which they sought to escape.

5

From the promenade-deck of the *Athlone Castle* I
look out again over the Mother City, framed by Devil's
Peak, Table Mountain and Lion's Head. Her life and
struggle are the life and struggle of South Africa. It goes on,
that struggle, all over South Africa, and indeed, all over
Africa south of the equator—the struggle for a European
foothold. If the South Africans weaken, that struggle will
be lost; and so once more, as so often in her ancient barbaric
glory, Africa will both throw out and absorb those outriders
of European civilisation that would build a Carthage on her
sands. To some observers it seems a pity that certain
irreconcilables among both Dutch and British, instead of
nursing their strength for this main task of nourishing
White South Africa, should fritter it away in wrangling
with one another. But these observers perhaps take too
seriously the hubbub and play-acting of the political hustings.

The so-called irreconcilables are a dwindling, cannibalistic brotherhood on the fringe of the people. These foolish few, devouring one another, argue about the rights and wrongs of the nineteenth century while the nation gets on with its present-day love of living, and presses eagerly forward towards a tomorrow of great promise and many problems.

Throughout the nineteenth century the farmers of the Cape were courageously busy with their discovery and colonisation of the unexplored highveld and lowveld that lay beyond the rivers and mountains of their frontiers. The British settlers of 1820, colonial reinforcements, voyaged in twenty ships straight from England to wrestle with disease and desolation along the eastern reaches of the Cape, agriculturally wooing the Zuurveld and beating off the frenzied assaults of the Kafirs. And the Dutch frontier farmers, who had already come to be called trek-Boers because of their passion for moving beyond any skyline that blotted out the smoke of their neighbour's chimney, now loaded up their tented ox-wagons; and in these, with their wives and children, they sought the solace of isolation far away among the fever-trees of the evil lowveld, along the malarial banks of the Limpopo, on the sun-baked plains of the Orange Free State, in the hostile hills of the Basutos, along the blood-drenched Transvaal trails of the wandering Matabele, and in the terror-filled valleys of the Zulus.

The weak or unlucky were killed off; the strong or fortunate ones survived. But not even the hardships endured by the British settlers in the Eastern Cape nor the sufferings imposed on the Dutch by the Great Trek could bring them together, during those rough days of each man for himself, in a mood of mutual sympathy. There were exceptions to this rule, even then: there were cases where the Boers and the Britons joyously joined forces against old Africa's ruthless bullying and against the warring Bantu tribes; but it remained generally true that they were reluctant to share their misfortunes and sorrows.

Yet they were, in fact, brothers in arms; for they were

fighting the same battle for the same prize. They were fellow protagonists in the stirring and dangerous drama of occupying the sub-continent. Like twin stars, their ordained courses kept them together. Obviously fate intended them to be blood brothers; but for many weary years they could not see this because the vast booty dazzled them. Each wanted it for himself. Today, after coming through the Valley of Blood and Tears, the Afrikaners and the British at last run in harness together; they are content, in a wiser economy, to divide the toil and the grazing.

At last the Boer's dream of a Promised Land, shut off from the Pharaohs of the world, fades in a waking sigh on the sunny plain beyond the well-thumbed pages of the Old Testament. And the Englishman's dream of a Colony where the Pax Britannica alone flourishes, lovely and beloved, is replaced by the present actuality of a separate country, a new nation crying its own wares and taking pride in its independence. It was these two dreams, for so long the stuff of South African life, that divided the loyalties of the Whiteman.

Tugged from her harbour, the *Athlone Castle* puts out to sea. The homes snuggling against the slopes of the mountains show bright in the sun, their windows winking and their families signalling *bon voyage* by flashing hand-mirrors. As we slant past Sea Point and Camps Bay, the Twelve Apostles, with white clouds tumbling about their heads like grey locks, stand at their eternal devotions. It is true that I am going back to London; yet I feel a sudden heart-pang as the great, streamlined ship carries me swiftly away from scenes and peoples I have known all my life. And so, as the Mother City and the mountains and the clouds, and all South Africa, grow misty before my eyes, I first murmur "*Hlala kahle!*" which is Zulu for "Rest gently!" or "God-bless!", and then "*Tot siens!*" which is Afrikaans for "See you again!"

INDEX

269